OECD Economic Surveys: Austria 2015

OECD
BETTER POLICIES FOR BETTER LIVES

This document and any map included herein are without prejudice to the status of or sovereignty over any territory, to the delimitation of international frontiers and boundaries and to the name of any territory, city or area.

Please cite this publication as:
OECD (2015), *OECD Economic Surveys: Austria 2015*, OECD Publishing, Paris.
http://dx.doi.org/10.1787/eco_surveys-aut-2015-en

ISBN 978-92-64-23819-0 (print)
ISBN 978-92-64-23828-2 (PDF)
ISBN 978-92-64-23831-2 (epub)

Series: OECD Economic Surveys
ISSN 0376-6438 (print)
ISSN 1609-7513 (online)

OECD Economic Surveys: Austria
ISSN 1995-3127 (print)
ISSN 1999-0189 (online)

The statistical data for Israel are supplied by and under the responsibility of the relevant Israeli authorities. The use of such data by the OECD is without prejudice to the status of the Golan Heights, East Jerusalem and Israeli settlements in the West Bank under the terms of international law.

Photo credits: Cover © iStockphoto.com/Arpad Benedek.

Corrigenda to OECD publications may be found on line at: *www.oecd.org/about/publishing/corrigenda.htm*.

Table of contents

Thematic chapters

Tables

Figures

This Survey is published on the responsibility of the Economic and Development Review Committee (EDRC) of the OECD, which is charged with the examination of the economic situation of member countries.

The economic situation and policies of Austria were reviewed by the Committee on 11 June 2015. The draft report was then revised in the light of the discussions and given final approval as the agreed report of the whole Committee on 23 June 2015.

The Secretariat's draft report was prepared for the Committee by Rauf Gönenç, Volker Ziemann and Isabelle Hassler, under the supervision of Andreas Wörgötter. Mathilde Mesnard (NAEC Unit), Monika Queisser and Willem Adema (ELS) provided valuable inputs. Research assistance was provided by Béatrice Guérard and secretarial assistance by Heloise Wickramanayake.

This Survey is published under the responsibility of the Secretary-General of the OECD.

The previous Survey of Austria was issued in July 2013.

Information about the latest as well as previous Surveys and more information about how Surveys are prepared is available at www.oecd.org/eco/surveys.

This book has...

StatLinks

A service that delivers Excel® files from the printed page!

Look for the *StatLinks* at the bottom of the tables or graphs in this book. To download the matching Excel® spreadsheet, just type the link into your Internet browser, starting with the *http://dx.doi.org* prefix, or click on the link from the e-book edition.

BASIC STATISTICS OF AUSTRIA, 2014

(Numbers in parentheses refer to the OECD average)[c]

LAND, PEOPLE AND ELECTORAL CYCLE

Population (million)	8.5		Population density per km^2	101.4	(34.9)
Under 15 (%)	14.3	(18.2)	Life expectancy (years, 2012)	81.0	(80.2)
Over 65 (%)	18.5	(16.0)	Men	78.4	(77.5)
Foreign-born (%, 2012)	16.2		Women	83.6	(82.9)
Latest 5-year average growth (%)	0.4	(0.6)	Latest general election	September 2013	

ECONOMY

Gross domestic product (GDP)			Value added shares (%)		
In current prices (billion USD)	437.2		Primary sector	1.3	(2.5)
In current prices (billion EUR)	329.1		Industry including construction	28.4	(26.6)
Latest 5-year average real growth (%)	1.3	(1.9)	Services	70.3	(73.1)
Per capita (000 USD PPP)[a]	45.8	(39.2)			

GENERAL GOVERNMENT

Per cent of GDP

Expenditure[a]	52.2	(41.9)	Gross financial debt (2013)	95.1	(110.3)
Revenue[a]	49.8	(37.7)	Net financial debt (2013)	57.5	(68.0)

EXTERNAL ACCOUNTS

Exchange rate (EUR per USD)	0.753		Main exports (% of total merchandise exports, 2013)		
PPP exchange rate (USA = 1)	0.845		Machinery and transport equipment	39.3	
In per cent of GDP			Manufactured goods	21.0	
Exports of goods and services	53.6	(49.2)	Chemicals and related products, n.e.s.	11.9	
Imports of goods and services	49.9	(46.0)	Main imports (% of total merchandise imports, 2013)		
Current account balance	0.8	(-0.1)	Machinery and transport equipment	33.2	
Net international investment position (2013)	-0.2		Manufactured goods	15.2	
			Miscellaneous manufactured articles	13.8	

LABOUR MARKET, SKILLS AND INNOVATION

Employment rate for 15-64 year-olds (%)	71.1	(65.7)	Unemployment rate, Labour Force Survey (age 15 and over) (%)	5.6	(7.3)
Men	75.3	(73.6)	Youth (6age 15-24, %)	10.3	(15.0)
Women	66.9	(57.9)	Long-term unemployed (1 year and over, %, 2013)	1.2	(2.7)
Participation rate for 15-64 year-olds (%, 2013)	76.1	(71.1)	Tertiary educational attainment 25-64 year-olds (%, 2013)	20.7	(33.3)
Average hours worked per year (2013)	1 623	(1 771)	Gross domestic expenditure on R&D (% of GDP)[a]	2.8	(2.4)

ENVIRONMENT

Total primary energy supply per capita (toe, 2013)	3.9	(4.2)	CO_2 emissions from fuel combustion per capita (tonnes, 2012)	7.7	(9.7)
Renewables (%, 2013)	29.9	(8.8)	Municipal waste per capita (tonnes, 2010)	0.6	(0.5)
Fine particulate matter concentration (urban, PM_{10}, µg/m^3, 2011)	28.4	(28.0)			

SOCIETY

Income inequality (Gini coefficient, 2011)[b]	0.282	(0.308)	Education outcomes (PISA score, 2012)		
Relative poverty rate (%, 2011)[b]	9.0	(11.1)	Reading	490	(496)
Median equivalised household income (000 USD PPP, 2010)	27.6	(20.4)	Mathematics	506	(494)
Public and private spending (% of GDP)			Science	506	(501)
Health care (2012)	11.1	(9.2)	Share of women in parliament (%, May 2015)	30.3	(27.0)
Pensions (2013)	13.9	(8.7)	Net official development assistance (% of GNI)	0.26	(0.36)
Education (primary, secondary, post sec. non tertiary, 2011)	3.6	(3.9)			

Better life index: *www.oecdbetterlifeindex.org*

a) 2013 for the OECD aggregate.

b) 2010 for the OECD aggregate.

c) Where the OECD aggregate is not provided in the source database, a simple OECD average of latest available data is calculated where data exist for at least 29 member countries.

Source: Calculations based on data extracted from the databases of the following organisations: OECD, International Energy Agency, World Bank, International Monetary Fund and Inter-Parliamentary Union.

Executive summary

- *Main findings*
- *Key recommendations*

Main findings

Austria possesses a dense fabric of successful large and medium sized export-oriented manufacturing firms which have provided employment, built social cohesion and supported GDP growth. Based on strong material foundations, well-being is widely shared and family networks and social policies are contributing to a high level of social cohesion. However, following remarkable resilience in the global crisis and a swift upturn thereafter, the Austrian economy has stagnated for the last three years and there has been some weakening in the traditional strength areas of well-being. Domestic demand has stalled, external demand has been weak and banks are exposed to volatile market developments in some central and eastern European economies. The large ongoing tax reform will boost household incomes and support consumption growth from 2016.

Limitations to competition in services are holding back productivity, distorting prices and raising costs for exporters, undermining their market share and limiting their ability to take further advantage of global value chains. Regulation and lack of start-up capital inhibit entry of innovative new firms, undermining economic dynamism. The education system shows weaknesses in integrating the most vulnerable socio-economic groups. Inefficiencies arising from a fragmented historically grown intergovernmental framework hamper reform efforts and undermine public finances. The labour tax wedge, though reduced by the tax reform, remains high, in particular for low-income earners.

Austria has in many respects led the way in gender equality, but its traditional model of separate gender roles of work, family and life arrangements is coming under strain. Study area choices made by young women are oriented towards professional tracks with lower earning potentials than those of men. Women with care obligations cannot participate fully in the labour force, and men do not participate enough in family life. As a result, Austria has one of the highest gender pay gaps in the OECD. This pattern is supported by a web of institutions, including the tax, care and educational systems. Reform of these institutions is central to providing women and men with equal lifetime opportunities and making full use of their talents. Progress in this direction would deliver significant growth gains in the medium-to-long term, helping support social institutions in the ageing society.

The gender pay gap

Annual gross earnings in thousand EUR by age cohort

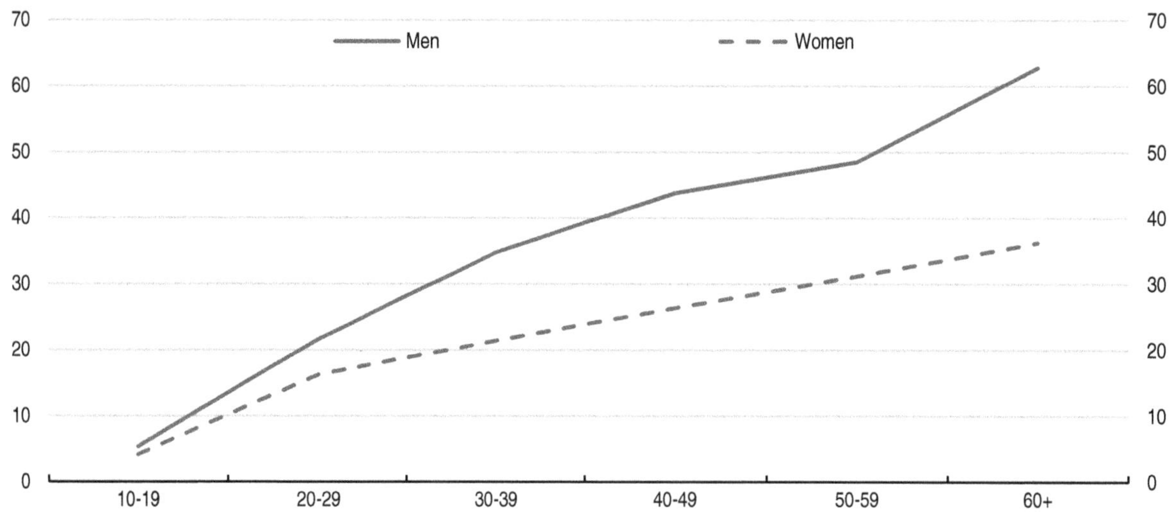

Source: Statistik Austria, administrative tax data 2013.

StatLink http://dx.doi.org/10.1787/888933251871

Key recommendations

Strengthening fundamentals

- Continue to curb expectations of implicit public guarantees to the banking sector by fully applying the EU Bank Recovery and Resolution Directive that requires the bailing-in of investors and creditors. Maintain close monitoring and supervision of banks.
- Encourage municipal mergers to exploit economies of scale. Align spending and financing responsibilities at different administrative levels by increasing the tax autonomy of sub-central governments.
- Further reduce the labour tax wedge for low income earners by partly or fully waiving social security contributions, financed by a broadening of the tax base and increases in consumption, environmental and recurrent property taxes.
- Increase effective retirement ages of both men and women and step up preparations for the convergence of the statutory retirement ages of male and female workers.
- Reduce barriers to competition in services by easing entry regulations, removing restrictions on capital shares and voting rights of foreign investors and strengthening the investigation power of competition authorities.
- Make schools and educational tracks more inclusive. Strengthen the early socialisation as well as language and cognitive development of children from disadvantaged backgrounds to improve their intergenerational education mobility.

Shifting to a more gender equal society

- Spur investment in high quality childcare facilities. Enhance the availability of full-day schools and care centres. Consider introducing legal entitlements for these services.
- Reduce the implicit taxation of transition from marginal and part-time to full-time employment and replace the sole-earner tax deduction by targeted transfers to families in need.
- Transform childcare allowance and parental leave schemes into a unique childcare account that allows parents to allocate subsidised absence from work flexibly over time. Reserve a sizeable part of this account, at least 33%, for the exclusive use of fathers.
- Raise awareness by publicising more information on innovations in study area choices of schoolgirls and schoolboys, earlier return to full-time work of mothers, and fathers' participation in care and household duties.
- Develop a comprehensive data base on social transfers or a comprehensive panel survey to assess the impact of alternative family policy schemes on labour supply, child care use and net budget costs, and adjust policy packages in the light of this information.
- The private sector should offer more family-friendly workplaces and more enabling working time options to employees of both genders. Policymakers should continue to support auditing and information campaigns to disseminate good practices.

Assessment and recommendations

- *The macroeconomic outlook is expected to improve after a prolonged period of weakness*
- *Towards a more robust economy*
- *Towards a more resilient economy*
- *Towards a more inclusive economy*
- *Towards a more environmentally sustainable economy*
- *Opening-up gender roles to improve well-being and growth*

Austria outperforms the OECD average in most well-being dimensions, but its relative position has weakened recently in some areas. Life satisfaction which used to be among the highest in the OECD, bolstered by particularly favourable outcomes for jobs and earnings, remains well-above OECD averages (Figure 1). A dense fabric of successful large and medium sized firms help attain a high level of GDP per capita, providing strong material foundations for individual and societal well-being and helping finance a generous social protection system. The environment is generally well preserved. However, air quality and the transition to a low-carbon society is undermined by the protection of energy intensive industries, urban sprawl, subsidies for car transport and fuel tourism. Housing conditions are also less favourable for certain groups. Perceptions about social connections, which used to be among the most positive in the OECD, have weakened relative to best performers.

Figure 1. **High material well-being and weaknesses in work-life balance**

Difference with respect to the OECD

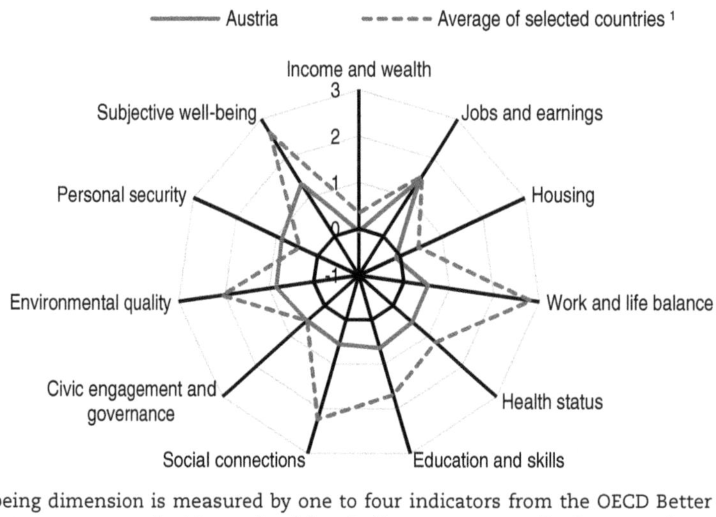

Note: Each well-being dimension is measured by one to four indicators from the OECD Better Life indicator set. Normalised indicators are averaged with equal weights. Indicators are normalised to range between 10 (best) and 0 according to the following formula: (indicator value - minimum value)/(maximum value – minimum value) multiplied by 10.

1. Selected countries are Denmark, Germany, the Netherlands, Sweden and Switzerland.

Source: OECD Better Life Index 2015.

StatLink http://dx.doi.org/10.1787/888933251881

The major well-being tensions, however, arise from poor work-life balances for men and women related to firmly entrenched separated gender roles. These typically emerge once the first child is born, with the fathers facing long working hours and women performing most of the unpaid household work. Health also exhibits strong gender patterns with women living considerably longer than men, though with relatively low self-reported health. The education system displays important gender-specific features and gaps, which weakens its overall performance, including in terms of adult skills.

Against this background, progress towards more gender equality would improve well-being through many different and important channels (Table 1). The potential for further improvement in education, labour market participation and earnings is particularly strong. A more gender-equal society would better mobilise the nation's talents and foster human capital. Better work-life balances and an increase in men's involvement in home care and home chores would facilitate child rearing decisions, in particular for well-educated women that, today, often have to choose between career and family.

Table 1. **Well-being implications of more gender equality**

Well-being dimensions	Outcomes	Channels
Education and skills	Increase in educational attainment	Open up educational tracks
	Improvement in intergenerational mobility	Open up educational tracks
	Better preservation and more diversification of skills	More post-formal education and on-the-job training for women
Jobs and earnings	Reduction of the gender pay gap	Reduction in structural asymmetries in the labour market
	More innovations	More gender diversity in managerial and entrepreneurial positions
	Creation of personal service sector jobs	Market supply of household services
	New work organisation challenges in enterprises	Reduction in hours worked by men
Income and wealth	Increase in family income	Stronger and more ambitious involvement of women in the labour market
	More financial independence for women	Higher earnings for women and a more even distribution of wealth
Health	Impact on women's health uncertain	Additional risks of stress for women, but also relief from care duties and less mental retirement
	Improvement in men's health	Fewer working hours for men and more time spent with the family
Work-life balance	Better work-life balance for both genders	Convergence in time spent on paid and unpaid work between genders
	Reduced strains at work and at home	Family-friendly work organisation and more formal childcare
	Improved child well-being, notably in vulnerable families	Stronger presence of father and better socialisation through kindergarten access
Life satisfaction	Realisation of broader life choices	Broader options for economic participation, earnings and family organisation
	Realisation of initial child rearing desires	Better reconciliation of child raising and professional aspirations

Long-term growth projections by the OECD suggest that stronger participation of women in the labour market, related improvements in human capital and the increase in fertility, could lift the country's potential output by about 13% by 2060. For comparison, pension and health expenditures are projected to increase by under 3% of GDP over the same horizon as a result of population ageing (European Commission, 2015). Stronger growth would generate more job creation opportunities for socially vulnerable groups, more resources for social cohesion policies, and would help secure the long-term sustainability of the well-developed health and pension systems. Additional fiscal costs of developing the necessary childcare infrastructure and full-day schooling can be expected to be more than recovered in the medium-term.

The gender equality agenda interacts with other policy priorities, such as overcoming socio-economic segregation due to the early streaming of students in the education system, better decision-making and resource allocation in the public sector through rationalisation in federal structures, and higher participation of immigrant children in early childhood education. Progress in these areas are top policy priorities which will help with strides in gender equality. Furthermore, gender policy goals affect different public institutions and levels and require a high degree of effective co-ordination. Stronger awareness across these agencies and levels on the potential of gender equality will facilitate action. High-quality monitoring and research on outcomes would help with efficient implementation. In this context, preserving options for all, including for those who consciously choose traditional roles, would help achieve consensus. At the same time, policy settings and care infrastructure bottlenecks should not restrict life choices – as they presently do- and should help open-up the separate roles model.

This survey reviews Austria's major structural challenges, including the transition to a more gender-equal society. In line with OECD's *New Approaches to Economic Challenges* (NAEC) initiative, it suggests measures to achieve stronger, sustainable and more inclusive growth. The 3 key messages are the following:

- Strengthen the fundamentals of the economy by completing the rehabilitation of the banking sector, fostering competition in services and reforming the intergovernmental fiscal framework.
- Further reduce the labour tax wedge. Increase effective retirement ages of both men and women and step up preparations for the convergence of the statutory retirement ages of male and female workers.
- Shift to a more gender-equal society by shifting to a tax-and-benefit system that encourages a more balanced distribution of work, providing more full-day schools and care centres, and sensitising the private sector for more family-friendly workplaces and working time models.

The macroeconomic outlook is expected to improve after a prolonged period of weakness

Economic activity has been very weak since the beginning of 2012 (Figure 2). Despite the increasing output gap and rising unemployment, inflation has been higher than in other euro area countries. Poor real disposable income growth has been partly offset by declining saving rates, helping to maintain consumption. Falling labour productivity, notably in services, has weakened international competitiveness and, despite real wages being still below pre-crisis levels, triggered substantial losses in export market shares and a decline in investment in the second half of 2014. Business and consumer confidence remained subdued despite the uptick of activity in the euro area in early 2015. In turn, bank lending growth has eased somewhat recently, but as lending standards have been stable in the past 12 months, this appears to reflect demand, rather than credit constraints.

Short-term macroeconomic prospects

The tax reform will boost private consumption despite some projected increase in the saving rate. External conditions have improved owing to stronger growth prospects in the euro area and price competitiveness gains *vis-à-vis* partners outside the euro area following the depreciation of the euro. In particular, the strong appreciation of the Swiss franc improves prospects for the Austrian tourism sector. In addition, the low real interest rate environment and the plunge in oil prices should strengthen domestic demand.

Figure 2. **Growth has stalled since 2012 and unemployment is rising**

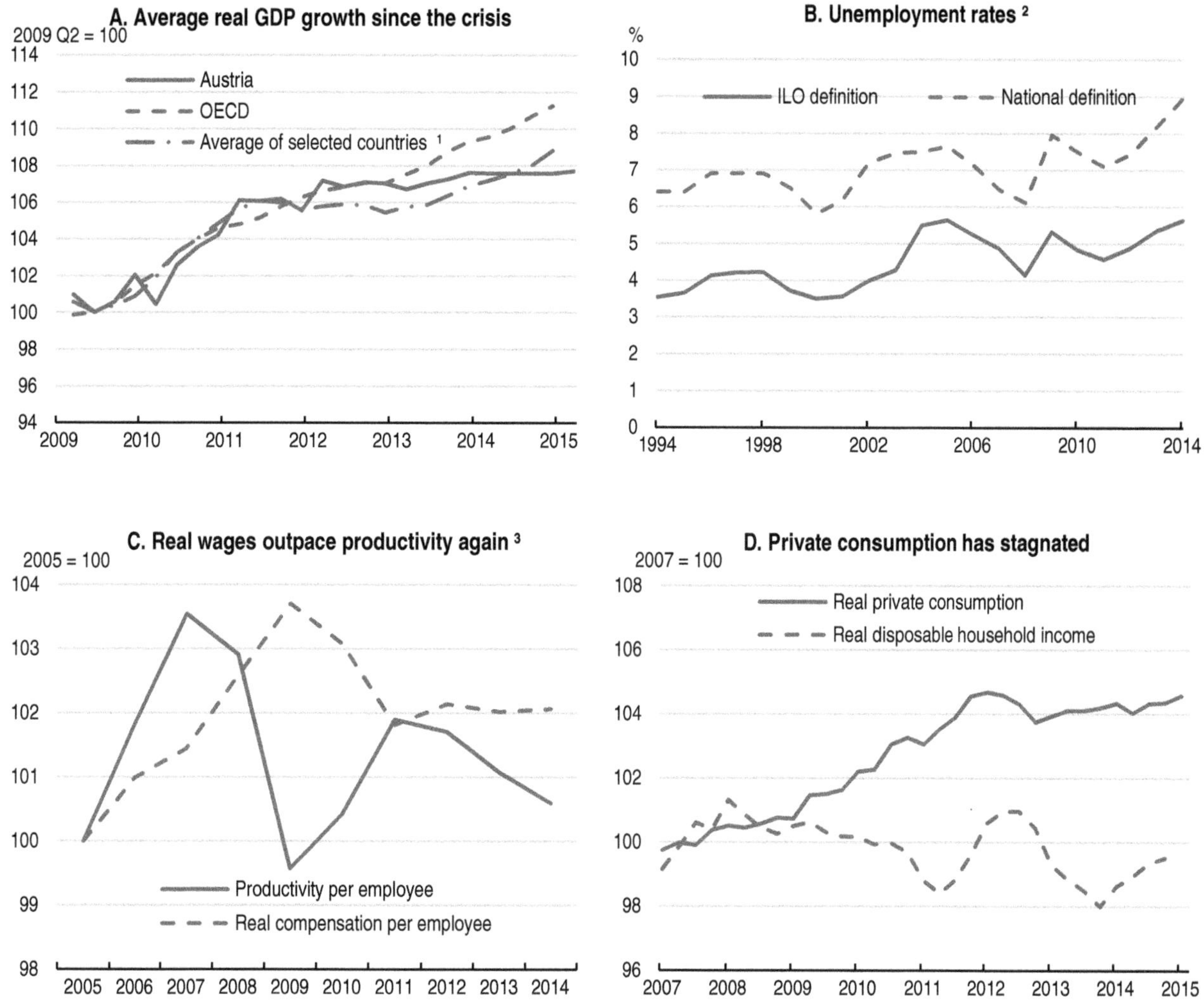

1. Denmark, Germany, the Netherlands, Sweden and Switzerland.
2. The ILO definition of unemployment is based on the labour force survey and comprises persons that are without work, currently available for work and seek work. The national definition of unemployment is based on registered unemployed persons.
3. Labour productivity and compensation per dependent employee in total economy. Real compensation is obtained as compensation divided by the private consumption deflator.

Source: *OECD Economic Outlook database*; Statistik Austria.

StatLink http://dx.doi.org/10.1787/888933251895

GDP growth is projected to increase gradually over the projection period driven by a pick-up in export and investment with an additional boost provided by private consumption (Table 2). Risks to this projection are balanced. If cost pressures increase further, Austria's exporters may benefit less than projected from the weakness of the euro. Uncertainty about bank balance sheet impairments also remains (see below). If this channel explains more of the current sluggishness of investment and consumer confidence than assumed, growth may prove more subdued than projected. On the other hand and on the upside, the tax reform could boost private consumption more if saving rates pick up less than expected. Second-round effects on employment and investment may also be stronger than anticipated. Finally, export performance may be stronger than projected if lost market shares are regained more swiftly.

Table 2. **Short-term Economic Outlook**

	2011	2012	2013	2014	2015	2016
	Current prices (EUR billion)	Percentage changes, volume (2010 prices)				
GDP at market prices[1]	308.7	1.0	0.1	0.4	0.6	1.7
Private consumption	165.6	0.6	-0.2	0.2	0.8	1.8
Government consumption	61.2	0.3	0.4	1.0	1.0	-0.6
Gross fixed capital formation	69.6	0.6	-1.4	0.4	-1.9	2.5
Final domestic demand	296.3	0.5	-0.4	0.4	0.2	1.5
Stockbuilding[2]	4.5	-0.1	-0.7	-0.2	0.5	-0.1
Total domestic demand	300.7	0.4	-1.0	0.2	0.7	1.3
Exports of goods and services	165.7	1.4	1.3	1.8	3.3	5.9
Imports of goods and services	157.7	0.8	-0.2	2.5	4.2	5.4
Net exports[2]	7.9	0.4	0.8	-0.2	-0.3	0.5
Memorandum items:						
GDP deflator	-	1.8	1.5	1.7	1.1	1.5
Harmonised index of consumer prices	-	2.6	2.1	1.5	0.6	1.6
Private consumption deflator	-	2.4	2.2	1.7	0.9	1.6
Unemployment rate[3]	-	4.9	5.4	5.7	5.8	5.7
Household saving ratio, net[4]	-	9.0	7.3	7.5	7.7	8.7
General government financial balance[5]	-	-2.2	-1.3	-2.4	-2.3	-2.1
General government gross debt[5]	-	96.7	95.1	96.3	97.6	97.8
General government debt, Maastricht definition[5]	-	81.4	80.9	84.5	85.7	85.9
Current account balance[5]	-	1.5	0.9	0.8	0.9	1.4

1. Based on seasonal and working-day adjusted quarterly data; may differ from official non-working-day adjusted annual data.
2. Contributions to changes in real GDP, actual amount in the first column.
3. Based on Labour Force Survey data.
4. As a percentage of disposable income.
5. As a percentage of GDP at market value.

Source: OECD Economic Outlook 97 database.

Towards a more robust economy

Reform the tax system to make it more growth-friendly

Austria exhibits one of the highest labour tax wedges in the OECD, in particular at lower incomes (Köppl and Schratzenstaller, 2015). Against this background, the Austrian government agreed upon a wide-ranging tax reform that will enter into force on 1 January 2016. The reform's main purpose is a sizeable reduction of income tax rates for low and medium income brackets (Figure 3, Panel A). The total tax relief amounts to EUR 5 billion and will boost disposable income by about 2.5% in 2016. While this will certainly buttress consumption in the short term, the labour tax wedge remains one of the highest in the OECD mainly owing to the size of social security contributions (Figure 3, Panel B). Also, the threshold effect that occurs at around EUR 13 000 with the transition from the income tax free zone to the first income bracket remains sizeable (Figure 3, Panel A). Therefore, additional steps to shift taxes further away from labour towards sources less detrimental to growth, such as consumption, environmental or property taxes, would broaden the revenue base and support currently weak employment growth.

Boost competitiveness, particularly in the service sector

Competitiveness has come under pressure. Unit labour costs have been on the rise and export prices increased by 1% over 2013-14, even as comparable prices in Austria's export markets declined by some 3%. Unit labour costs were mainly driven by productivity losses

Figure 3. **Tax reform was significant but the tax wedge at low-incomes remains high**

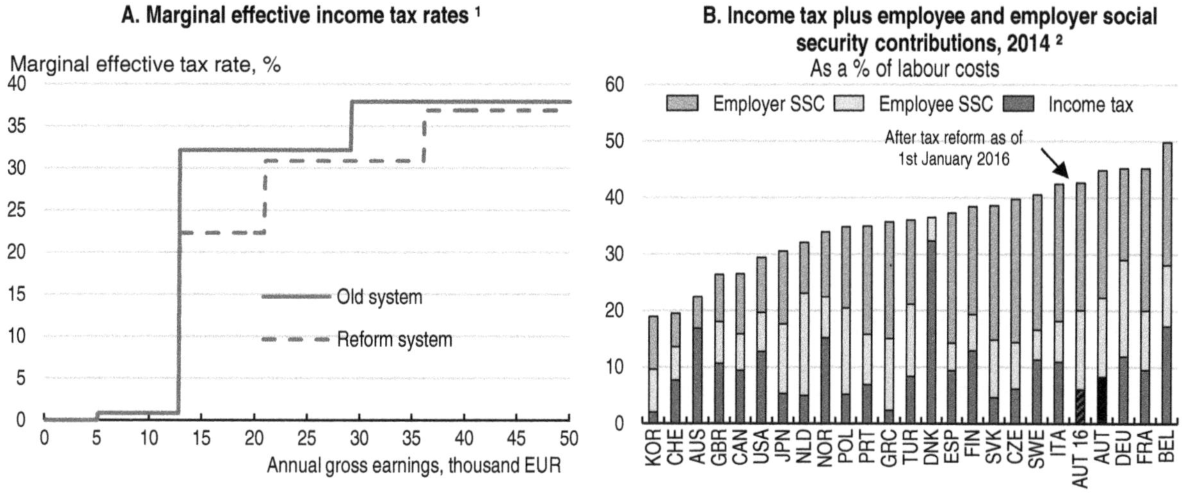

1. Marginal effective tax rates are shown. Annual earnings typically are paid out as 12 regularly monthly instalments and 2 additional bonus and holiday payments. The conducted tax reform will modify the tax rates for the 12 monthly instalments but not the tax rates of bonus and holiday instalments. Effective tax rates are obtained by decomposing annual earnings into 14 equal payments, 12 of which are taxed according to the regular tax scheme and 2 of which are taxed according to the bonus and holiday income tax scheme.
2. Single individual without children at the 67% income level of the average worker. Includes payroll taxes where applicable.

Source: Calculations based on marginal rates on regular instalments as of April 2015 as communicated by the Austrian government; and OECD, *Taxing Wages database*.

StatLink http://dx.doi.org/10.1787/888933251908

Box 1. **The 2015/16 tax reform**

In March 2015, the government agreed upon a wide-ranging tax reform that is expected to be legislated by mid-2015 and will enter into force on 1 January 2016. Public consultation is still ongoing and the parliamentarian process has not started yet. The most prominent of the measures planned is a reduction of lowest income bracket tax rate by 11.5 percentage points from 36.5% to 25%. Earners with income below the first income bracket, who do not pay income taxes, will be eligible for a reimbursement of half of their social security contributions, up to EUR 400 per year. Pensioners will benefit from a similar provision, but limited to EUR 110 annually. Child allowances are to rise from EUR 220 to EUR 440 annually. Finally, in order to finance certain research and education investment projects, a new top tax rate of 55% for income above EUR 1 million will be in force for five years. Tax deductions for employees investing in their companies' shares will increase from EUR 1 460 to EUR 3 000 per year.

Tax increases are foreseen in the area of capital gains taxes (all capital gains taxes except on general savings accounts are increased from 25 to 27.5%), value added tax (for various products and services subject to a reduced rate, the tax rate will be raised in direction of the normal rate), tax on capital gains from property sales (a rate increase from 25 to 30% is foreseen) and by reducing the general depreciation rates for buildings. Furthermore, an environmentally motivated tax disincentive for company cars emitting more than 120 g/km CO_2 (value decreasing over time) is planned.

The government estimates that this reform will have a fiscal cost of more than EUR 5 billion, but expects it to be fully financed. It is assumed that the stimulating effect of the package on economic activity will raise EUR 850 million in revenues; that measures to fight tax fraud will raise EUR 1.9 billion; and that various tax increases will raise EUR 1.15 billion. Cost reductions in the public administration are expected to produce savings of EUR 1.1 billion.

while real wages remained robust. Despite strong non-price competitiveness underpinned by a highly innovative and diversified manufacturing sector, Austria's exporters have lost more than 5% of their market share since 2012 (Figure 4). Measured in nominal terms, Austria lost 3.3 percentage points of market share on its most important export market, Germany (OeNB, 2015). Preserving competitiveness and further consolidating positions in global value chains (GVCs) will be essential in maintaining the export sector as a growth engine of the Austrian economy over the medium term.

Figure 4. **Export performance undermined by unit labour cost pressure**

Indices, Q1 2012 = 100

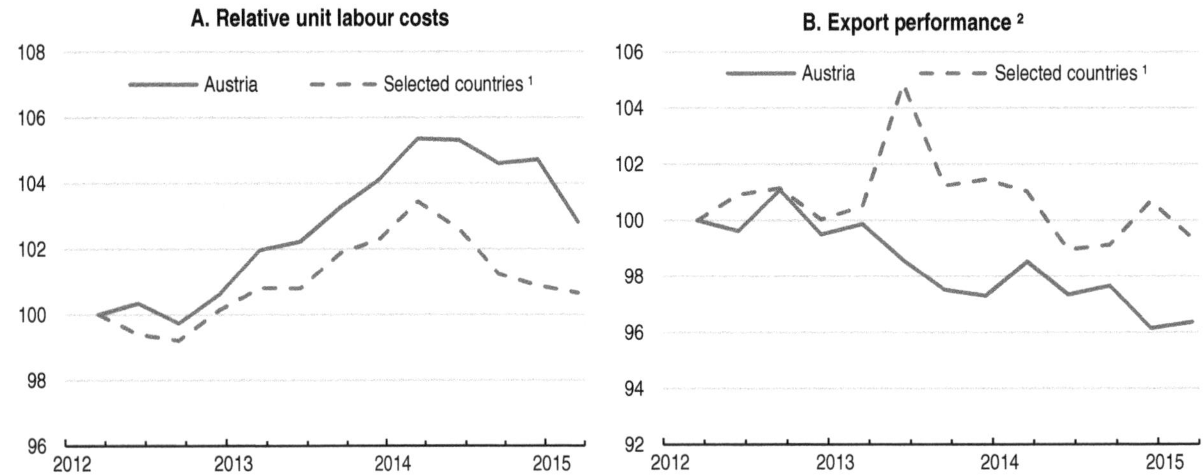

1. Selected countries are Denmark, Germany, the Netherlands, Sweden and Switzerland.
2. Export performance is measured as actual growth in exports relative to the growth of the country's export market.

Source: OECD Economic Outlook database.

StatLink http://dx.doi.org/10.1787/888933251911

Services play a key role for global value chains. They account for almost 30% of Austria's gross exports and for almost 50% of the value-added in exports, underpinning the importance of strong domestic services that can provide cost-efficient intermediate inputs and facilitate the diffusion of new technologies (OECD, 2015b). While Austria has made impressive progress in deregulating product markets (Figure 5, Panel A), regulations for certain services, in particular entry regulations, are still among the most stringent in the OECD (Figure 5, Panel B). Limitations to competition in incumbent-dominated services (Figure 5, Panel C), such as retail trade, hamper labour productivity and could partly explain the downward rigidity of prices: nearly three quarters of the inflation differential with respect to the euro area and Germany can be ascribed to services. In certain sectors such as legal services, accounting and broadcasting, caps on capital shares and voting rights make entry for foreign competitors more difficult. A more dynamic service sector would open new opportunities for entrepreneurs, strengthen economic growth, and help with job creation and social cohesion. More proactive competition advocacy in services by the competition authority would provide additional stimulus (Figure 5, Panel D).

Increase the financing capacity of the real economy

Investment rates of Austrian companies have declined recently albeit from high levels in international comparison. The share of intellectual property investment has risen markedly after the crisis and has partly offset declines in the share of business

Figure 5. **Service sector regulations should be eased**

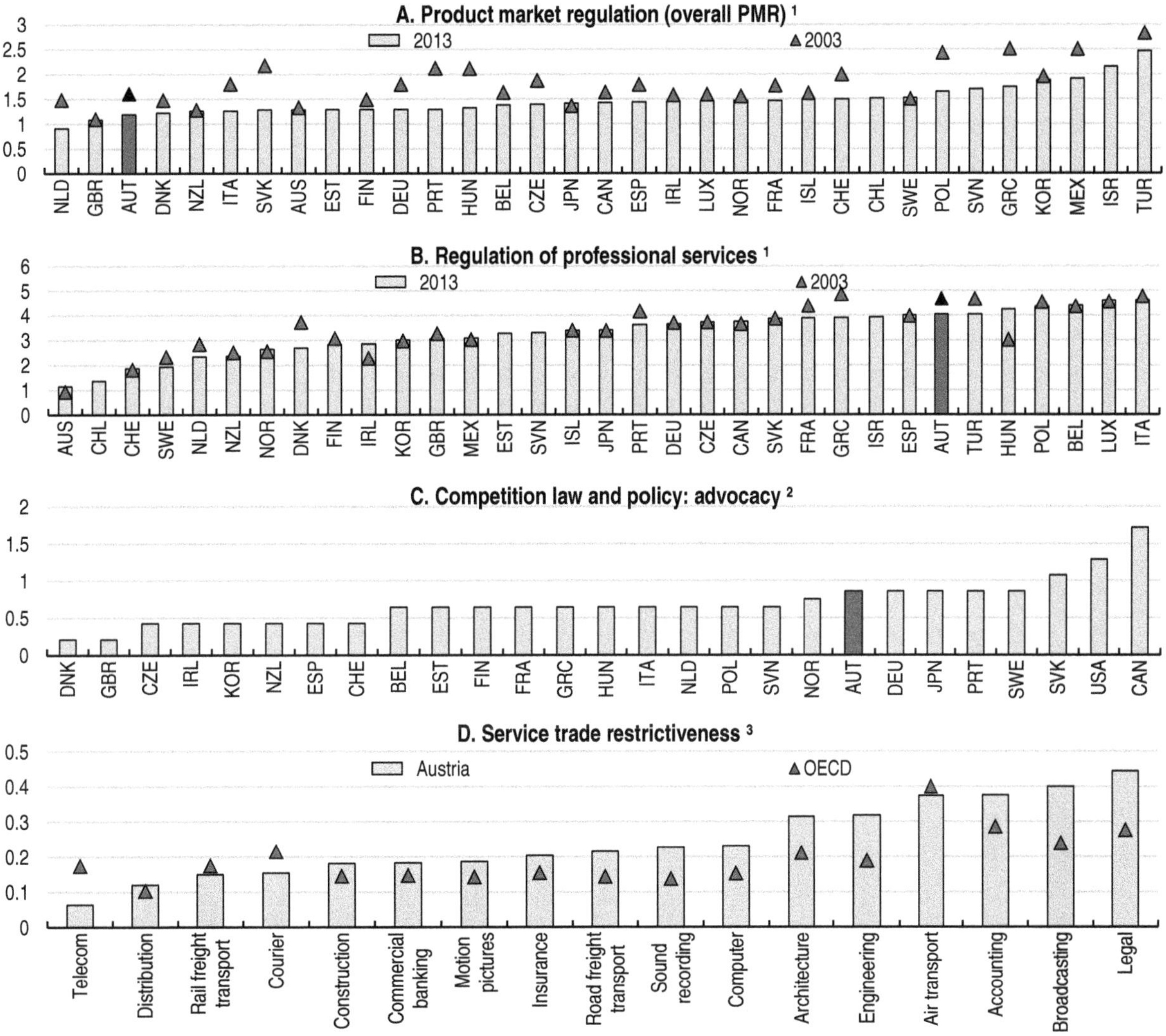

1. Index, scale 0-6 from least to most restrictive.
2. Index in 2013, scale 0-6 from the most to the least conductive to competition.
3. STRI indices take values from 0 to 1, where 0 is completely open and 1 completely closed.

Source: OECD, *Product Market Regulation database, www.oecd.org/economy/pmr* and *Regulatory Database for Services Trade Restrictiveness, www.oecd.org/tad/services-trade/regulatory-database-services-trade-restrictiveness-index.htm.*

StatLink http://dx.doi.org/10.1787/888933251925

investments in buildings, structures and ICT equipment. Despite progress over the past 10 years, Austrian SMEs still have very low equity ratios compared to other European countries (OeNB, 2014). The recent development of bond markets for medium-sized firms heralds a welcome diversification toward market sources. Government initiatives towards the support of venture capital and crowdfunding have the potential to boost entrepreneurship and business investment. These initiatives should be carefully monitored and evaluated to provide insights for future policies.

Towards a more resilient economy

Controlling the rise in public debt through pension reforms and adjustments in fiscal federalism

Public debt is considerably higher than in other small open advanced European economies and Germany (Figure 6, Panel A). It has also risen more since 2008, mainly driven by participation capital and liquidity boosting funds provided to Austrian banks, three of which have been nationalised and are being wound down. Fiscal consolidation efforts and strong post-crisis growth brought down the general government deficit from 5.3% in 2009 to 1.5% of GDP in 2013, and Austria exited the excessive deficit procedure in spring 2014. However, in 2014, the general government deficit widened again to 2.4% of GDP owing to outlays for the restructuring of Hypo Group Alpe Adria (a mid-sized provincial mortgage institution which had expanded into the Balkans), weak economic environment, and failure to fully implement legislated spending cuts. Indeed, expenditure targets in successive Stability Programmes (SP) have been constantly revised upwards (Figure 6, Panel B). The 2015 SP projects total expenditures of 51.2% of GDP in 2016, against 50.0% in the 2014 SP and 48.9% projected in the 2013 SP. The revision mainly stems from overshooting in social transfers, the compensation of government employees and intermediate consumption.

Figure 6. **Public debt continues to rise as expenditures turn out to be higher than expected**

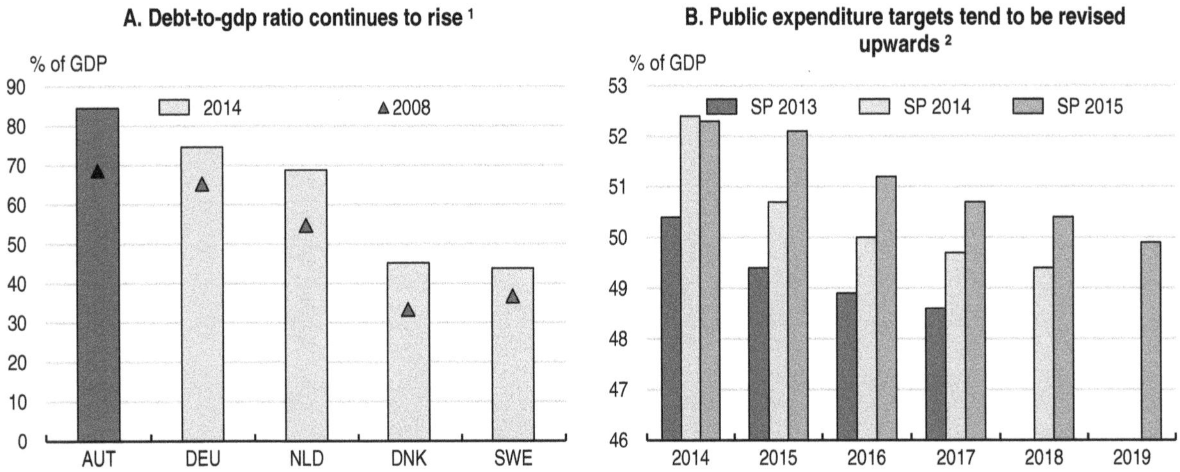

1. Gross public debt, Maastricht definition, in percentage of GDP.
2. Total general government expenditures in percentage of GDP. SP refers to "Stability Programme".

Source: OECD *Economic Outlook database* and European Commission.

StatLink http://dx.doi.org/10.1787/888933251930

In particular, the effective retirement age is increasing only very slowly (Figure 7), calling for a swifter removal of early retirement schemes and substantive preparations for the planned increase in women's retirement age. Currently age related differences in employment protection for men and women hamper a voluntary prolongation of working lives for women by phasing out employment protection at statutory retirement age (OECD, 2005). Consideration should be given to align age related employment protection to ease the convergence of male and female retirement ages. One option to ensure longer-run cost control would be to link the parameters of the pension system more directly to life expectancy. Long-term projections by the European Commission imply that total

Figure 7. **Senior workers' employment has improved but average age of withdrawal remains low**

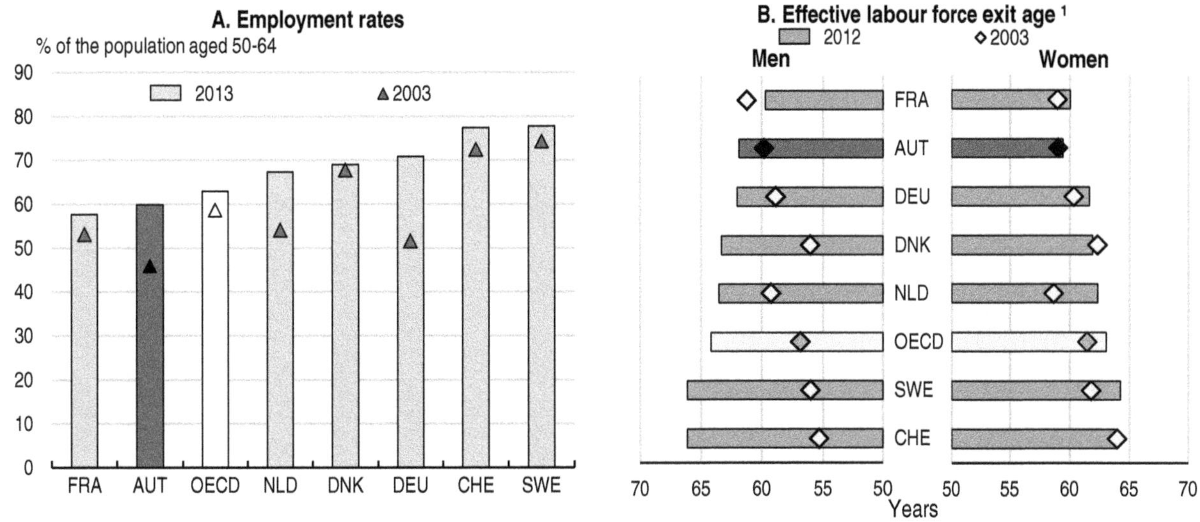

1. Effective exit age over the five-year periods 1998-2003 and 2007-12. The effective exit age (also called the effective age of retirement) is calculated as weighted average of the exit ages of each five-year age cohort, starting with the cohort aged 40-44 at the first date, using absolute changes in the labour force participation rate of each cohort as weights.

Source: OECD, *Labour Force Statistics database*; and OECD estimations based on data from national labour force surveys and from OECD *Education database*.

StatLink http://dx.doi.org/10.1787/888933251947

pension spending will increase from 13.9% of GDP in 2013 to 14.4% of GDP in 2060 (European Commission, 2015). The government defined a target path and timetable for increasing the rate of employment of older persons and their effective retirement age until 2018, and agreed on new measures to this end. According to the envisaged path, the rate of employment of men aged 55-59 is to be raised from 68.1% in 2012 to 74.6% in 2018, and that of men aged 60-64 from 21.6% in 2012 to 35.3% in 2018. The rate of employment of women aged 55-59 is to be raised from 47.9% to 62.9% and their actual retirement age from 58.4 to 60.1 years. Convergence to these targets will reviewed by a semi-annual pension monitoring programme, and immediate, binding measures will be taken if significant deviations occur.

Curbing public expenditures is hard given Austria's intergovernmental framework. The existing multi-layer organisation of the government makes decision making difficult in many areas, including key service sectors. This creates inequalities between residents living in different parts of the country and inflates costs. Reforms to streamline service responsibilities at different levels have long been on the cards but limited progress was achieved so far. In particular, the present framework suffers from a misalignment between spending and tax attributions (Austrian Fiscal Advisory Council, 2014). Intergovernmental grants and tax-sharing are the main revenue sources of sub-central governments while their share of own taxes is among the lowest in the OECD (Figure 8, Panel A). The resulting vertical imbalances soften the budget constraints of local and state governments and also explain the exceptionally high level of guarantees issued by subnational governments (Figure 8, Panels C and D), which may be seen as implicitly guaranteed by the federal government, further weakening budget constraints. These guarantees are provided to financial institutions, especially public ones and have fuelled excessive risk-taking at some *Länder*-controlled banks.

Figure 8. **Weak tax autonomy of sub-central governments and fragmentation undermine fiscal discipline**

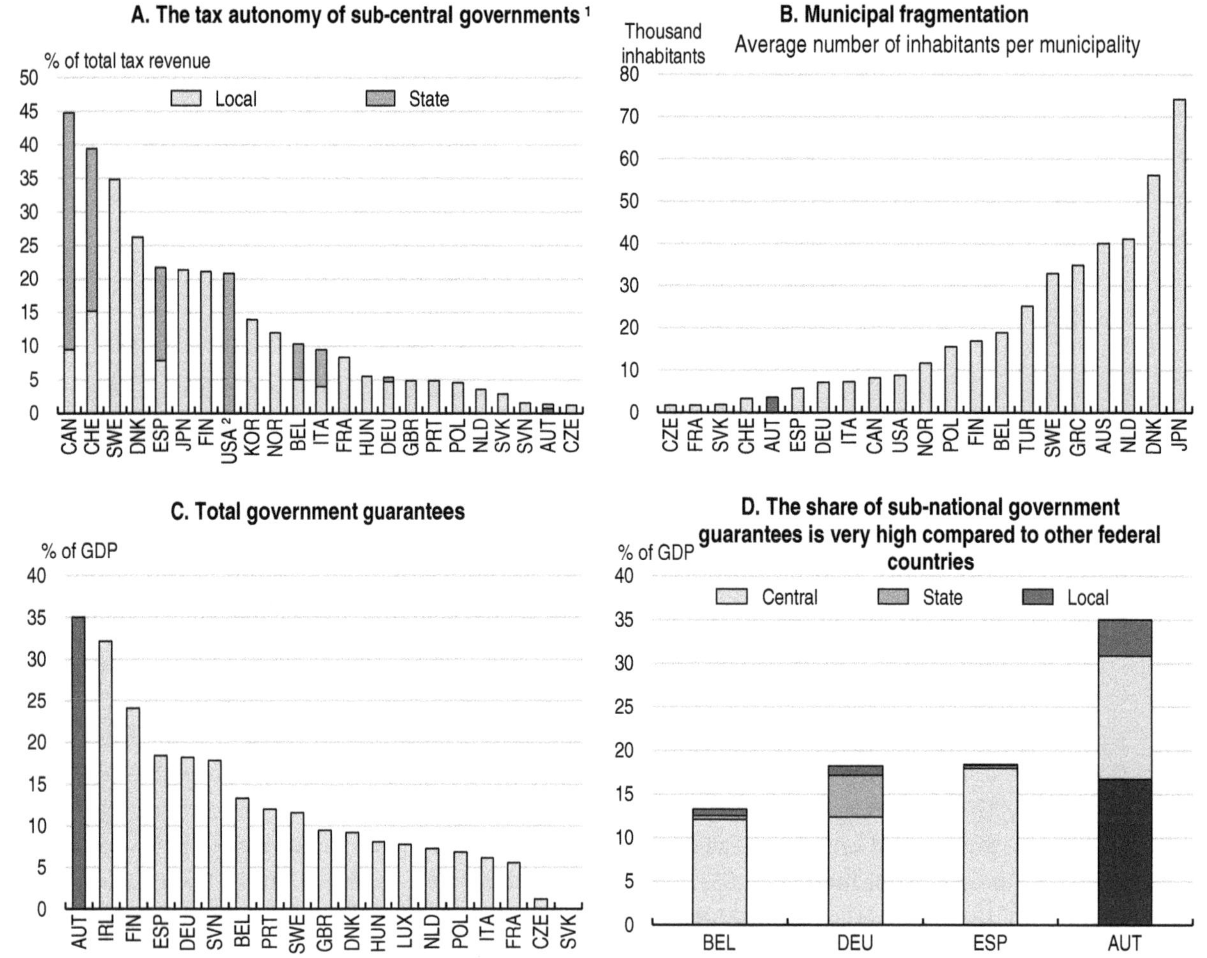

1. Taxes where sub-central governments have power to set the tax base and/or tax rates, 2011.
2. Local governments in the United States have a wide variety of taxing powers but it is not possible to identify the share of each.

Source: OECD Fiscal Decentralisation database; OECD (2013), *Subnational Governments in OECD Countries: Key Data* (brochure), *www.oecd.org/regional/regional-policy*; and Eurostat.

StatLink http://dx.doi.org/10.1787/888933251954

The large number of small municipalities (Figure 8, Panel B) reduces spending efficiency further by limiting the scope for economies of scale in the provision of public services. In this regard, the recent reform in Styria, which halved the number of municipalities and raised their average population from 1 750 to 3 300 inhabitants, is encouraging. Overall, the average municipality in Austria has still only 3 600 inhabitants against 9 100 in the OECD. Austria could rely on international best practices, such as the successful municipal merger programme implemented in Denmark, and encourage mergers through financial and advisory assistance. In 2011, the government approved the Austrian Internal Stability Pact that includes expenditure ceilings and structural deficit limits at all government levels from 2017 onwards. If duly implemented, this reform has the potential to reduce overspending.

Enhancing financial stability

Like a number of other small open economies, Austria has a large banking sector relative to the size of its economy. Intense competition and low profit margins in the domestic market have pushed major banks to expand abroad, in particular in Central, Eastern and South-Eastern Europe (CESEE), where subsidiaries long delivered large profits, but also took high credit, exchange rate and geopolitical risks. The banking sector was hard hit as these risks materialised during and after the global crisis. Non-performing loans increased sharply and the government had to provide substantial financial support to three of the major banks. The ongoing rehabilitation of the financial sector weighs on public finances and limits the room for public policy initiatives to back growth and social cohesion.

The financial supervisors, the Austrian National Bank and the Financial Market Authority responded. From 1 July 2016, large banks will have to hold additional capital buffers according to their business model and risk exposure, and new lending of subsidiaries will be closely monitored to make sure that local lending activities are in line with local refinancing. Austria also transformed the EU Bank Recovery and Resolution Directive into national law on 1 January 2015 which, in particular, provides for bailing-in bank shareholders and bond holders. The Austrian authorities imposed a moratorium on all principal and interest payments by HETA Asset Resolution, a bad bank created as part of the winding-up process of the former Hypo Alpe Adria. This has reduced expectations of implicit federal government guarantees (Schich and Aydin, 2014) and should help to settle banks' funding costs at non-subsidised, market-based levels. According to OeNB (2014), reduced funding costs due to implicit federal government guarantees accounted for between 25% and 40% of Austrian banks' profits in 2006-13.

Exposure to some more volatile Central European and South-Eastern European (CESEE) countries has already been reduced and exposure to more stable ones has risen (Table 3). The Vienna Initiative 2, which brings together key international financial institutions, relevant EU institutions and the principal cross-border banking groups to ensure the orderly deleveraging process of CESEE banks, will also help to restore trust and to stabilise the sector in Austria.

Table 3. **Claims of Austrian banks on CESEE countries**

	EUR billion in 2014	% change since 2011	% share in 2014	% share in 2011
Czech Republic	45.4	-20	15.2	14.1
Romania	26.1	-18	8.8	8.0
Slovak Republic	25.5	3	8.5	6.4
Croatia	20.0	-34	6.7	6.9
Poland	16.6	28	5.6	3.1
Hungary	16.2	-71	5.4	7.2
CESEE-6	***154.8***	***-14***	***50.2***	***45.7***
Russia	12.1	-1	4.1	3.2
Ukraine	2.8	-61	0.9	1.8
Total foreign claims	**298.2**	**-30**	**100.0**	**100.0**

Note: CESEE-6 denote the Czech Republic, Romania, the Slovak Republic, Croatia, Poland and Hungary.
Source: BIS. Consolidated foreign claims of Austrian banks, immediate borrower basis, yearly averages of quarters.

The share of variable-rate loans is considerably larger in Austria than in other euro area countries and has increased further recently. This would make households more vulnerable to interest rate increases. In addition, a considerable, though declining, share of loans is still denominated in foreign currencies. Currency risk recently materialised with the sharp appreciation of the Swiss franc. Austrian bank supervisors should continue to curb foreign exchange rate lending to largely unhedged households and SMEs. In this regard, it is welcome that Austria is currently one of the few countries to fully comply with the seven European Systemic Risk Board recommendations on lending in foreign currencies.

All large Austrian banks (except for OeVAG, which is to be wound down) passed the ECB stress test in fall 2014. Nevertheless, Austrian banks have the lowest operating profit ratios in the European Union, due to high provisions and impairments (Figure 9, Panel A). Despite improvements in recent years, their risk-weighted capitalisation still lags behind comparable European banks, due to more risky exposures, in particular in CESEE countries (Figure 9, Panel B). An intensification of geopolitical tensions would raise their risk still further. Cost pressures are also a problem. Cost-to-income ratios are considerably higher than in other countries. A defragmentation of the large net of units in the co-operative sector would yield economies of scale and reduce operating costs. As a first welcome step, the currently more than forty primary institutions of the Volksbank-sector are to be merged into eight regional and two specialised banks.

Figure 9. **Low profitability and capital ratios**

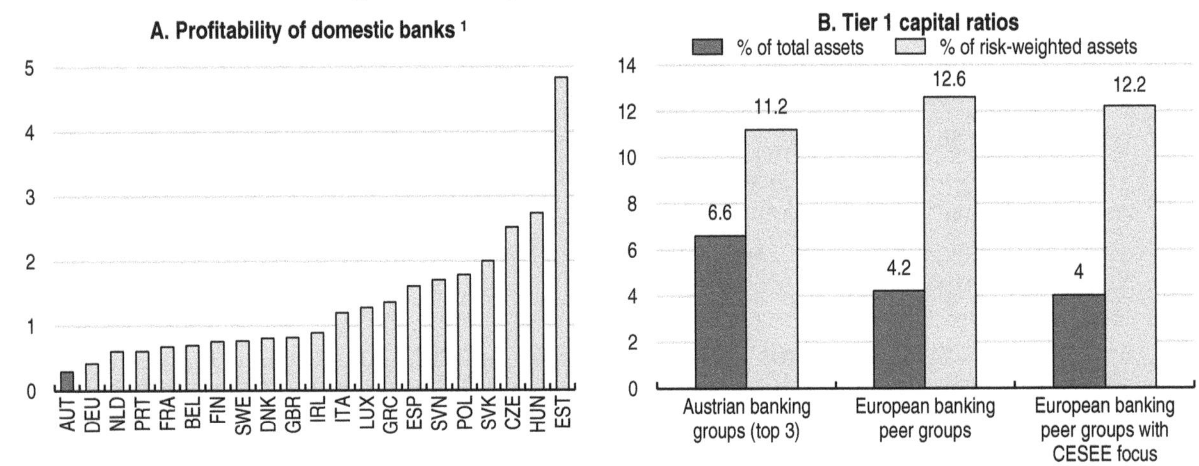

1. Operating profits as a percentage share of total assets.
Source: OeNB. Reference period is between end-June 2013 and end-June 2014.

StatLink http://dx.doi.org/10.1787/888933251961

Towards a more inclusive economy

A pillar of Austria's high living standards and well-being is the quality of its social networks. Strong family structures and a prominent role for community life provide extensive local social support (OECD, 2013a). Eighty-nine per cent of Austrians report that they could count on relatives or friends in case of trouble, putting Austria above OECD average in the "community" well-being dimension of the OECD Better Life Index (Figure 10, Panel A). Another backbone of social cohesion is low income inequality and a strong perception of fairness. The Gini coefficient, a measure of inequality of disposable incomes, is among the lowest and redistribution is among the largest in OECD countries

Figure 10. **Social cohesion**

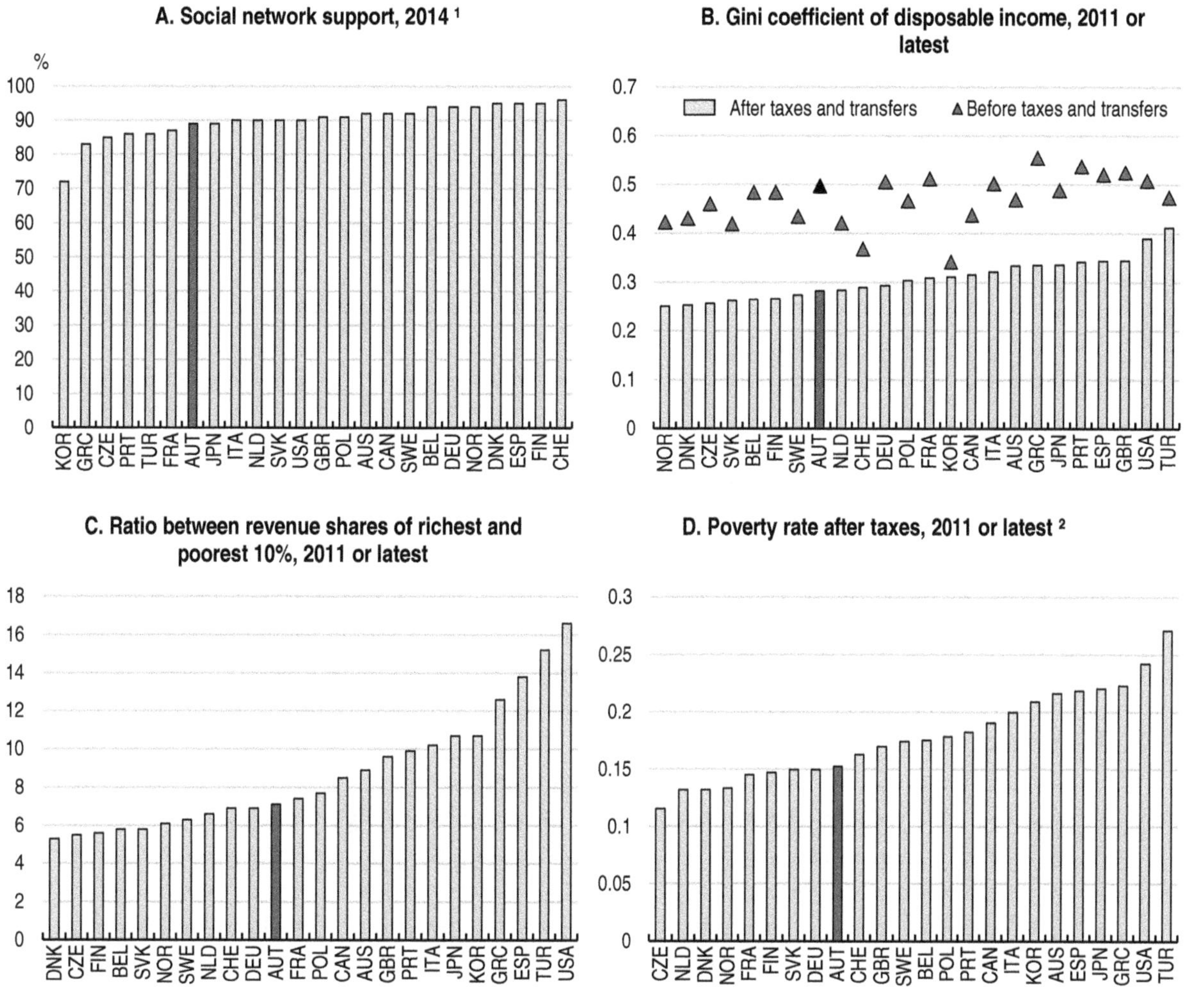

1. Percentage of people reporting that they could count on relatives or friends in case of need. The reference year is 2014 for all countries with the exception of 2013 for Japan, Korea, Norway, Switzerland, and the United States.
2. The poverty rate is the ratio of the number of people who fall below the poverty line which is set at 60% of median household income.

Source: OECD Better Life Index and *OECD Income Distribution and Poverty database.*

StatLink http://dx.doi.org/10.1787/888933251972

(Figure 10, Panel B). Revenue shares of the richest and poorest (Figure 10, Panel C) and relative poverty rates (Figure 10, Panel D) further illustrate Austria's strong commitment to equity.

Promote labour integration of low-skilled workers

Recent labour market developments have tended to reduce social cohesion. Inactivity and unemployment have increased. Low-skilled workers have been affected more than higher-skilled ones, and men more than women. Both developments are more pronounced for immigrants, which underlines the importance of improving their social inclusion through upskilling and greater labour force participation (Figure 11). Further measures should promote the labour market integration of low-skilled groups. Additional tax cuts and social security reductions for low-income earners (on top of those introduced with the 2015 tax reform) would stimulate labour supply and demand. Additional in-work benefits may be

Figure 11. **Unemployment rates by level of education, sex and family background**

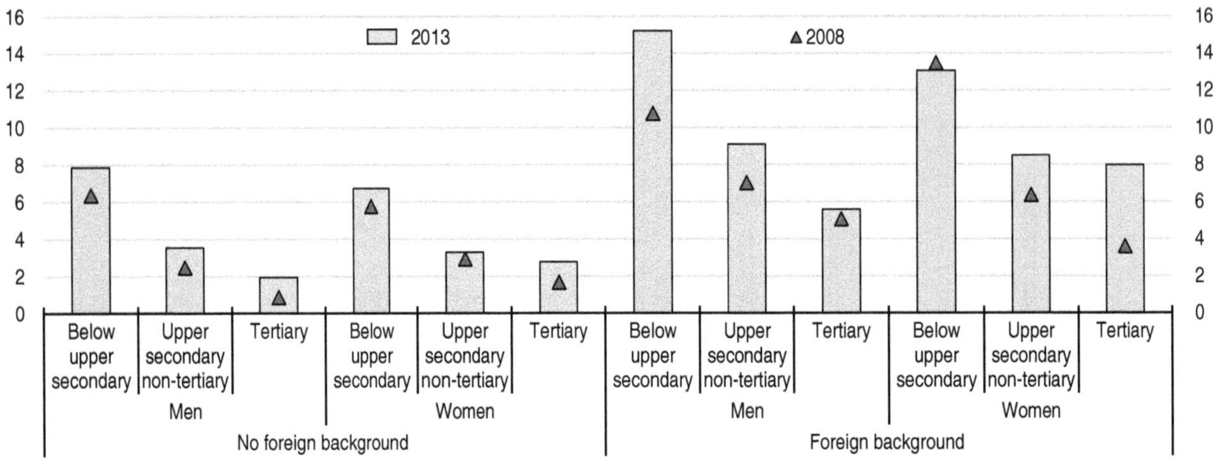

Note: An individual with a foreign background has both parents born abroad.
Source: Statistik Austria, Microcensus.

StatLink http://dx.doi.org/10.1787/888933251983

considered as in other OECD countries. Concurrently, work availability requirements combined with up-skilling schemes should continue to be actively implemented for the recipients of social transfers to back their attachment to the labour market.

Better integrate migrants

According to survey results, trust in people and the perception of solidarity and helpfulness have weakened somewhat, albeit from relatively high values (Bertelsmann, 2014). Austria's overall ranking in social cohesion is still high, but the acceptance of diversity has weakened over the past 10 years. This notably seems to hint at tensions with respect to the integration of immigrants. The Austrian government has launched several initiatives to attract foreign workers amid low fertility and growing shortages of skilled labour. In 2011, the Red-White-Red (the Austrian national colours) and EU blue cards have been introduced, both with the view to facilitate immigration.

Austria has one of the largest population groups with immigrant origin among OECD countries. Education and labour market characteristics of some of these groups are clearly weaker than those of native Austrians. These exhibit lower levels of skills, lower employment rates and higher unemployment rates. Recent PISA results indicate that the Austrian school system tends to perpetuate differences of educational outcomes between socio-economic groups across generations. In particular, the socio-economic characteristics of students attending the same school are less diverse than in most other OECD countries. This hinders the educational mobility of immigrant groups with weak human capital.

To better integrate immigrants and head off socio-economic tensions, policies to increase the inflow of skilled workers (OECD, 2014) should be flanked by targeted measures improving the educational and labour market outcomes of previous waves of immigrants. Opening up all educational tracks to disadvantaged groups and making schools more inclusive would foster social inclusion. Opening social partnership platforms to immigrants to enhance their awareness and ability to support their children's health, education and other needs may also help (OECD, 2013a). A critical step in this regard would be to increase the participation of immigrant children in early childhood education before the compulsory pre-school age of five. Enrolment is currently very low for certain groups, and increasing it would help with the early socialisation and language development of children, as well as the labour market participation of their mothers.

Towards a more environmentally sustainable economy

The quality of natural assets contributes importantly to Austria's well-being and attractiveness. Most environmental indicators are good. Water quality is very high and Austria's system for identifying hazardous chemicals to be included in the REACH (Regulation on Registration, Evaluation, Authorisation and Restriction of Chemicals) system is a model for other countries (OECD, 2013c). There are nevertheless areas of concern. Increased commuting and heavy freight traffic, mainly transit traffic, contribute to a relatively high concentration of particulate matter in the air in some areas. They also result in high greenhouse gas (GHG) emissions (Figure 12). While Austria is currently on

Figure 12. **Road transport weighs on CO_2 emissions**

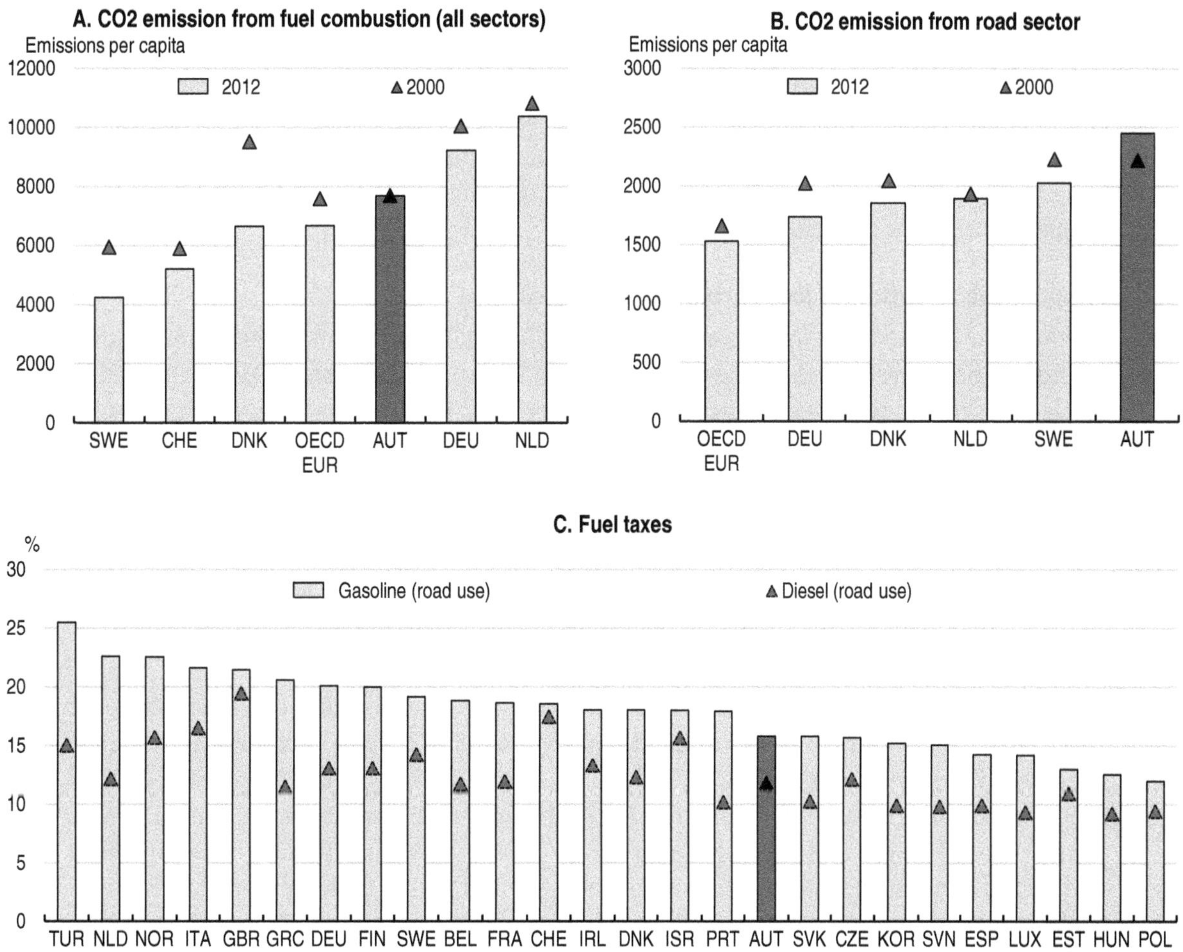

Source: OECD, *Energy database*; OECD (2013), *Taxing Energy Use: A Graphical Analysis*, OECD Publishing, Paris, *http://dx.doi.org/10.1787/9789264183933-en.*

StatLink *http://dx.doi.org/10.1787/888933251993*

track to meet its renewable energy target of 34% by 2020 (renewable energy already supplied more than 30% of final energy consumption in 2012 and slightly less than 30% of primary energy supply in 2013) it is projected to miss its GHG emission target by as much as 7%, mainly because of the transport sector. Nevertheless, Austria remains committed to honor its European Union climate change mitigation obligations.

Remove adverse incentives

Low fuel taxes (Figure 12, Panel C) encourage fuel use and, in particular, fuel tourism. Fuel exports – measured as the difference between domestic fuel sales and domestic fuel consumption – accounted for 30% of total GHG emissions in 2012. The CO_2 emissions from fuel tourism need to be offset by the purchase of carbon credits. As credits have been cheaper than the corresponding fuel taxes, Austria in effect gains by arbitraging the inconsistent carbon pricing at European level. The authorities should consider whether these gains are worth the local deterioration in air quality due to additional particulate matter.

The government could also remove other adverse incentives in the transport sector, notably tax breaks for company cars and commuting costs. Tax incentives for company cars will be reduced from 2016 onwards. Motivated partly by the idea of compensating workers for costs outside their control, these subsidies in effect encourage private car use, long-distance commuting and urban sprawl, to which housing subsidies also contribute (OECD, 2013c). This compounds the initial problem, increases fuel consumption and GHG emissions, as well as emissions of local air pollutants, and generates greater noise, congestion and risk of accidents.

Support the adoption of low carbon technologies

Austria has already made good progress in phasing out some fossil-fuel related subsidies and many tax reliefs have been allowed to expire. The most relevant remaining one is a tax refund for energy-intensive industries. Next to transport, heavy industries, in particular steel and cement production are still major and growing sources of GHG emissions. To protect these industries and maintain their viability, the government should refocus its intervention from low taxation to support for the adoption of low carbon technologies. Until GHG emissions in these industries face a reasonable price, however, take-up of low carbon technologies, which will be necessary to meet Austria's longer-term commitments, will remain low. The government has plans to give the energy sector a stronger role within its strategy on research, technology and innovation.

Austria has been the third-largest buyer of carbon credits under the Kyoto Protocol (after Japan and Spain), buying up to 71.4 million tons of CO_2-equivalent (Mt CO_2-eq.), roughly all its GHG emissions in 2011. The cost since 2007 has been more than EUR 442 million (IEA, 2014). Austria should build on the impressive capacity and experience it has created with the Austrian JI/CDM Programme (which buys emission reductions generated by Joint Implementation (JI) and Clean Development Mechanism (CDM) projects to meet its Kyoto target in accordance with the National Climate Strategy). However, domestic measures should be prioritised within the national strategy plan to reach the 2020 targets.

Recommendations for a more robust, resilient, inclusive and sustainable economy

Key recommendations

- Continue to curb expectations of implicit public guarantees to the banking sector by fully applying the EU Bank Recovery and Resolution Directive that requires the bailing-in of investors and creditors. Maintain close monitoring and supervision of banks.
- Encourage municipal mergers to exploit economies of scale. Align spending and financing responsibilities at different administrative levels by increasing the tax autonomy of sub-central governments.
- Further reduce the labour tax wedge for low income earners by partly or fully waiving social security contributions, financed by a broadening of the tax base and increases in consumption, environmental and recurrent property taxes.
- Increase effective retirement ages of both men and women and step up preparations for the convergence of the statutory retirement ages of male and female workers.
- Reduce barriers to competition in services by easing entry regulations, removing restrictions on capital shares and voting rights of foreign investors and strengthening the investigation power of competition authorities.
- Make schools and educational tracks more inclusive. Strengthen the early socialisation as well as language and cognitive development of children from disadvantaged backgrounds to improve their intergenerational education mobility.

Other recommendation

- Increase the low fuel taxes which encourage fuel use and fuel tourism. Phase out tax breaks for CO_2-emitting company cars.

Opening-up gender roles to improve well-being and growth

The 2013 *OECD Economic Survey of Austria* (OECD, 2013a) investigated the key dimensions of well-being in Austria and identified gender equality as an area of tension. Services provided inside families play indeed a more important role in Austria than in comparable countries, and family patterns involve separate and asymmetric gender roles (Berghammer, 2014; Buber-Ennser et al., 2014). This model has been supported, rather effectively, by public policies and infrastructure (Schratzenstaller, 2015). Achieving gender equality requires providing more opportunities to leave the separate gender role model in order to broaden work-life balance options for all, which would improve well-being and bolster economic growth.

In Austria, men and women's labour force participation diverge when the first child is born. Upon graduation from school, the majority of young women and men, living in a couple or not, tend to work full-time and perform household tasks. However, the birth of a child triggers a divergence of roles which widens as the child grows up, further children are born and responsibilities for caring for elderly parents rise. In 2014, 90% of childless young men and 91% of childless young women were in the labour force, whereas following the birth of a child 95% of young fathers but only 76% of young mothers were. The separation of roles, which differs from comparable countries, tends to follow a two-stage pattern (Figure 13):

- After the birth of a child, the mother generally withdraws entirely from the labour force for about two years. In close to 70% of families with children less than 2 years old, there is only one working parent.

Figure 13. **The birth of children drives the parting of gender roles**

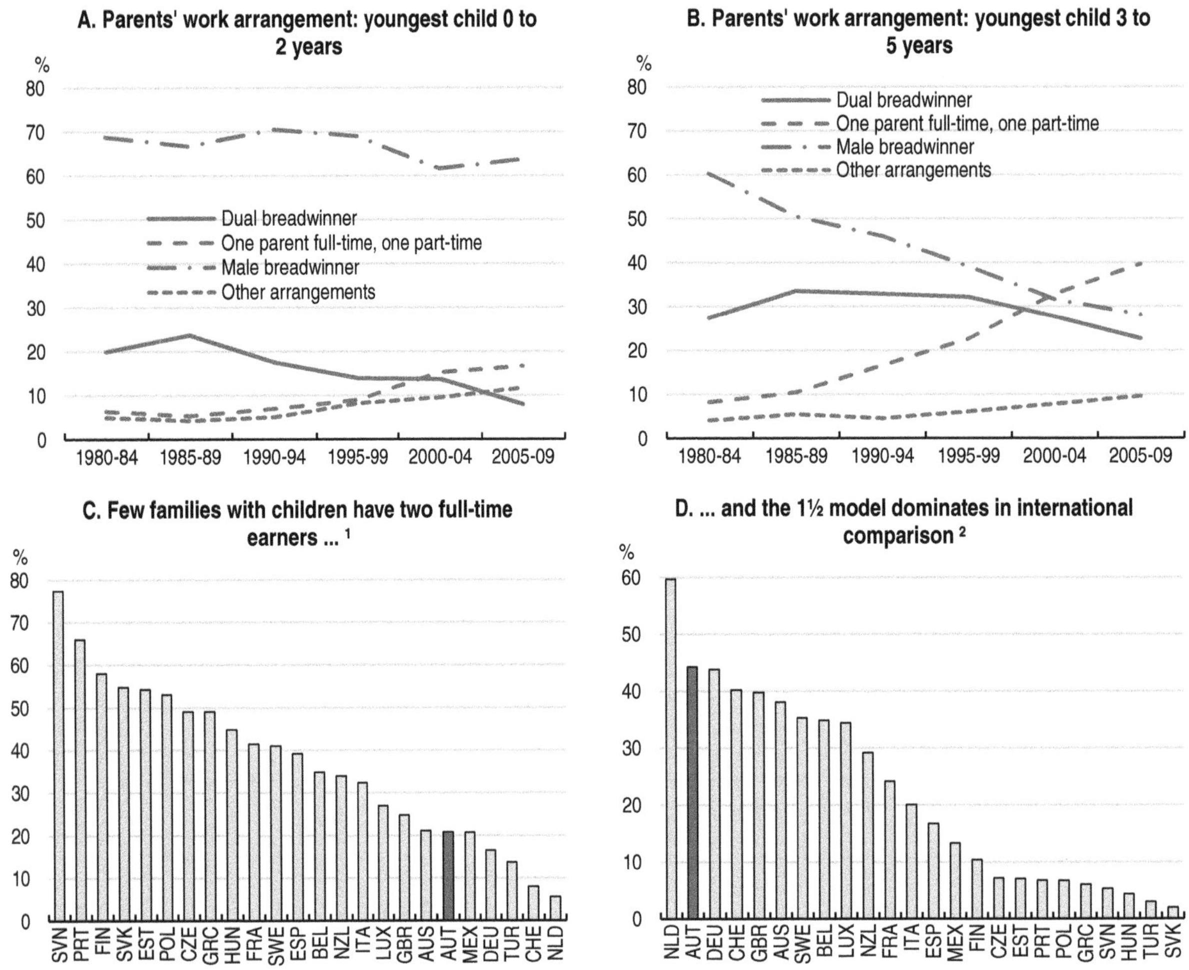

1. Proportion of couple families with children aged 0-14 with both parents working full-time, in 2011 except for Mexico, Sweden and Switzerland referring to 2010.
2. Proportion of couple families with children aged 0-14 with one parent working full-time and the other part-time, in 2011 except for Mexico, Sweden and Switzerland referring to 2010.

Source: Berghammer, C. (2014), "The Return of the Male Breadwinner Model? Educational Effects on Parents' Work Arrangements in Austria, 1980-2009", *Work, Employment and Society*, Vol. 28, No. 4; OECD (2014), *OECD Family database, www.oecd.org/social/family/database.htm*.

StatLink http://dx.doi.org/10.1787/888933252007

- Once the child reaches the age of 2, many mothers take a part-time job. A combination of one full-time and one part-time working parent then dominates (the "1½ model"). Only 20% of families with children below five have two full-time working parents.

This model is backed by parts of the public policy framework, in three main respects (Statistik Austria, 2010; Lutz and Schratzenstaller, 2010):

- **The tax and benefit system.** Taxation is personal, not family based, and therefore does not penalise the second earner. Also, child allowances are universal, and thus do not penalise work. These two features contribute to non-discriminatory family taxation. However, the income tax has a "sole earner deduction" for families with children, unless the annual taxable income of the second earner exceeds EUR 6 000. Further, workers enjoy a social security contribution exemption if their income is below a cap corresponding roughly to 7 hours of work per week at average hourly wages. The loss of this benefit penalises extra work. The marginal tax rate for the lowest income bracket is high, even after the recent tax reform, and second earners become liable for it if they work more than part-time (at average hourly wages, Figure 14). Bonus payments for overtime work, mainly provided by the main breadwinner, are partly tax exempt and provide an additional premium to the separation of roles.

- **The care infrastructure.** Childcare is highly subsidised and thus supports working parents. However, places are limited for children aged 0-2 in the vast majority of *Länder* (Figure 15). From age 3, almost all children are enrolled in day care facilities, but most day care facilities are half-day and out-of-day care facilities hours are long. Thus, a carer is still needed at home. Care for the elderly is also well subsidised, but the vast majority of dependents are cared for in their, or their families', home under the responsibility of families. Institutional care often involves using the elderly person's wealth, including real estate property, to cover the cost.
- **Workplace organisation.** In principle, parental leave allows working parents of either gender to stay with newly born children for up to two years, and to work part-time for up to seven years, both of these are long by OECD standards. But leave is used almost solely by mothers. Moreover, enterprises are prepared to extend part-time contracts to their female employees, and as a result most mothers work part-time for up to 15 years. In contrast, parental leave reserved for the exclusive use of fathers is short. Paternity leave, paid or not, does generally not exist in the private sector. In the public sector, only 12% of the fathers make use of the one-month unpaid leave that was introduced in 2011.

Figure 14. **The tax and subsidy system penalises dual earners more than in other countries**

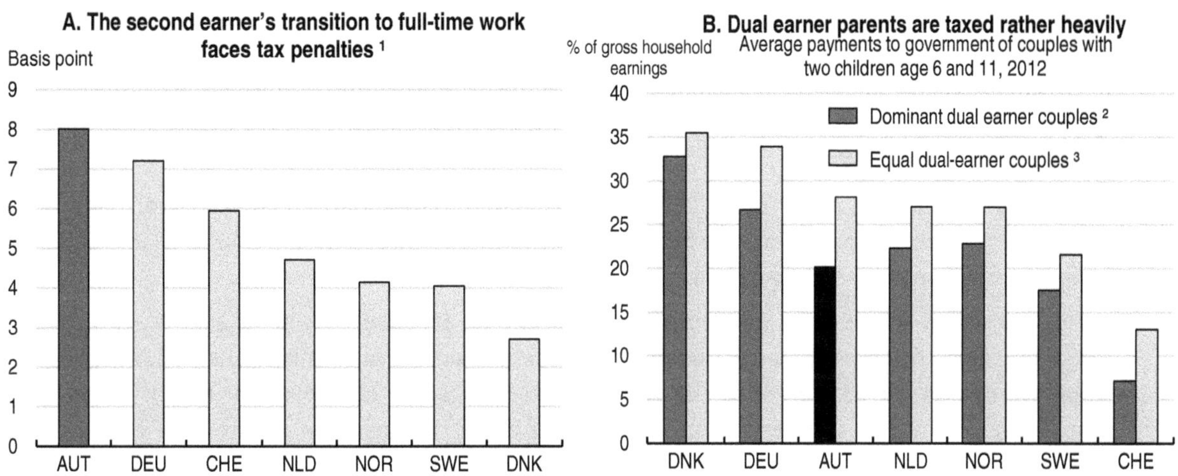

1. Difference in average payments to government in per cent of gross household earnings for a couple with two children aged 6 and 11, when the second earner transits from 33% to 100% of average earnings with the first earner earning 100% of average income.
2. Couples with income equal to 100% and 33% of average worker earnings.
3. Couples with both income equal to 100% of average worker earnings.

Source: OECD (2014), *OECD Family database, www.oecd.org/social/family/database.htm.*

StatLink http://dx.doi.org/10.1787/888933252018

Figure 15. **Care infrastructure is weak**

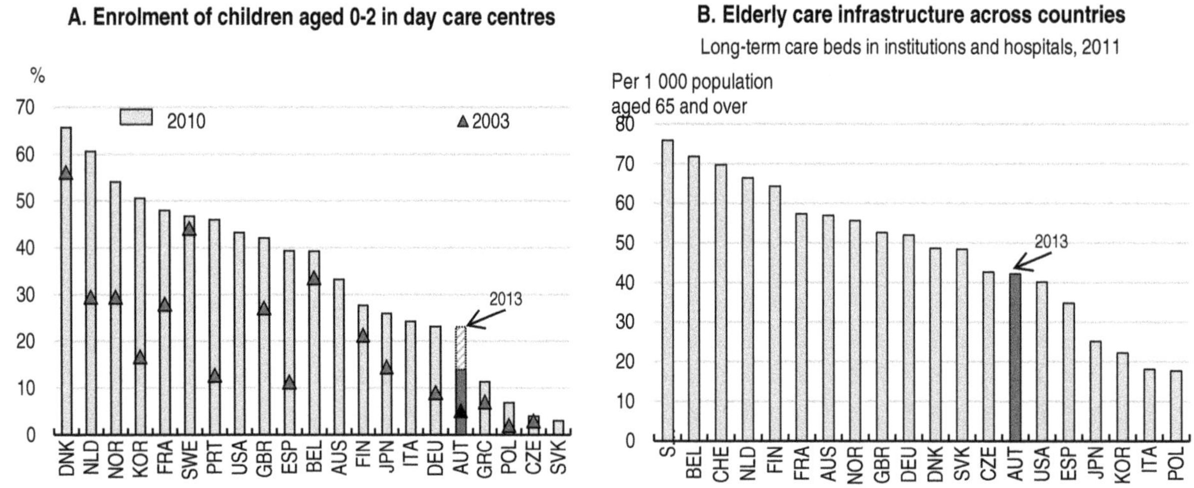

Source: OECD (2014), *OECD Family database*, *www.oecd.org/social/family/database.htm*; OECD (2013), *Health at a Glance 2013: OECD Indicators*, OECD Publishing, Paris, *http://dx.doi.org/10.1787/health_glance-2013-en*; and Statistik Austria.

StatLink http://dx.doi.org/10.1787/888933252026

The divergence of gender roles affects several dimensions of well-being

Although women already surpassed men in years of educational attainment, they are underrepresented in the most financially rewarding professions (Lassnigg et al., 2014). Interests for areas of study diverge by gender early in life, and persist through formal education and lifelong learning. Men tend to make choices and take professional tracks with higher earning potentials than women. In contrast, 50% of girls taking apprenticeship education specialise in one of three branches among 250 (office management, retail trade and hairdressing), and those proceeding to tertiary education typically graduate in non-technical fields (Figure 16). Early streaming of students in the education system consolidates this divergence.

Career paths and occupational responsibilities differ between men and women. The share of women at managerial level and top senior positions is particularly low in international comparison (Figure 17).

In contrast, women are particularly numerous in atypical jobs such as part-time, fixed-term and temporary agency work, which help them fulfil family tasks (Figure 18). Gaps are deeper for women with children. When engaged in entrepreneurial activities, women generally run smaller ventures (in one-third of the cases on a part-time basis). These differences in employment patterns affect their pension entitlements, pushing many women in sole households into relative poverty at old age (Geisberger, 2014; Böheim et al., 2013; Mader et al., 2014).

As a consequence of differences in professional specialisation, lesser responsibilities and less standard full-time employment, gender gaps in hourly wages and take home pay are much larger than in other countries (Figure 19). Analysis in Geisberger (2014) suggests that more than half of the hourly wage gap in Austria is left unexplained after controlling for age, education, sector, region, occupation, full/part-time work, seniority and the size of the enterprise. This earnings gap results in substantial poverty risks for women, in particular the risk of old-age poverty and poverty in the case of divorce.

Figure 16. **Education and skill gaps**

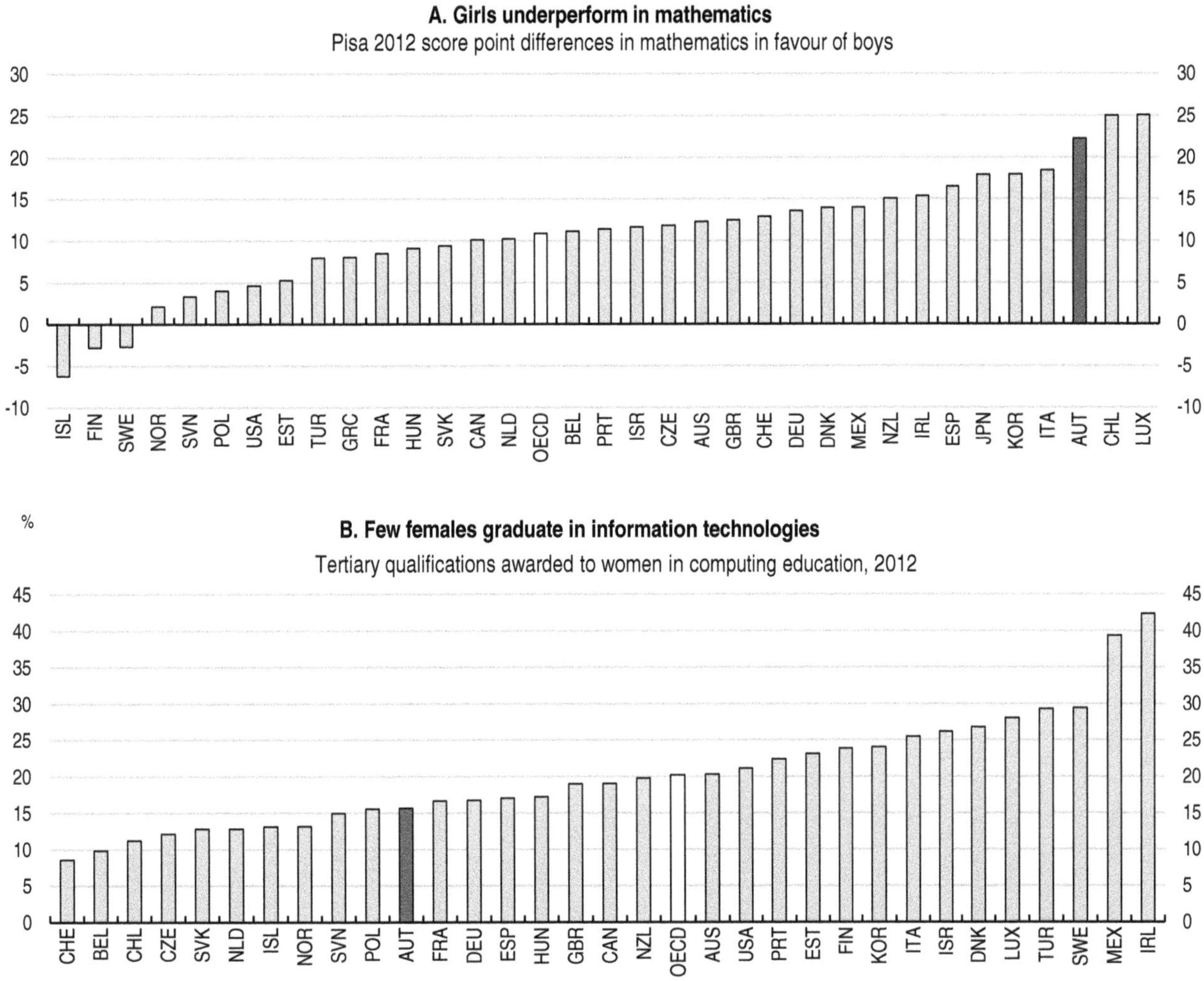

Source: OECD, *PISA 2012 database*; OECD (2014), *Education at a Glance 2014: OECD Indicators*, OECD Publishing, Paris, Table A3.3 online only, *http://dx.doi.org/10.1787/888933115388.*

StatLink http://dx.doi.org/10.1787/888933252031

Austrian men work very long hours, including overtime. Part-time working women also work more hours than part-time working women in other countries, in order to support family budgets which are strained by the 1½ model. As a result, Austrian women deliver a higher total of paid and unpaid work than in other countries.

According to an econometric estimation of the drivers of subjective well-being, earned incomes play a bigger role for men's life satisfaction in Austria than women's, and; the gap is larger than in other OECD countries (Chapter 1). Also, the majority of women without children, including highly educated women, declare drawing more satisfaction from voluntary part-time work than in comparable countries. Contrary to comparable countries, the presence of children reduces Austrian women's reported subjective well-being, perhaps reflecting the tensions inherent in the 1½ model.

Figure 17. **Gender gaps in management**

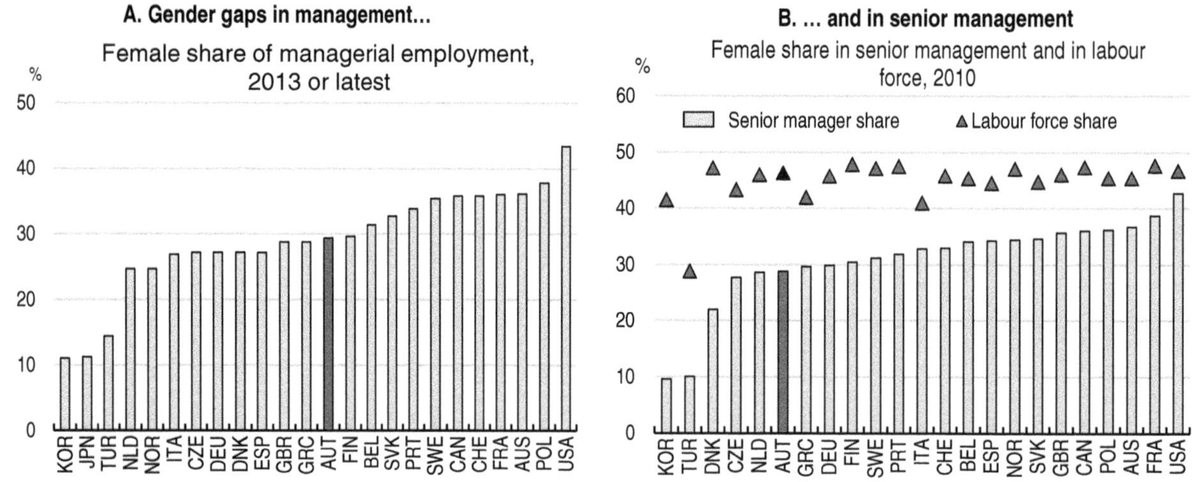

Source: OECD (2014), *OECD Family database, www.oecd.org/social/family/database.htm*; OECD (2012), *Closing the Gender Gap: Act Now*, OECD Publishing, Paris, *http://dx.doi.org/10.1787/9789264179370-en*.

StatLink http://dx.doi.org/10.1787/888933252048

Figure 18. **Gender gaps in employment quality**

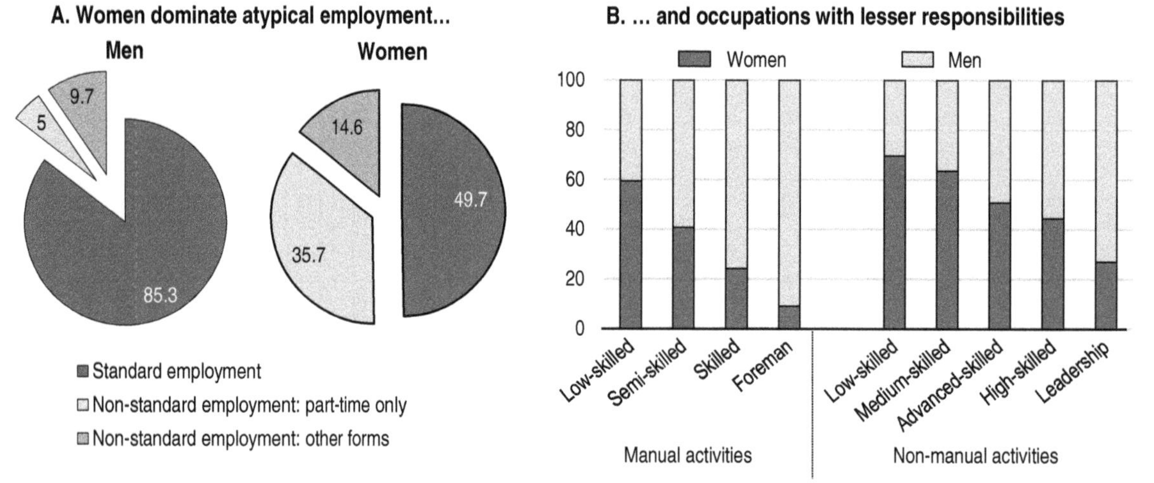

Source: Statistik Austria, Labour Force Surveys 2013 and Microcensus on labour 2008.

StatLink http://dx.doi.org/10.1787/888933252052

The prevailing model faces tensions

Today, the 1½ model faces three major tensions: i) men's long working hours crowd out their family life, including with respect to their relations with children, an outcome deplored by a large share of the population; ii) a sizeable proportion of women working part-time would prefer to work longer hours, notably to increase family incomes and pursue more ambitious careers, but do not have the necessary support infrastructure; and iii) households willing to move towards the dual breadwinner model face many practical complications in combining work and family lives.

The population living outside the 1½ model finds more restricted support for work and life arrangements than elsewhere. Notably, Austria has a larger share of sole parents with dependent children than in many other OECD countries. These sole parents, mostly

Figure 19. **Gender pay gaps**

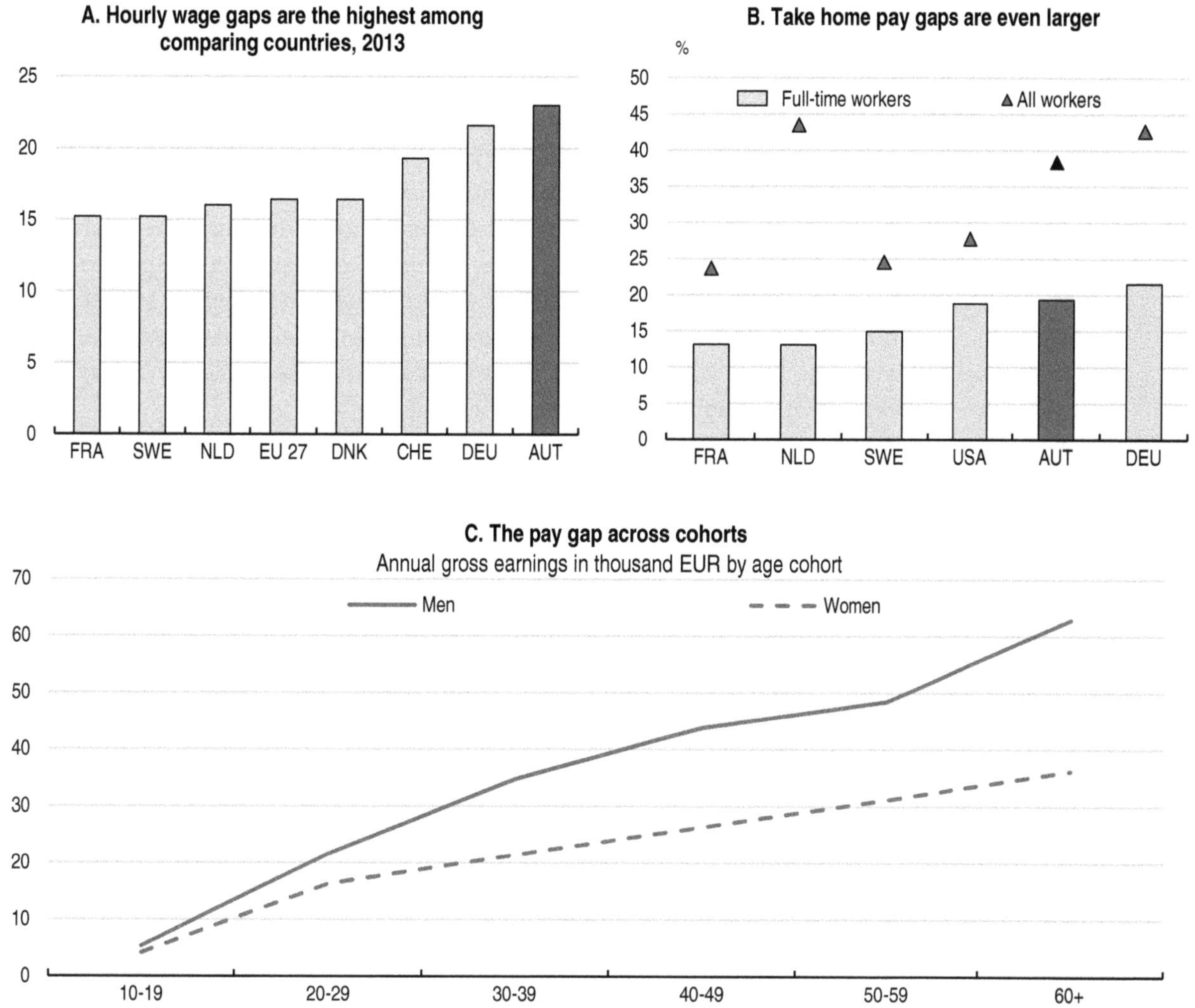

Source: Eurostat; OECD (2012), *Closing the Gender Gap: Act Now*, OECD Publishing, Paris, *http://dx.doi.org/10.1787/9789264179370-en*; and Statistik Austria, administrative tax data 2013.

StatLink *http://dx.doi.org/10.1787/888933252064*

women but also men, face particularly difficult conditions in reconciling child raising and work. They, as well as full-time working parents, do not benefit from the same quality of support from public infrastructures as the "1½" families.

Consequently, many households stay childless, as women seem to feel they need to choose between the career and children. According to the latest demographic forecasts, 20% of women in current adult cohorts will remain childless through life, against less than 10% who opt for this as an initial preference (Buber-Ennser et al., 2014). This is a serious gap between life aspirations and outcomes and therefore a major loss of well-being. It also deprives society from dynamic demographics, stronger growth and lower old-age dependency ratios.

Policy initiatives to reduce gender inequalities

Many initiatives have been taken in Austria to reduce gender inequalities. In the early 2000s, Austria was considered a leading country in the EU in this area (Heinrich Böll Stiftung, 2014). An Act on the Equal Treatment of Women and Men was adopted in 1979, and subsequent amendments broadened its scope. This Law was instrumental in reducing explicit wage discrimination. Gender mainstreaming was adopted as a key government goal from 2000 to "improve policy processes so that a gender equality perspective is incorporated at all levels and stages of policy-making" (Federal Chancellery, 2015). This particularly helped gender career paths converge in the public sector. A major further step was the *National Action Plan: Gender Equality in the Labour Market* in 2010, which included more than 50 detailed measures in various fields. Performance benchmarks were established for each measure, the measures were to be implemented in four years, and *ex post* formal evaluation was to be carried out.

More recently, "gender budgeting" has put gender policies at the centre of fiscal policy. As part of an ambitious fiscal framework reform and transition to performance-based budgeting, every line ministry is required to set at least one gender equality performance target. An annual government report evaluates if the objectives in the previous budget have been achieved. The report is transmitted to parliament in time for the debate on the next budget. Gender performance goals include "achieving a better distribution of paid and unpaid work between women and men on the basis of an adequate tax system" (Ministry of Finance), "stronger re-involvement of women in the labour force after career breaks" (Ministry of Labour), "strengthening women's competencies in business" (Ministry of Economy) and "improvement of equality of opportunities in education" (Ministry of Education and Women Affairs). The rules of regulatory impact assessment have also been extended to gender goals. Since 2013, before the adoption of any new law, regulation, government directive and other large public project, the expected impact on "effective equality of women and men" must be documented.

In 2013, the coalition government established after the 2013 legislative elections adopted a programme which included a large set of gender equality objectives (Federal Government, 2013). It emphasises two overall goals: "increasing the employment of women and improving their income opportunities" and "ensuring that work involved in looking after the family is held in high regard, that there is a real choice between work and family". Related targets occupy a large place in the government programme. The build-up of successive layers of gender equality initiatives has strengthened this agenda, but calls for a clearer co-ordination of policies around priorities, as suggested in the OECD Council Recommendation on Gender Equality in Education, Employment and Entrepreneurship (OECD, 2013b).

Higher and more evenly shared awareness among different parts and levels of government about the significance and benefits of gender equality would facilitate the evaluation of the existing efforts with a view to their prioritisation. Recent delays in the production of the evaluation reports of the National Action Plan for Gender Equality in the Labour Market hint at shortcomings in this regard. The two-yearly report to Parliament on gender equality could become a surrogate, providing a regular review of the main gender gaps and a comprehensive evaluation of ongoing initiatives. Such a reference document would help foster and maintain awareness throughout the policymaking community and the society as a whole.

Setting priorities for faster progress

Make the tax and benefit system less gender role biased

The tax penalty associated with second earners' transition from marginal to normal, and from part-time to full-time work should be cut, and the rate of taxation of dual earners be reduced. The recent tax reform addresses some of these traps (see above) and is a welcome step forward. Still, several features of the tax and subsidy system continue to penalise young mothers' return to work. These include the highly symbolic "sole earner deduction" (see above). The poverty reduction goals of this scheme should be pursued by targeted transfers to families in need. A higher share of child subsidies should be allocated to parents who increase their labour force participation. All factors determining working parents' net return from employment must be taken into account – which encompasses a complex range of elements for which internationally comparable up-to-date information is hard to obtain.

The current parental leave and child allowance schemes, which are governed by different rules and administrations, should be aligned to give more consistent and transparent options to working parents. The longest variant among the available childcare allowances options (30 months for the mother with an additional 6 months reserved for the father) should be phased out. Current plans to transform the parental leave entitlement into a more flexible time account are welcome. Childcare allowance and parental leave schemes could be transformed into a unique childcare account that allows parents to allocate subsidised absence from work flexibly over time. This would allow parents to return earlier to work without losing entitlements. A sizeable part of this account, at least 33%, should be reserved to the exclusive use of fathers to strengthen labour market attachment of both fathers and mothers without jeopardising care and family commitments.

To assess the impact of alternative family policy schemes on labour supply, child care use and net budget costs, and adjust policy packages accordingly, a comprehensive micro-data base or panel survey is necessary. It would enable policymakers to analyse the efficiency of various tax and subsidy instruments. Family policies could then be refined on the basis of actual experience. If such a full-fledged administrative database cannot be implemented, a comprehensive survey could be put in place as a substitute, along the model of the German Socio-Economic Panel. Germany launched a comprehensive investigation of the efficiency of its family policies on the basis of this information; Austria could undertake a similar exercise.

A "one-stop shop" for all present and future parents, completing the existing Ministry of Family website on child allowances, could provide additional information on available workplace options, public incentives and time-off possibilities. This would include support at sub-federal (*Länder* and municipal) levels. It can possibly take the form of a physical network (located for example in employment agencies), or of a user-friendly website. Importantly, it should provide information on the long-term employment, earning and pension implications of the choices made by parents.

Reconcile work and family lives by extending infrastructure

The care infrastructure could better support working parents. Expanding the availability of day care centres for children aged 0-2, full-day kindergarten for children aged 3-5, and full-day school services for children aged 5-15 in all *Länder* would all make it possible for parents to have full-time jobs. More investment in early childhood education and care facilities would not only support labour supply and foster gender equality, it would also strengthen children's cognitive development, in particular in vulnerable families. In addition, providing out-of-school care would make better use of existing school buildings.

The care infrastructure for dependent elderly should also be reinforced with a more complete range of services responding to the needs of persons with and without family support. It will be important to preserve a high degree of flexibility between family, home-based, ambulatory, institutional and temporary care services, as availability of choice in this area is highly appreciated in Austria and may be fiscally more efficient than massive recourse to institutional care.

The delivery channels of services could include public, non-profit and commercial providers. To ensure the expansion of high-quality services, national quality and capacity plans should be put in place. The pricing of services on an economic basis (reflecting costs), together with a targeted subsidisation of eligible beneficiaries (through for example means-tested vouchers successfully utilised in Swiss cities such as Lucerne and Bern) could facilitate the development of supply sources on a level playing ground.

The fragmentation of federal, *Länder* and municipal responsibilities in the funding and provision of services generates artificial borders in service delivery and access. The criterion of "main place of residence", which currently governs the allocation of federal funds and the selection of beneficiaries, makes access to services more difficult. Funding and provision rules should be redesigned to reflect the increasing mobility of the population – care receivers and caregivers alike.

Encourage more flexible workplace practices

The private sector has also a major responsibility in promoting gender equality. Workplaces should be made more supportive of better balanced earner/carer arrangements. Priorities include broadening working-time options for fathers, keeping mothers of young children more attached to their careers, and providing more support to both men and women with care responsibilities:

- Fathers should be helped to better balance paid and unpaid work. Overtime work should be reduced to the extent possible and should not be tax-subsidised as at present. Work schedules should better fit family life patterns, for example by providing more flexi-time arrangements and longer leaves for special caring circumstances. Parental leave exclusively reserved for fathers (at an adequate level of wage compensation) should be increased.
- Parental leave and shortened working hours should be made less penalising for the professional status and careers of both mothers and fathers. Other countries' business practices and policy frameworks which yield better results, such as the flexible and intermittent leave practices which have been effective in Scandinavian countries, should be examined.

- More enabling time management options along the life cycle should be offered to employees of both genders. They help accommodate evolving family circumstances and preferences through the life cycle (Stock et al., 2012). Related international innovations, such the "time-banking" schemes introduced in Germany to help accumulate credit hours for longer leave periods, should be monitored as a repertory of good practices.
- A number of countries are striving to overcome the dichotomy between full and part-time work. In several instances, intermediary arrangements can help to reconcile work and family requirements. Austria has started, but still offers less flexibility along these lines than other OECD countries, and the share of partial working time arrangements in total employment remains lower (Figure 20). The range of available options should be expanded.
- Social partners can contribute to these efforts by helping to develop practices that facilitate the reconciliation of family obligations and work responsibilities while preserving the enterprises' productivity and competitiveness. Wage negotiations should aim at reducing the gender wage gap.

Figure 20. **Making work organisation more supportive of dual earner families**

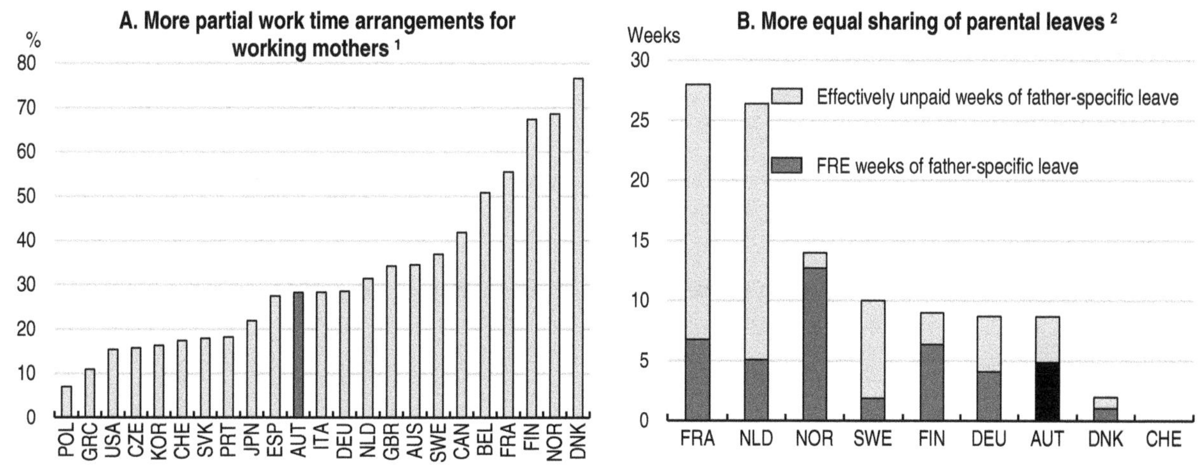

1. Proportion of women working between part and full-time (30 to 39 hours per week).
2. Paid leave entitlements for fathers that cannot be transferred to mothers. Full-rate equivalent (FRE) is defined as the duration of leave in weeks multiplied by the payment rate (as per cent of average wage earnings).

Source: OECD (2014), *OECD Family database*, *www.oecd.org/social/family/database.htm.*

StatLink http://dx.doi.org/10.1787/888933252070

Foster awareness to back reforms

Wider awareness in Austria on persisting gender gaps, their sources and their impact on various dimensions of well-being would help policymakers, families and enterprises gain support to change the tax-benefit system, fill the holes of the care infrastructure and promote gender-equality in the workplace. The highest priority is to overcome the stereotypes regarding the desirable family organisation for child raising, notably by making clear that more active participation of fathers is essential for the well-being of children and mothers, and that women can return to work much earlier and fully than at present, without prejudice to the child, provided that high-quality care is available.

Long-term growth gains

Progress towards gender equality will raise GDP growth. A stylised simulation by the OECD Secretariat based on a long-term growth accounting framework illustrates that gender-equality affect long-term growth through three direct channels: i) increase in labour utilisation; ii) increase in human capital; and iii) increase in fertility:

- Increase in labour utilisation. The incidence of part-time work is five times higher for Austrian women than men. Overall female participation is lower in Austria and Austrian men work longer than the OECD average. Total hours worked would rise by 3.5% if these differences were evened out by raising female labour force participation from 71% to 75%, reducing the proportion of women working part time from 33% to 21%, and reducing weekly hours worked by men from 43.5 to 41.8.
- Increase in human capital. Narrowing gender gaps in education and the labour market would channel young people to educational tracks that better match their skills and interests. As a result, enrolment in higher education would increase and raise average years of schooling to the level of Denmark by 2060, which corresponds to an increase from 11.8 years in 2014 to 14 years in 2060.
- Increase in fertility. Eurostat population projections provide both a baseline and a low-fertility scenario. By extrapolating the differences for each age cohort, a high-fertility scenario is obtained for Austria. It entails a gradual increase in the average fertility rate from 1.45 births per woman in 2013 to 1.9 in 2060, against 1.6 in the baseline and 1.3 in the low-fertility scenario.

Taken together, these three effects could raise GDP by 13%. Per capita GDP would increase by 8.3% and the total population by 4.7% (Figure 21).

Figure 21. **Long-term growth gains from opening up gender roles**

Ratio of more gender equal scenario over baseline projection

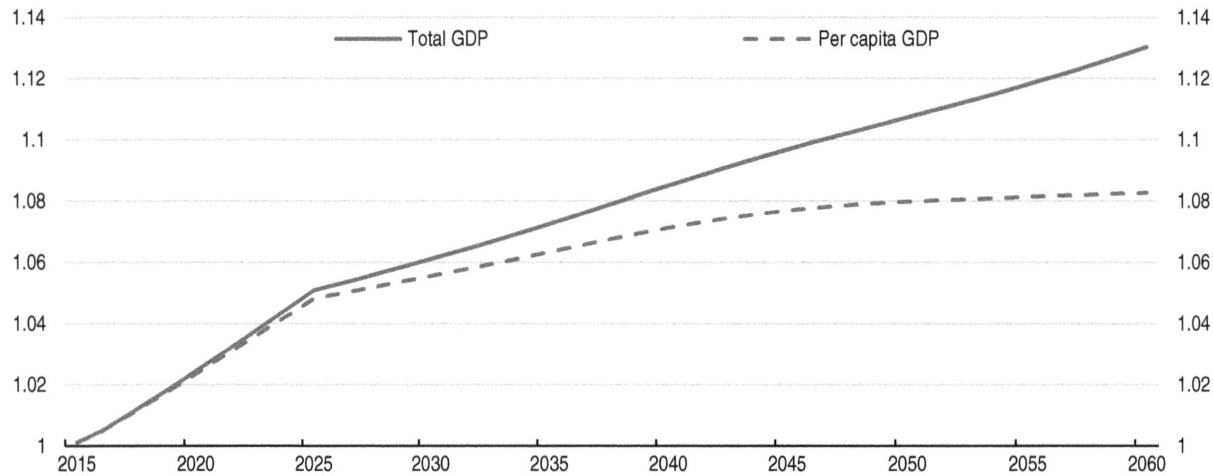

Source: Calculations based on the OECD's long-term growth model. Ratio of more gender equal scenario over baseline projection.

StatLink http://dx.doi.org/10.1787/888933252082

Recommendations to promote gender equality

Key recommendations

- Spur investment in high quality childcare facilities. Enhance the availability of full-day schools and care centres. Consider introducing legal entitlements for these services.
- Reduce the implicit taxation of transition from marginal and part-time to full-time employment and replace the sole-earner tax deduction by targeted transfers to families in need. Open active labour market programmes also for part time workers.
- Transform childcare allowance and parental leave schemes into a unique childcare account that allows parents to allocate subsidised absence from work flexibly over time. Reserve a sizeable part of this account, at least 33%, for the exclusive use of fathers.
- Raise awareness by publicising more information on innovations in study area choices of schoolgirls and schoolboys, earlier return to full-time work of mothers, and fathers' participation in care and household duties.
- Develop a comprehensive data base on social transfers or a comprehensive panel survey to assess the impact of alternative family policy schemes on labour supply, child care use and net budget costs, and adjust policy packages in the light of this information.
- The private sector should offer more family-friendly workplaces and more enabling working time options to employees of both genders. Policymakers should continue to support auditing and information campaigns to disseminate good practices.

Other recommendations

- Social partners should help develop practices that facilitate the reconciliation of family obligations and work responsibilities while preserving the enterprises' productivity and competitiveness. Wage negotiations should aim at reducing the gender wage gap.
- Promote gender diversity in leadership positions in private companies.
- Widen access of part-timer workers to active labour market programmes.

Bibliography

Austrian Fiscal Advisory Council (2014), "Current Fiscal Performance and Recommendations by the Fiscal Advisory Council on Austria's Budget Policy and Budget Financing in 2015", 10 December.

Bank Austria (2015), "Die Einkommenssteuerentlastung 2016 und ihre Gegenfinanzierung", Analysen, March.

Berghammer, C. (2014), "The Return of the Male Breadwinner Model? Educational Effects on Parents' Work Arrangements in Austria, 1980-2009", *Work, Employment and Society*, Vol. 28, No. 4.

Bertelsmann (2014), *Social Cohesion Radar*, Bertelsmann Stiftung.

Böheim, R., K. Himpele, H. Mahringer and C. Zulehner (2013), "The Gender Wage Gap in Austria: Eppur si Muove!", *Empirica*, Vol. 40, No. 4.

Buber-Ennser, I., N. Neuwirth and M. Testa (2014), *Families in Austria 2009-2013: Descriptive Findings on Partnerships, Fertility Intentions, Childbearing and Childrearing*, Vienna Institute of Demography, Vienna.

Eiffe, F. and K. Gärtner (2014), "Distribution and Determinants of Subjective Well-Being in Austria", mimeo based on *Statistische Nachrichten 2014*, No. 1, Statistik Austria, Vienna.

European Commission (2015), "The 2015 Ageing Report – Economic and Budgetary Projections for the 27 Member States 2013-60", Brussels.

Federal Chancellery (2015), "Guidelines for Gender Mainstreaming in Legislation", website of the Federal Chancellery of Austria, *www.bka.gv.at/site/6823/default.aspx*.

Federal Government (2013), Work Programme of the Austrian Federal Government, Vienna.

Geisberger, T. and T. Glaser (2014), "Geschlechtsspezifische Verdienstunterschiede – Analysen zum Gender Pay Gap auf Basis der Verdienststrukturerhebung 2010", *Statistische Nachrichten* 2014, No. 3, Statistik Austria, Vienna.

Guigon, P. (2010), "Voluntary Carbon Markets: How can they Serve Climate Policies", *OECD Environment Working Papers*, No. 19, OECD Publishing, Paris, *http://dx.doi.org/10.1787/5km975th0z6h-en*.

Heinrich Böll Stiftung (2015), *Feminism and Gender Democracy*, Austria, *www.gwi-boell.de/en/2012/02/07/austria*.

IEA (2014), *Energy Policies of IEA Countries: Austria 2014*, IEA, Paris, *http://dx.doi.org/10.1787/9789264209602-en*.

Köppl, A. and M. Schratzenstaller (2015), "The Austrian Tax System – Perspectives for Reform", WIFO *Bulletin*, No. 6.

Lassnigg, L., A. Kulhanek and P. Wejwar (2014), "Quantitative Information About Sex and Gender Issues in the Austrian National Education Report", mimeo, Institute for Advanced Studies (IHS), Vienna.

Leoni, T. and R. Eppel (2013). "Women's Work and Family Profiles over the Lifecourse and their Subsequent Health Outcomes", *WWW For Europe Working Paper*, No. 28, *https://ideas.repec.org/p/feu/wfewop/y2013m7d0i28.html*.

Lutz, H. and M. Schratzenstaller (2010), "Mögliche Ansätze zur Unterstützung von Familien durch die öffentlichen Haushalte", *WIFO Monatberichte*, No. 8.

Mader, K., A. Schneebaum, K. Hollan and P. Kopf (2014), "Vermögensunterschiede Nach Geschlecht: Erste Ergebnisse für Österreich" (Wealth Differences: First Results for Austria), *Document on Economy and Society*, No. 129, Arbeitkammer, Vienna.

OECD (2005), *Ageing and Employment Policies/Vieillissement et politiques de l'emploi: Austria 2005*, OECD Publishing, Paris, *http://dx.doi.org/10.1787/9789264010093-en*.

OECD (2007), *Babies and Bosses – Reconciling Work and Family Life: A Synthesis of Findings for OECD Countries*, OECD Publishing, Paris, *http://dx.doi.org/10.1787/9789264032477-en*.

OECD (2011), *Doing Better for Families*, OECD Publishing, Paris, *http://dx.doi.org/10.1787/9789264098732-en*.

OECD (2012), *Closing the Gender Gap: Act Now*, OECD Publishing, Paris, *http://dx.doi.org/10.1787/9789264179370-en*.

OECD (2013a), *OECD Economic Surveys: Austria 2013*, OECD Publishing, Paris, *http://dx.doi.org/10.1787/eco_surveys-aut-2013-en*.

OECD (2013b), *Recommendation of the Council on Gender Equality in Education, Employment and Entrepreneurship*, OECD, Paris, 29 May, *www.oecd.org/gender/C-MIN(2013)5-ENG.pdf*.

OECD (2013c), *OECD Environmental Performance Reviews: Austria 2013*, OECD Publishing, Paris, *http://dx.doi.org/10.1787/9789264202924-en*.

OECD (2014), *Recruiting Immigrant Workers: Austria 2014*, OECD Publishing, Paris, *http://dx.doi.org/10.1787/9789264226050-en*.

OECD (2015a), *Stakeholder Consultation on the draft Recommendation of the Council on Gender Equality in Public Life* (unpublished).

OECD (2015b), *The Future of Productivity*, Working Party No. 1 on Macroeconomic and Structural Policy Analysis (unpublished).

OeNB (2014), *Financial Stability Report*, No. 28, Österreichische Nationalbank, December.

OeNB (2015), *Gesamtwirtschaftliche Prognose für Österreicht 2015 bis 2017*, Österreichische Nationalbank, June.

Schich, S. and Y. Aydin (2014), "Policy responses to the issue of implicit bank debt guarantees: OECD survey results", in *OECD Journal: Financial Market Trends*, Vol. 2014/1, OECD Publishing, Paris, *http://dx.doi.org/10.1787/fmt-2014-5jxzbv3r1x9x*.

Shratzenstaller, M. (2015), "Familienpolitische Leistungen in Österreich im Überblick" (Family Benefits in Austria – An Overview), *WIFO-Monatsberichte*, No. 88(3).

Statistik Austria (2010), *Frauenbericht (Women Report)*, Vienna.

Statistik Austria (2014), *Vertiefende Analysen der PIAAC-Erhebung 2011/12 (In-depth PIAAC Analyses)*, Vienna, *www.statistik.at/web_de/statistiken/bildung_und_kultur/piaac/vertiefende_analysen_der_piaac_erhebung_2011_12/index.html*.

Stock, G., H. Bertram, A. Fürnkranz-Prskawetz, W. Holzgreve, M. Kohli and U. Staudinger (2012), *A Future with Children: Fertility and the Development of Society in Germany, Austria, and Switzerland*, Campus Verlag.

Wifo (2015), Monatsberichte 05/2015, forthcoming.

ANNEX

Progress in structural reform

This annex summaries key recommendations made in previous Surveys *and main actions taken since the* OECD Economic Survey on Austria *published in July 2013.*

Fiscal and financial policy

Recommendations in previous *Surveys*	Action taken
Let automatic stabilisers operate freely around the announced structural consolidation path towards a balanced budget.	According to government calculations, the structural fiscal balance will improve by 0.25 percentage points of GDP between 2013-15. This amounts to a broadly neutral fiscal stance as recommended.
Internationally active banks should be required to present clear strategies to strengthen their capital base taking into account the need to repay government capital. The restructuring of the nationalised banks should be pursued.	The internationally active banks have gone through and passed the comprehensive assessment by the ECB. Their joint core capital ratio increased and approached 12% by end 2014. *Kommunalkredit Austria* is being liquidated. ÖVAG will also be liquidated after a restructuring. Some parts of *Hypo Alpe Adria* are being sold while consideration is given to bailing in some of its creditors.

Public governance and policy formation

Recommendations in previous *Surveys*	Action taken
Fully implement performance-based budgeting, regulatory impact assessment and long-term public spending simulations and extend them to the whole general government sector.	A comprehensive system of performance based budgeting and regulatory impact assessment has been implemented in 2013. An evaluation report on the new budgeting system at the federal level has been completed recently and identified areas for improvement. Its proposals will be discussed in Parliament. The federal government aims at extending the new budgeting rules to the entire general government sector.
Make sure that increasingly available indicators on different dimensions of well-being are integrated in the policy formation process. Encourage social partners to aim for representation of all stakeholders.	The project "*Wie geht's Österreich*" ("How is Austria") by Statistik Austria established a set of indicators on different dimensions of well-being. The publication which was developed in close co-operation with all relevant ministries as well as research institutes, social partners and other stakeholders is online; it is regularly updated and discussed.

Ageing, work/family obligations and the integration of migrant groups

Recommendations in previous *Surveys*	Action taken
Reduce all remaining obstacles to the employment of older workers and close the remaining loopholes into early retirement. Reflect changes in life expectancy more directly in the sustainability mechanisms of the pension system. Calculate the "redistributive" and "deferred saving" elements in the system in order to improve the evidence basis for future measures.	A new "Employment Initiative 50 plus" initiative supports the employment of older workers with wage subsidies, in-work benefits and temporary employment opportunities in social firms. It has a budget of EUR 370 million for 2014-16 and is backed by an awareness campaign. Quantitative targets spelled out in the Government programme 2013-18 (effective retirement ages for both genders) are monitored on a semi-annual basis. If outcomes deviate from goals additional measures will be implemented.
Make high quality institutional child care available and affordable for children at all ages. Subsidies should be granted on a level-playing field between public, non-profit and private providers to stimulate entry and innovation in the sector.	The enrolment-rate of children up to age 3 increased to 25% and the *Barcelona target* agreed at the level of the European Union for children aged 3-6 was met. To reach the *Barcelona target* for children below age 3, and increase the quality of care, a budget of EUR 440 million will be spent over the period 2014-17. Subsidies to the operating expenses of public and private child care providers are granted by *Länder* and municipalities. In several *Länder* full-time child care is free of charge, or fees are adjusted to the income level of parents. Negotiations about an additional compulsory kindergarten year (free of charge) are starting. A pilot project in 70 locations aims at improving the quality of education for young children via an integrated curriculum across the last kindergarten year and the first 2 years of primary school. This approach will be generalised in the entire country in 2016-17.

Recommendations in previous *Surveys*	Action taken
Improve the dialogue with communities with migrant background to foster the education and labour market prospects of the next generation.	To improve language and reading capacities of children with migrant background, the recently introduced two-year language courses at kindergarten level (on the basis of a special agreement between Federal and *Länder* governments) are being extended to 2015-16. New projects enhancing the intercultural dialogue between migrants and the host society are subsidised by the Federal government, including projects supporting immigrants' language skills and labour market integration. Around EUR 3.5 million was dedicated to these projects in 2014.

Environmental sustainability

Recommendations in previous *Surveys*	Action taken
Price externalities stemming from road transport better. Increase diesel taxes to reflect externalities. Consider extending the road pricing system. Abolish the favourable taxation of company cars and phase out the commuting subsidy.	The 2015/16 tax reform reduces tax incentives for the use of CO_2-emitting company cars from 2016 onwards. Other tax incentives are offered for non-CO_2-emitting company cars (e-cars),
Develop instruments to improve co-ordination between the regional, *Länder* and federal levels to promote denser settlements well connected to public transport. To increase land supply in designated areas, raise property taxes by updating land values on which they are levied.	The Federal and *Länder* governments agreed on "minimum standards for accessibility by public transport", based on number of inhabitants per settlement. This aims at "re-densifying" existing settlements in order to improve the quality of services. The *Austrian Conference on Spatial Planning* (ÖROK) issued new planning recommendations for settlements. The 2015/16 tax reform changes the tax base for real estate transfers from the outdated cadaster value to an updated value.

Responding to globalisation challenges

Recommendations in previous *Surveys*	Action taken
Support the modernisation of corporate governance in family firms, notably in order to facilitate generational transmissions, and further foster venture capital supply. Reduce entry barriers for services, including social services, without reducing high quality standards and consumer protection.	A 2013 amendment to the Trade Act facilitated the intergenerational transmission of businesses, including provision of a transition period for full compliance with the requirements of the Trade Act. To foster the growth of start-ups and young businesses, new government schemes are offered to facilitate their financing in early and growth stages, and improve their long-term financial stability. Austria participates in the *Transparency Initiative* according to the EU Directive on professional qualifications. This covers all regulated professions with qualification rules and will provide, by the end of 2015, an overview of possible areas of overregulation. Austrian authorities emphasise the importance of formal qualification requirements for maintaining strong incentives for dual (apprenticeship) and vocational education.
Implement policies to preserve high quality and labour market relevant education as the main driver of Austria's well-being in the future as in the past, as set out in the 2009 Survey and in the OECD's Skill Strategy.	30% of all school places are planned to offer day-long education by 2018-19. New schemes to improve education quality are being introduced, including a standardised school leaving exam from 2015, a new teacher training scheme also from 2015, and compulsory "quality management" systems to be applied in all schools. A *Higher Education Action Plan* was adopted, providing "a mapping process" for Austrian higher education. Performance agreements between the Ministry of Science, Research and Economy and individual universities will settle focal competence areas to improve the employability of graduates. The development of *Universities of Applied Sciences* continues to offer highly labour market-relevant tertiary curricula.

Thematic chapters

Chapter 1

Austria's separate gender roles model faces tensions

Austria has a model of "separate gender roles" in work, family and life arrangements which persists despite efforts to better balance these roles. Irrespective of their education level – which is higher for new generations than men's – the majority of women with children withdraw fully or partly from the labour force until their children reach school age, and beyond. This pattern has provided the Austrian population with generally high quality family services, but buttressed gender inequalities, and deprived society from the activation of existing talent, and therefore from additional household incomes, fiscal revenues and potential output. Gender differences in life-time career and income paths, well-being, and participation patterns in public life generate increasing dissatisfaction in growing segments of society, among both women and men.

Introduction: Specific gender roles restrict choices

Austria's prevailing work, family and life arrangements are based on distinct "gender roles", notwithstanding recent progress towards better balance. The model has supported well-being outcomes, but now faces tensions. It allows families to provide extensive "in house" services to the population, in particular to the children and the elderly, but at the cost of a deep asymmetry in men's and women's unpaid and paid work responsibilities and career and income paths. Limiting aggregate labour force participation, it restricts choice between market and household services, and between private and public services. The model therefore reduces the opportunities for specialisation and productivity growth, which are key for maintaining living standards and a strong supply of social services for an ageing society.

This chapter describes the main features of the prevailing work, family and life arrangements and static and dynamic implications on Austria's main well-being dimensions according to the OECD's "How's Life?" framework. Gender differences which result from separate roles are reviewed in detail. The second chapter of this Survey discusses how this model can be "opened up", to achieve more gender justice, better balance in well-being and faster economic growth.

Austria's separate gender roles model

The special role of families

As underlined in the previous *OECD Economic Survey of Austria*, families play a particularly important role in Austria's economic and social organisation (OECD, 2013c). They have fulfilled this function through a separation of gender roles so far, which associates men with primarily breadwinning activities, and women, who generally participate only partly in the labour market, primarily with child rearing and family responsibilities. According to many indicators reviewed in this Survey, Austria is the most gender-differentiated among comparable countries – taken here as the other small, high-income European economies.

In all OECD countries families are the central unit of social organisation. "As the source of home production, they create economies of scale for people living together. They redistribute resources in cash, in-kind and time, and are an instrument of solidarity among individuals, households and generations. They provide protection and insurance against hardship" (OECD, 2011). Most Austrian households are couple families (53%), the majority of which (about 60%) have children. Nearly half of these families have one child, 40% two children and 15% three or more. Couples are more widespread in the prime age population: three quarter of persons in the age group 18-49 live in couple. The share of families with three children or more, which potentially help approach the minimum demographic replacement rate of 2.1 children per family, is particularly low.

The birth of children drives the parting of gender roles

Separation of gender roles emerges principally after the birth of children. Upon graduation from school, the majority of women and men, living together or not, start to work full-time and experience little asymmetry in household tasks. Only a minority engage in traditional marriage with a male breadwinner and a female homemaker. The aggregate labour force participation of young women and men between 25 and 34 is one of the highest in the OECD: in 2014, 84% of young women and 91% of young men were in the labour force.

The birth of a child often triggers the separation of labour market roles. In 2014, 90% of childless young men and 91% of childless young women were in the labour force. After the birth of a child the rate increased to 95% for young fathers but declined to 76% for young mothers. Participation rates remain different as the child grows up, further children are born, and part of the population faces care responsibilities for elderly parents. The typical life cycle of mothers with young children is characterised by a long period of parental leave, followed by a long period of part-time work, at least until the youngest child completes compulsory school. During this period, mothers bear the bulk of child-rearing duties. Survey results show that 82% of them stay with children in case of illness, 71% are the primary help for children with school homework, and 63% of the mothers take children to school (Buber-Ennser et al., 2014).

Whereas for couple families without children home tasks (including cleaning, shopping, doing dishes, etc.) are rather evenly shared (except in the area of cooking where women prevail more frequently), the birth of a first child triggers a separation of roles in non-child related areas as well. Recent surveys show that in up to 70% of families with children, shopping, vacuum-cleaning, etc. tasks are today carried out by mothers. Women generally perform the role of supplier of family services, which persists when they resume part- and then full-time work. The separation of roles goes well beyond what is found in comparable countries (Figure 1.1).

Figure 1.1. **Family services are provided by women**

Percentages

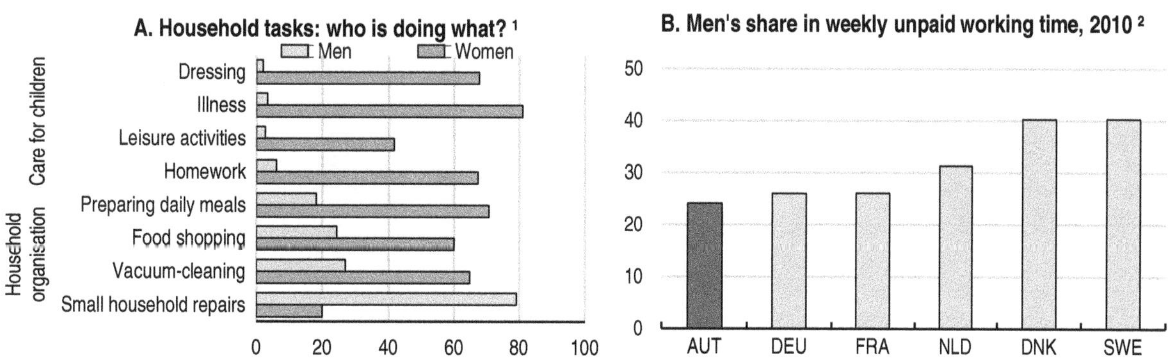

1. Share of respondents who stated that the task is always or usually done by her/him.
2. European Working Condition Survey 2010; Unpaid work is calculated for 7 days a week and includes hours of caring for and educating own children (included are persons with children aged less than 18 living in the same household) as well as hours for household/cooking-tasks; EWCS includes only persons in employment/self-employment.

Source: Generations and Gender Survey Austria Wave 1; European Commission (2012), *The Role of Men in Gender Equality – European Strategies and Insights*, DG Justice, December, Brussels.

StatLink http://dx.doi.org/10.1787/888933252094

This pattern is more prevalent in certain regions than in others (Figure 1.2). In Vienna for example, mothers re-enter the labour market more rapidly, transiting more swiftly from maternity leave to part-time work, and from part-time to full-time employment. However, subsequent to the birth of the second child, the national pattern prevails in Vienna as well. In other *Länder*, more mothers stay away from employment and for longer. The regional spread of separate gender roles appears inversely proportional to the availability of out-of-family care and education units for children. Only in Vienna is the majority of children are in care places compatible with full-time work of parents, in other *Länder* a very small share of children are enrolled in such facilities[1] (Figure 1.2).

Figure 1.2. **Child raising separates gender roles**

Estimates of employment shares according to full-time/part-time and number of children, 2013, in %

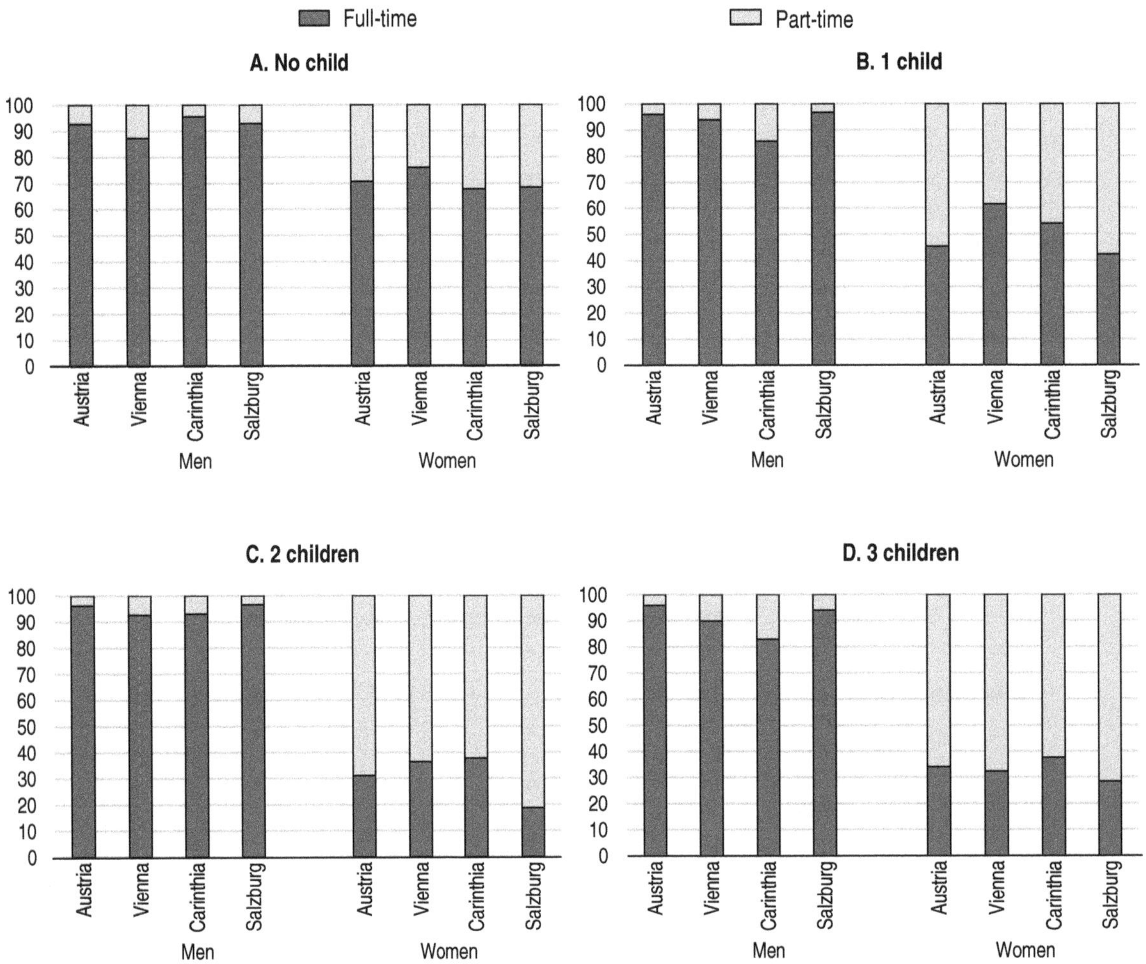

Source: Estimates by the OECD Secretariat on the basis of Labour Force Surveys microdata from Statistik Austria.

A consequence of this divergence of roles is fathers' limited involvement in the development of their children. The Austrian Institute of Family Studies reports that fathers' share in total parental leave days taken is less than 5%, significantly less than in comparable countries (Buber-Ennser and Panova, 2014). Less than one fifth of fathers take some parental leave, and when they do it is of short duration. The ratio of fathers to mothers using their entitlement to parental leave is 10%, while it reached respectively 75%,

60% and 48% in Sweden, the Netherlands and Denmark. Austria has at present the highest prevalence of the opinion that children are being excessively deprived of their fathers' presence. An EU study identified Austrian fathers as outliers in this area (European Commission, 2012a).

These separate roles in families can be characterised by a two-stage pattern (Figure 1.3):

i) After the birth of a child, the mother withdraws entirely from the workplace for about two years. In up to 70% of families with children below 2, there is only one working parent. The proportion of part-time working mothers at this stage is only 15%.

ii) Once the child reaches age 2, most mothers take a part-time job. Across couple families, a combination of one full-time and one part-time working parent then dominates. The share of families with two full-time working parents (with children below five) contracted steadily over the past two decades and is now below 20%.

Figure 1.3. **The two-stage separation of gender roles**

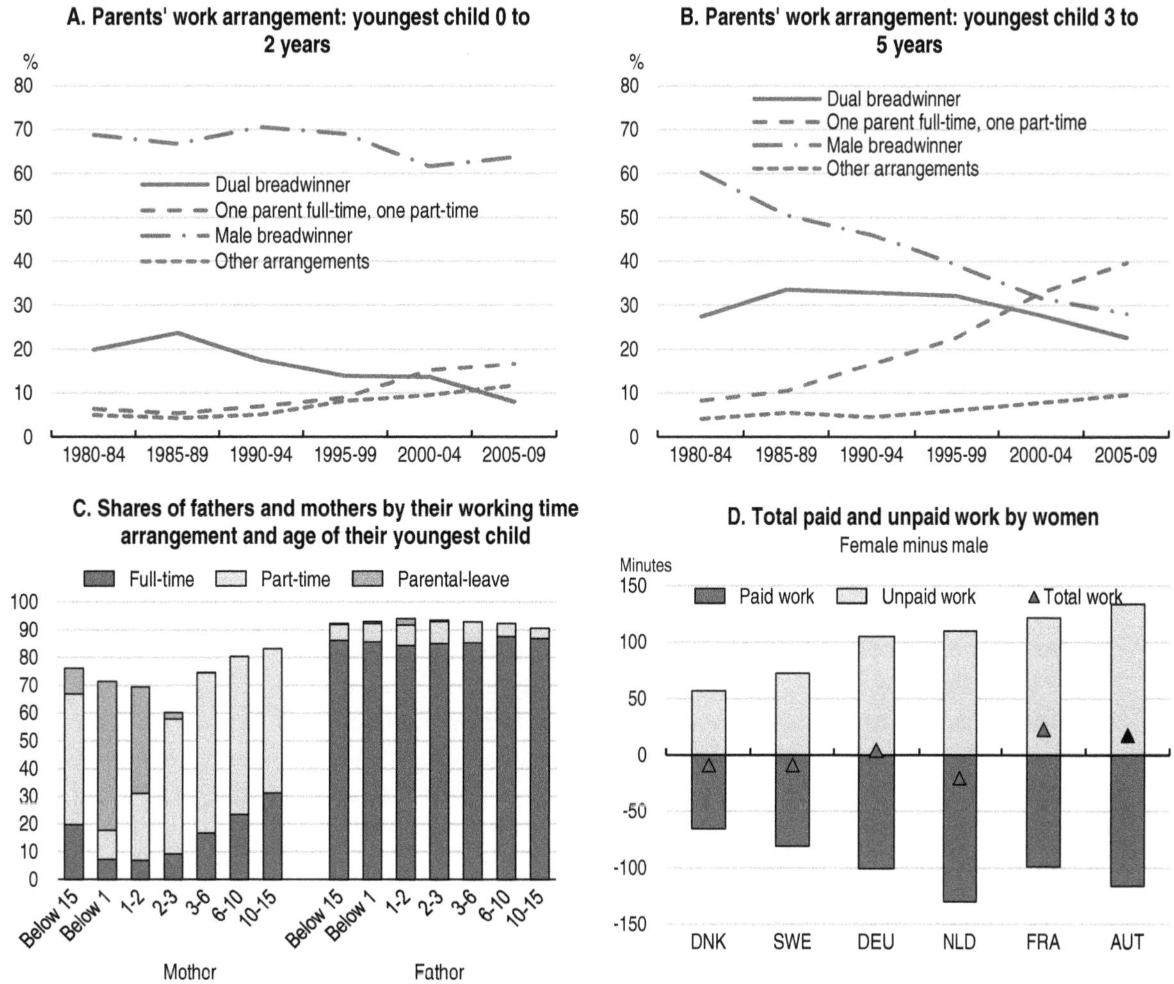

Source: Berghammer (2014), "The Return of the Male Breadwinner Model? Educational Effects on Parents' Work Arrangements in Austria, 1980-2009", *Work, Employment and Society*, Vol. 28, No. 4; Statistik Austria; OECD (2012), *Closing the Gender Gap: Act Now*, OECD Publishing, Paris, *http://dx.doi.org/10.1787/9789264179370-en*.

StatLink http://dx.doi.org/10.1787/888933252108

This model pertains to families in all socio-economic conditions, irrespective of the educational background of parents (Figure 1.3, Panels A and B). It stays in place for a long period in the life cycle of the family, usually until the youngest child completes secondary education at about age 15. In families with children below 15, the majority of mothers continue to work part-time (Figure 1.3, Panel C). Even at compulsory school age, education support from family – from the mother in practice – is needed as a result of Austria's typical half-day schooling schemes. In particular in small, rural municipalities, few extra-curricular activities are available because of budget constraints.

The separation of roles determines the structure of employment at the macroeconomic level. Austria has the second largest share of one full-timer and one part-timer families in the working population among all OECD countries (Figure 1.4). The share of families with one breadwinner, at 30%, is also the highest among comparable countries.

Figure 1.4. **The one full-timer/one part-timer family model prevails in Austria**

Employment patterns among couple families with children aged 0-14, 2011[1]

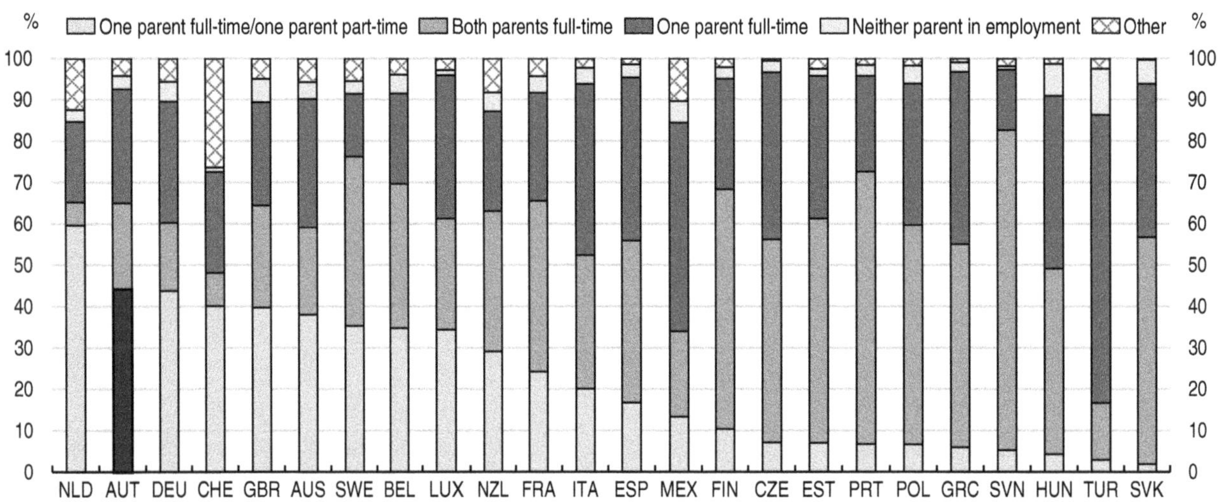

1. Data refer to 2010 for Mexico, Sweden and Switzerland.

Source: OECD (2014), *OECD Family database, www.oecd.org/social/family/database.htm.*

StatLink http://dx.doi.org/10.1787/888933252117

As partners in couple families reach age 40-45, care responsibilities for elderly parents come into play. The majority of dependent elderly are taken care of in home settings, requiring a substantial amount of attendance by family members and bearing on their work and life arrangements (European Commission, 2014c).[2] According to one survey, around 7% of Austrians in the age group 40-44, 9% of those between 45 and 49, and more than 10% of those between 50 and 80 had elderly care duties (Hörl, 2005). The Chamber of Labour reports that, on average, 10% of working age women, and 6% of men, care for an elderly dependant (Chamber of Labour, 2014). In addition, many households have organisation and supervision responsibilities for rotating home carers who play a particularly important role in Austria (home carers for the elderly are generally of foreign origin and alternate three week-long stays with families with three week absences). With the ageing of the population, and the seemingly enduring preference of all involved for home-based care (less than 20% of dependents were in institutional care in 2013) these responsibilities will likely continue to be borne by women. There are indications that women with such responsibilities are more intensely involved than men. On the other hand about 39% of women working part-time point to care responsibilities (for children or elderly) as a major reason for working part-time, against only 4% for male part-timers (European Commission, 2015).

In addition, there is overlap between work and grandparenthood responsibilities. This principally concerns grandmothers providing mostly care for grandchildren. In general daughters receive support from their mothers – childcare remaining therefore a female responsibility across generations. According to EU's Surveys of *Health, Ageing and Retirement (SHARE)* and *Generations and Gender (GGP)*, more than half of all grandparents in Austria contribute to the family tasks of their offspring. This is facilitated by the stability of family settlements, notably in "rural" areas where more than 55% of the Austrian population live.[3] One third of grown-up children continue to live in the same dwelling as their parents and 85% of grandparents have at least one grown-up offspring living closer than 25 km.

The divergence of gender roles alters the balance between paid and unpaid work at the level of society. According to *Statistik Austria*, total work effort provided by the working age population is still slightly biased toward unpaid work (for 51% in 2009). This keeps households' effective labour force participation, earned incomes, purchase of services and aggregate GDP at a lower level than in alternative arrangements which prevail in comparable countries. Even if time use surveys do not permit comprehensive international comparisons in this area, indirect indicators highlight that a different balance between market and household services prevails in Austria (Figure 1.4).

The separation of gender roles is, however, not the only form of work and life organisation in force in Austria. Many women and men do not fit into the prevailing model, even if these alternative arrangements do not benefit from the same institutional and infrastructural support:

i) There are many sole adult households Single person households (including elderly survivors) account for 34% of households, against an OECD average of 28%. Sole parents with dependent children form a larger group in Austria than in comparable countries (accounting for about 10% of households, against 6% in Germany and 5% in Denmark and Switzerland, according to the *OECD Family database*). Single mothers use more time for paid work and less for child care (Statistik Austria, 2009).

ii) Households with dependent children with two full-time workers. The share of such families is about 20%. This is significantly below the OECD average of 37%, but remains above certain comparable countries (these households represent 9% of families with children in Switzerland and 5% in the Netherlands).

iii) Childless households. This is a varied group, including households with grown-up children and households with no children. Their share in all households is above 60%. According to the Austrian Institute of Family Studies, 20% of women born in the 1970s are projected to remain childless, half of them against their initial will. In 2009, only less than 10% of people below age 40 wished to remain childless (Figure 1.5).

Migrant families have more segregated gender roles

Migrant families now account for a sizeable share of Austria's population. Many of these families display deeply separate gender roles, often with the support of Austria's prevailing institutional and infrastructural framework. Many migrant women, especially those with a low educational background, do not participate in the labour market at all and

Figure 1.5. **Voluntary and involuntary childlessness**

Persons childless and their intention to have a child, 2009, per cent per age cohort

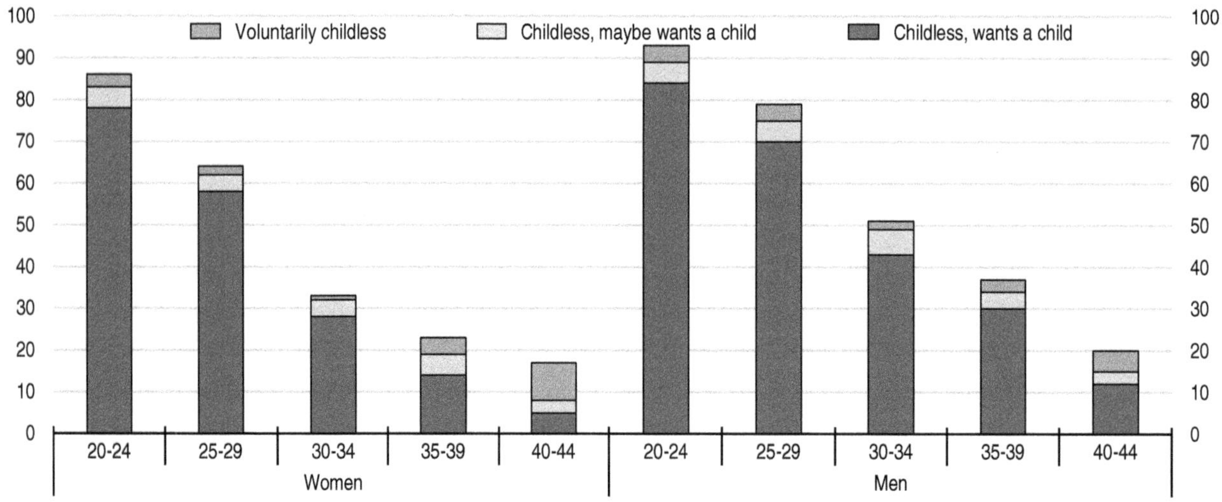

Source: Buber-Ennser et al. (2014), *Families in Austria 2009-2013: Descriptive Findings on Partnerships, Fertility Intentions, Childbearing and Childrearing*, Vienna Institute of Demography, Vienna.

StatLink http://dx.doi.org/10.1787/888933252125

children are raised entirely within families until the compulsory pre-school age of five. Until 2010, compulsory school started in the Fall following a child's sixth birthday, an additional compulsory pre-school year was introduced in 2010.

As parents may be less well equipped than their Austrian counterparts to provide a fully adequate education for the social and economic integration of children (in particular with respect to adequate language development), this raises a special challenge (Knittler, 2011). Groups facing the largest difficulties appear to be migrants from Turkey and former Yugoslavia. More than 60% of women with a Turkish migration background are inactive on the labour market and those working generally have a low-paid job. Their absolute poverty rate is high at 20%, against less than 5% for Austrian women. The early socialisation and education of their children in an exclusively family context risks perpetuating human capital disadvantages.

How Austria compares internationally on gender equality

Separate roles in work and family life have a bearing on Austria's ranking in international gender equality comparisons. Austria regularly stands out as a very "gender unequal" country in these comparisons, even if available indexes capture only imperfectly the existing gaps (Figure 1.6). The following section reviews if and how these inequalities affect key well-being dimensions as identified in OECD's "How's Life?" framework.

Gender-specific well-being outcomes and emerging tensions

Concerning gender gaps in well-being outcomes in advanced countries, the OECD's latest synthesis report suggests that "despite extraordinary achievements in the status of women over the last century, changes were neither uniform nor universal, and gender equality remains an unattained goal" (OECD, 2013b). This diagnosis applies well to Austria: there has been far-reaching gender convergence in many dimensions of well-being, but major gaps persist.

Figure 1.6. **Gender equality in Austria in international comparison**

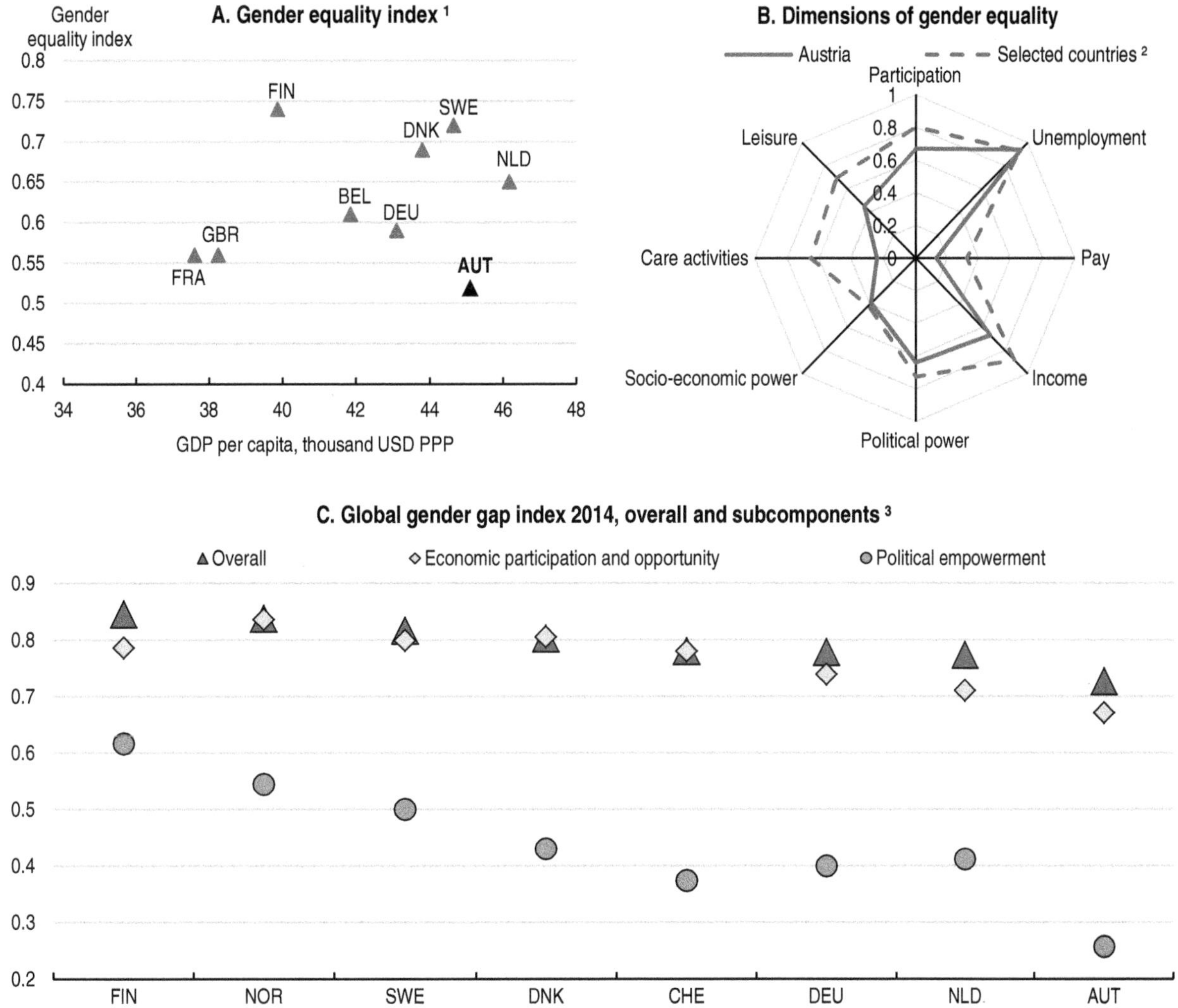

1. A higher score means more gender-equal. This indicator has been computed in Plantenga et al. (2009). It is based on eight indicators: labour force participation, which measures the gap in employment rates between men and women; unemployment, which compares their rate of unemployment; wages and earnings, which captures the average gap between men's and women's hourly earnings; income, which tracks the difference in absolute poverty rates in single households; political participation which is based on the share of men and women in parliament; socio-economic power, which represents the gender gap in the number of senior officials and managers; distribution of care responsibilities, which reflects the difference in caring time for children; and access to leisure, which measures the gap in daily time spent on leisure.
2. Average of Denmark, Finland, Germany, the Netherlands and Sweden.
3. The Global Gender Gap Index was first introduced by the World Economic Forum in 2006 as a framework for capturing gender-based disparities and tracking their progress. It examines the gap between men and women in four fundamental categories: economic participation and opportunity, educational attainment, health and survival, and political empowerment. These subindexes cover 14 different variables. The overall index is an un-weighted average of each subindex score. Economic participation and opportunity subindex contains three concepts: the participation gap, the remuneration gap and the advancement gap. The political empowerment subindex measures the gap between men and women at the highest level of political decision-making. The economic participation and political empowerment dimensions capture most of Austria's gap.

Source: *OECD National Accounts database*; and Plantenga et al. (2009), "Towards a European Union Gender Equality Index", *Journal of European Social Policy*, Vol. 19; World Economic Forum (2014), *The Global Gender Gap Report 2014*, Geneva.

StatLink http://dx.doi.org/10.1787/888933252132

Austria has achieved rather good performances in all of the 11 dimensions of OECD's Well-Being framework, as highlighted in the 2013 *OECD Economic Survey*. This Survey focuses on six dimensions from a gender perspective: i) education and skills; ii) employment and entrepreneurship; iii) income and wealth; iv) work-life balance; v) health; and vi) life satisfaction.

Education and skills

Educational achievements shape life opportunities and drive many other well-being outcomes. They not only determine employability and earnings, but also widen life options, enhance health, and foster civic participation.

Women's educational performance lagged that of men's over most of the 20th century, but there has been steady convergence in recent decades. Young women now surpass young men in terms of tertiary enrolment, and do better on several indicators of academic proficiency. Yet, they are under-represented in education areas that offer the most financially rewarding job opportunities. Gender-specific educational achievements and the divergence of gender roles in society seem to mutually reinforce each other. The segregation in education can be illustrated by gender-differences in: i) educational enrolment; ii) academic proficiency; iii) study area choices; and iv) life-long education and adult skills.

Enrolment

Austrian men's historically higher educational attainments have now faded out. The youngest girl cohorts have approached boys in upper secondary enrolment and surpassed them in tertiary enrolment. With a lag, this convergence affects the educational attainment profile of the entire working age population (Figure 1.7).

This convergence in enrolment has however taken place with a low degree of social mobility. According to OECD (2014a) Austria has still a particularly large gender gap in social mobility in educational attainment: 33% and 25% of men and women have respectively attained higher educational levels than their parents, against OECD averages of 40% and 38%. Austria is at present one of the only two OECD countries where women's intergenerational educational mobility is inferior to men's (Schneebaum et al., 2013).

Proficiency

Girls' reading skills now exceed those of the boys in Austria, but boys perform better in mathematics (Figure 1.8). Over the past decade girls' superiority in reading has weakened, and their handicap in mathematics increased. Austria is the OECD country where girls' relative position eroded most between 2003 and 2012 (OECD, 2015a).

Study area choices

Girls and boys tend to select different study areas in Austria at all levels of education (Figure 1.9). These differences have changed little over the past 30 years and some of them have widened rather than narrowed. The inertia in interest areas may reflect the strong emphasis on gender roles from early school years. For example, boys and girls used to attend separate handicraft and needlework lessons until 1979,[4] and are still split for physical education classes. Their focus seems to diverge relatively early. For example, Austria is the OECD country where the gap between girls and boys in "reading enjoyment" is the widest. When asked about professional expectations, 15 years olds express highly

Figure 1.7. **Gender differences in educational attainment have disappeared**

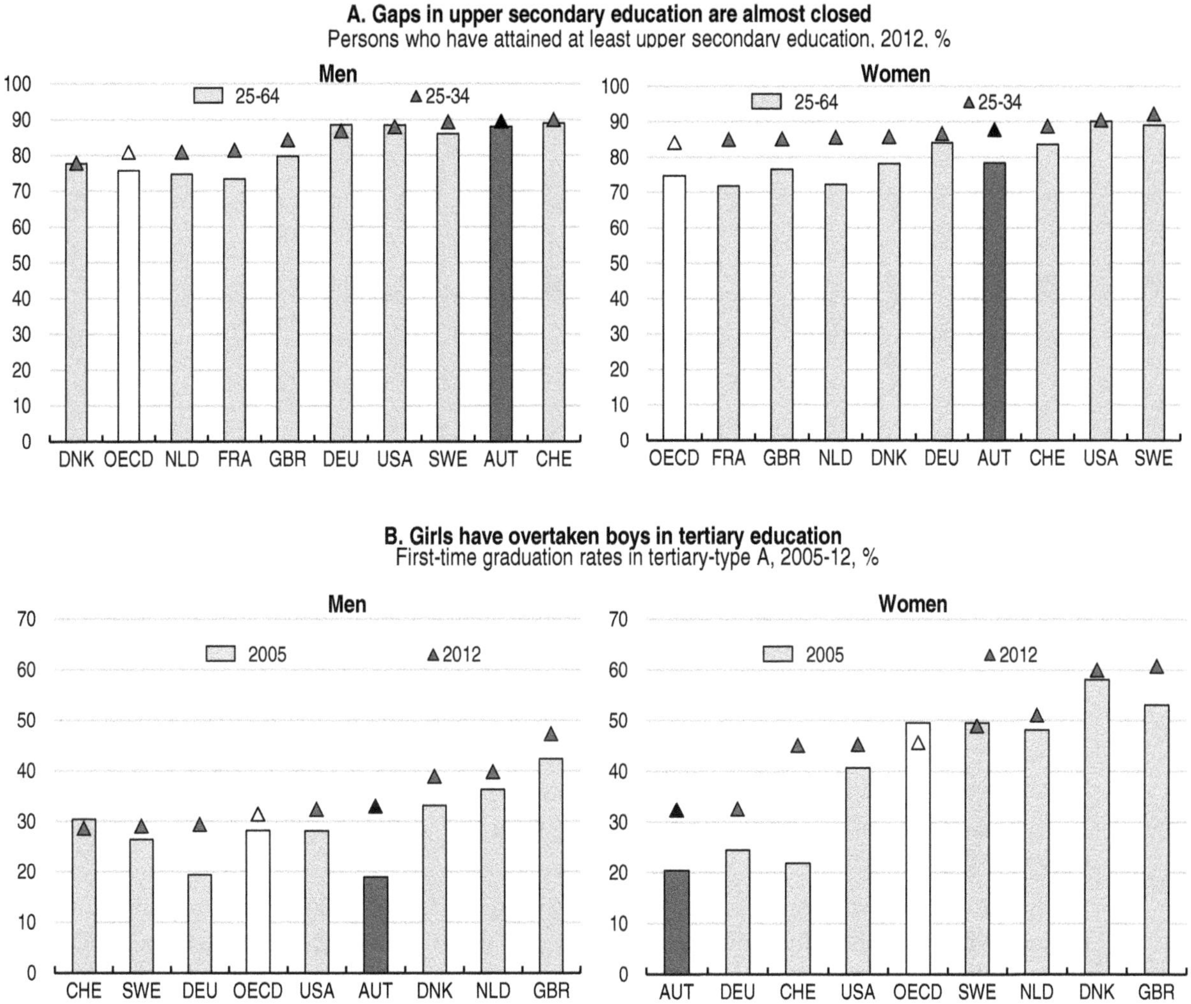

Source: OECD *Education database.*

StatLink http://dx.doi.org/10.1787/888933252142

different inclinations: boys show much more interest for technical and research areas and girls for social, artistic and language-related fields (Eder, 2012). These differences seem to have become more pronounced in the 2000s (Lassnigg et al., 2014) and a recent study confirmed their persistence in tertiary choices (Freisinger et al., 2014).

In part, these divergences reflect anticipated gender roles. Boys lean toward fields with higher and safer revenues, while for girls, professions with multiple employment opportunities (across geographical areas) and those compatible with career interruptions and part-time work may be more attractive. Indeed, a study documented the restrained geographical mobility of married women, which hinders their employability and earnings (Mairhuber, 2009). At the time of that study, the public employment service classified 50% of registered female unemployed as "hard to place"; in 65% of the cases this was due to their "restricted geographical mobility".

Figure 1.8. **Girls and boys have different academic achievements**

Difference in Pisa score points (boys' scores minus girls' scores), 2012

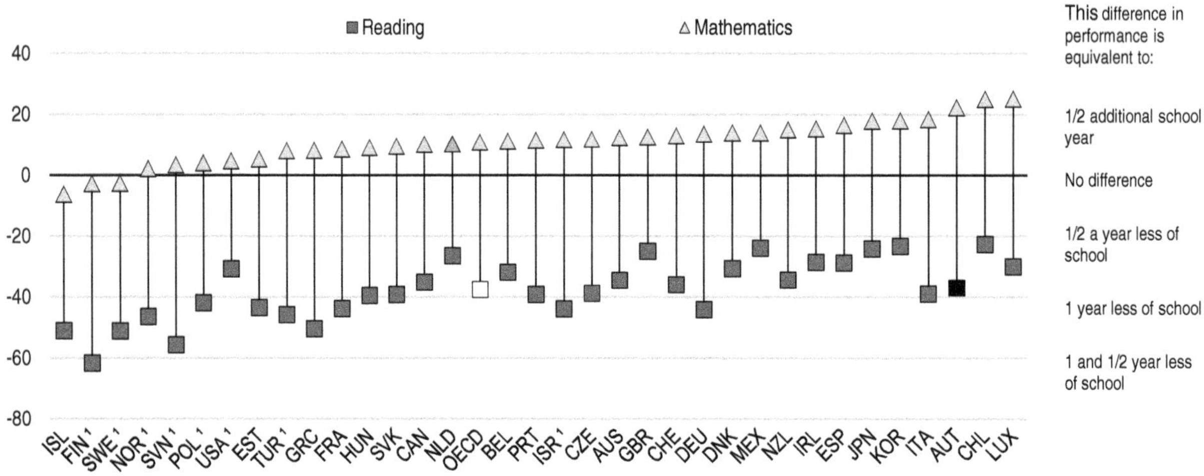

1. Pisa scores difference in mathematics is not statistically significant for this country.

Source: OECD (2015). *The ABC of Gender Equality in Education: Aptitude, Behaviour, Confidence*, PISA, OECD Publishing, Paris, *http://dx.doi.org/10.1787/9789264229945-en.*

StatLink http://dx.doi.org/10.1787/888933252155

The divergence of study fields occur in apprenticeships, secondary vocational education and tertiary education:

- In apprenticeships (which remain the largest education stream in Austria) choices are highly gender-specific. Half of all girl apprentices are in retail trade, office work, and hairdressing, while more than half of young men are in technical fields (Figure 1.9, Panel A).
- Study fields are equally gender-specific in secondary vocational education. The share of female graduates in childhood education, social work and support services is 95%, 93% and 90% respectively, but it falls below 20% in engineering. Some 75% of technical school students are boys while 80% of economic school students are girls (Figure 1.9, Panel B).
- Girls and boys make very different area choices in tertiary education as well. Girls mostly enter health, education and social professions, but are utterly underrepresented in engineering and computer sciences. The proportion of female graduates in scientific areas is one of the lowest in OECD (Figure 1.9, Panel C).
- An OECD review found that study areas in Austria are excessively driven by student demands and not enough by labour market needs (Musset et al., 2013). Austria has a particularly high share of over-qualified workers, whose occupation does not match their field of study. This especially concerns women.

Life-long education and adult competencies

The qualification profile of the working age population reflects individuals' earlier education and subsequent professional experience. The OECD PIAAC survey revealed the following characteristics of Austrian adults' labour market skills, which echo separate gender roles:

- Average adult proficiency is below OECD average in reading, above OECD average in numeracy, and at about OECD average in problem-solving (Figure 1.10, Panel A).

Figure 1.9. **Study areas differ by gender**

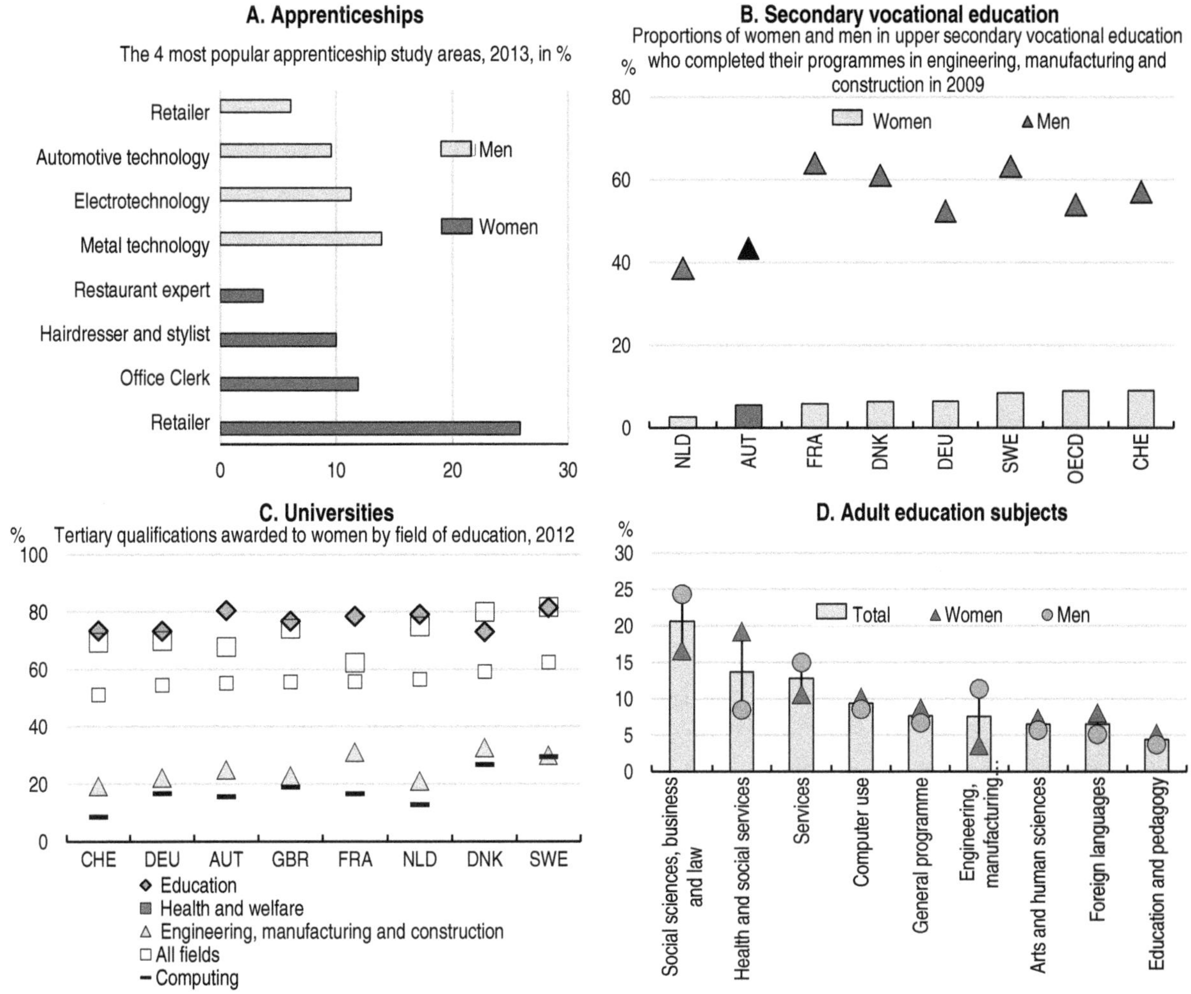

Source: Statistik Austria; OECD (2012), *Closing the Gender Gap: Act Now*, OECD Publishing, Paris, *http://dx.doi.org/10.1787/9789264179370-en*; OECD (2014), *Education at a Glance 2014: OECD Indicators*, OECD Publishing, Paris, Table A3.3 online only, *http://dx.doi.org/10.1787/888933115388*; Statistik Austria, *Erwachsenenbildungserhebung 2011/2012 (AES)*.

StatLink http://dx.doi.org/10.1787/888933252167

- Women's average skills are weaker than men's, with a similar gender gap as the OECD average, but a larger difference than in comparable countries.
- Gaps across age groups are steeper in Austria than in comparable countries. The best qualified cohorts are the youngest ones, skills then erode sharply, especially for women.
- Average skills are much stronger for childless adults than for those with children. The gap is larger for women (mothers) and larger in Austria than in comparable countries. This may be related to their longer absences from professional life (Figure 1.10, Panel C).
- Adult skills are more evenly distributed than in comparable countries, as reflected in the Gini distribution of skills and the distance between high and low performers. The share of the lowest-skilled is smaller than in comparable countries, in particular among women. The adult population appears therefore well-equipped for life-long education (Figure 1.10, Panel B).

Figure 1.10. **Adult skills**

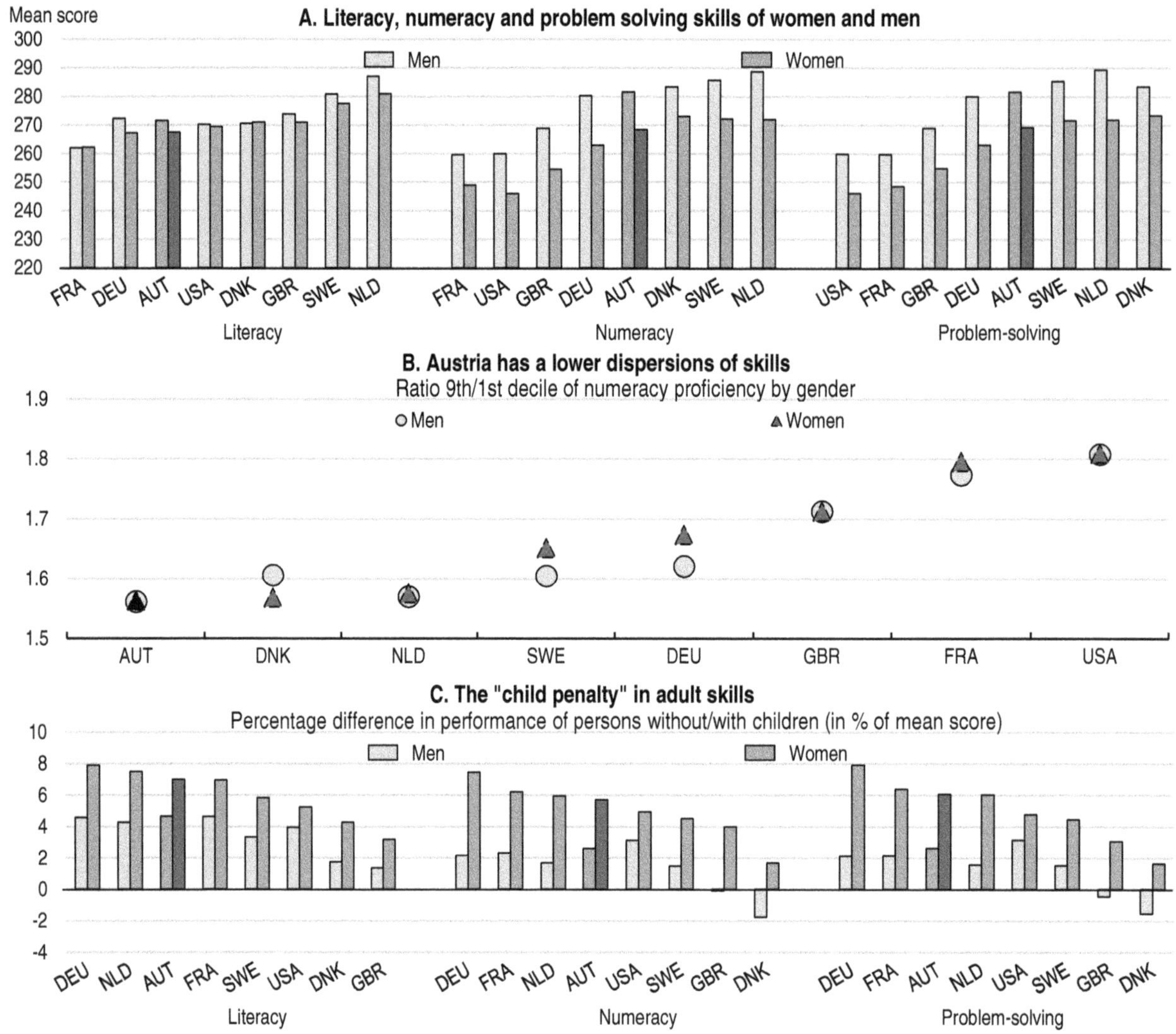

Source: Calculations from OECD PIAAC data.

StatLink http://dx.doi.org/10.1787/888933252171

Life-long education is increasing in Austria. It is offered through active labour market schemes, on-the-job training and personal participation in educational programmes. It has some distinct gender characteristics:

- In the past, men were more active in adult education than women, with a larger gender gap than in comparable countries. However, policy initiatives permitted a convergence in life-long education. Enrolment in adult education grew more rapidly than in the rest of Europe, and more rapidly for women than men. According to Eurostat's latest Adult Education Survey in 2011, 48.7% of male workers and 47.6% of female workers had participated in some formal or informal life-long learning in the last twelve months (Eurostat, 2011).
- Still, many women declare not having access to adult education, mainly because of family responsibilities. This obstacle is reported more frequently in Austria than in other small European countries. *Statistik Austria* confirms that availability for adult education

seems to be below comparable countries because of family duties invoked by women and workload invoked by men (Statistik Austria, 2014a).

- There is a gender asymmetry in subject choices. Men seek further skills more frequently in engineering, production and construction, while women do so in health, pedagogy and foreign languages (Statistik Austria, 2007).
- There is common interest for new technology programmes. Attendance rates are gender balanced in computer and life sciences. Women show active interest for re-qualification schemes to help them engage in new professions.

Employment and entrepreneurship

Having a job that matches one's interests and pays well is an universal aspiration. Jobs provide income, help develop new skills and create opportunities for social and professional relationships (OECD, 2013b). In contrast, unemployment undermines physical and mental health, and subjective well-being. Labour market behaviour of Austrian women confirms that access to employment is a widely-shared goal.

Despite high female participation rates at prime age, women's effective labour force participation subsequently falls short of men's (Figure 1.11). For the relatively younger cohorts, this results from the prevalence of part-time work after the birth of children and the uneven share of unpaid work as discussed above. For the more senior cohorts, it reflects the low statutory and effective retirement ages, as well as high invalidity rates. At present, the *de facto* retirement age for old-age pensions is 59 for women against 62 for men. Both are lower than in other OECD countries, but the gap with comparable countries is particularly large for women (Figure 1.11, Panel D).

In the years following the global crisis Austria's gender gaps in employment diminished. This resulted from severe job losses in trade-exposed and male-dominated manufacturing, in contrast with more resilient employment in female-dominated services (Figure 1.12). Major differences persist nonetheless in the respective employment characteristics of the genders.

Beyond the bifurcation into full and part-time employment (Figure 1.11), the types of jobs occupied by men and women differ considerably. Gaps are found in the distribution of contract forms (standard vs. atypical), hierarchical positions and types of entrepreneurial activities.

The overwhelming majority of Austrian men are in standard full-time jobs, against only half of women (Figure 1.13, Panel A). In 2014, 47% of all female workers and 74% of female workers with children below 14 worked part-time (Statistik Austria, 2015). About 80% of part-time workers in the public sector are women (OECD, 2014c). One sixth of all female workers hold other atypical jobs, including the so-called "marginal jobs" (defined as those paying less than EUR 406 per month) and fixed-term, temporary agency and free-lance jobs.

While men dominate traditional manufacturing activities which have standard employment patterns, women dominate in services with special/atypical activity arrangements. Many women with child care responsibilities appear to be forced into non-standard working times because during such periods other family members may be available to look after children. Health, retail trade, tourism and cleaning services are typical of such areas with a majority of female workers. A recent survey of the cleaning sector revealed that nearly 50% of employees work very early in the morning, about 40%

Figure 1.11. **Employment patterns follow the separation of gender roles in the life-cycle**

Ratio of employed persons in age cohort by gender and type of working-time arrangement in percentage of the population of same age cohort and gender, 2013

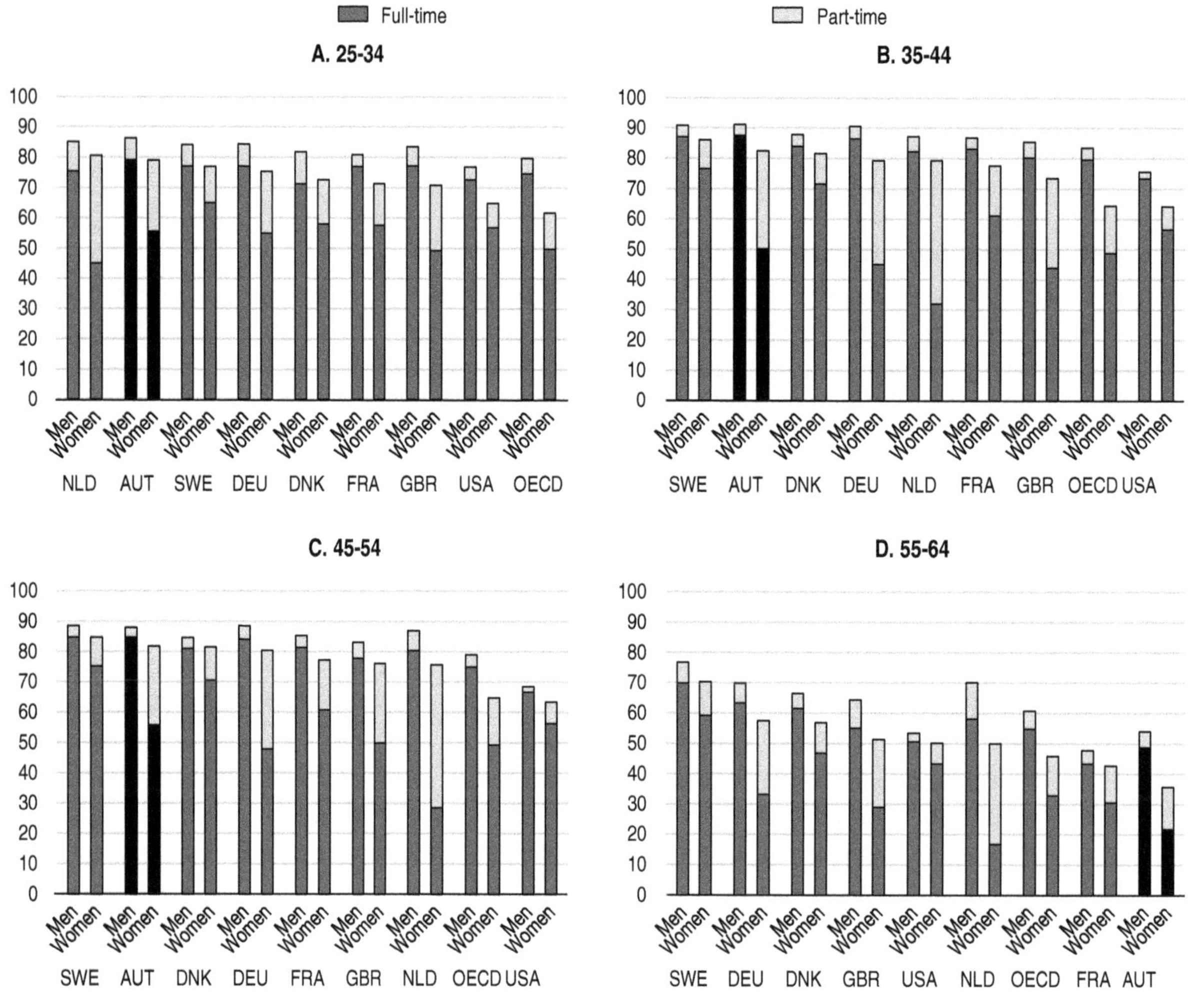

Note: Data presented in this figure do not include persons working less than 30 hours per week in their main job.
Source: OECD, *Labour Force Statistics database*.

StatLink http://dx.doi.org/10.1787/888933252188

have divided schedules, and 10% work during weekends (Arbeiterkammer Wien, 2013). According to the Chamber of Labour, in half of Austrian households at least one parent works outside routine hours (Chamber of Labour, 2014).

The leaky pipeline

Men's and women's access to career progress is uneven. These gaps are bigger than differences in educational backgrounds, and wider than similar gaps observed in comparable countries. They arise at low, middle, and high hierarchical levels:

- Women are overrepresented in low-qualified positions. They occupy the majority of "non-qualified" jobs in manufacturing, despite their minority weight in aggregate manufacturing employment. They also hold the majority of "low-qualified" and "middle-qualified" jobs in services (Statistik Austria, 2010) (Figure 1.13, Panel B).

Figure 1.12. **Female employment has been more resilient after the global crisis**

Index, 2007 = 100

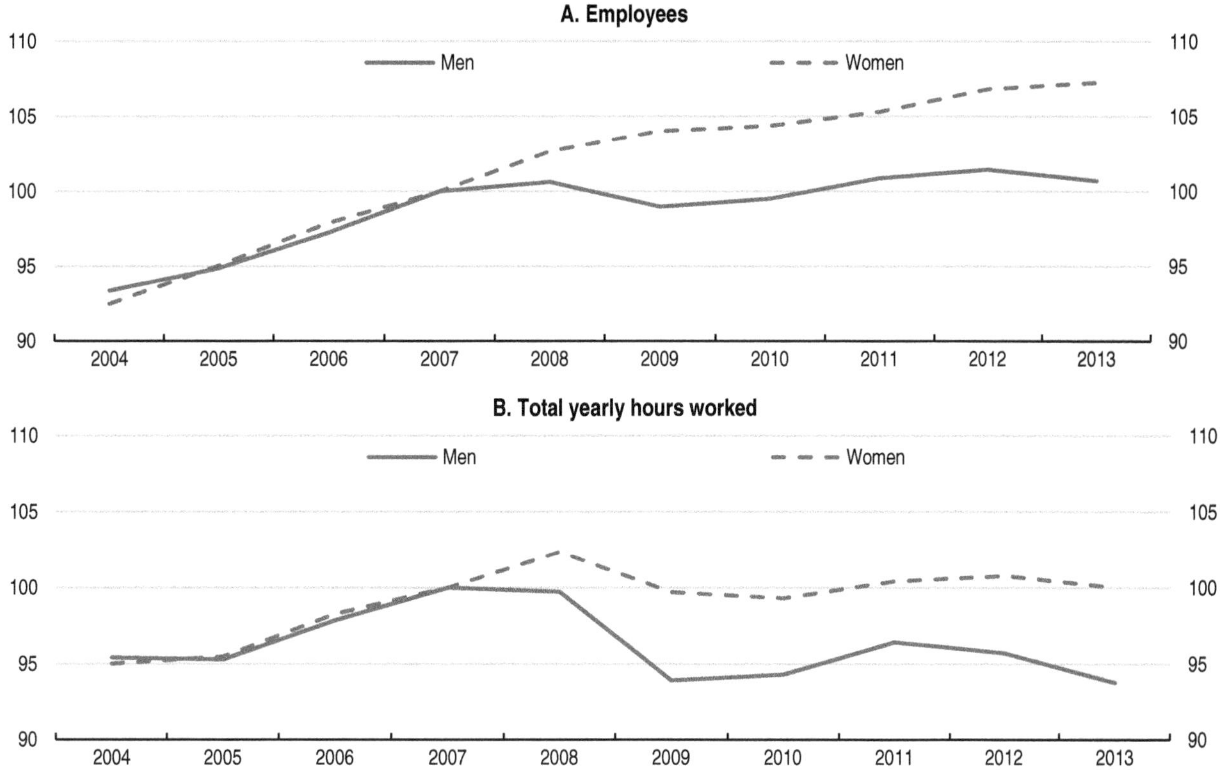

Source: Statistik Austria.

StatLink http://dx.doi.org/10.1787/888933252198

- Women are underrepresented at intermediary management levels. Men and women with similar educational backgrounds, notably those who graduated from upper secondary education attain uneven hierarchical positions (Table 1.1). Available international data suggests that Austria has a lower proportion of female middle-managers than in comparable countries (Figure 1.13, Panel C).
- At senior management levels, women are found in even smaller numbers. According to a recent review, women's share in executive management (6%) and boards (14%) of the 200 largest companies was lower than in comparable countries. Only 3% of stock market-listed companies had a woman CEO. When all firms are taken into consideration, women's presence in top management remains very low: 18% in executive management and 23% on boards (Austrian Court of Audit, 2013). The gap between women's share in total labour force and their share in senior management is one of the highest in the OECD (Figure 1.13, Panel D).
- Similar gender differences exist in the public sector, even if the women's share in high level positions in public services has constantly increased (Chapter 2). In 2011, women's share of federal administration positions was 55%, but their share in the highest positions was 22% – the third largest gap in the OECD (OECD, 2013c). Among comparable countries, women's share in top public sector jobs is still the lowest, and their share in secretarial jobs is the highest (OECD, 2014c). In the judiciary, 55% of the judges and 68% of the judicial authorities in the *Länder* were women in 2013, but their share declined to 29% in the Supreme and Constitutional Courts, and to 25% in the High

Figure 1.13. **Gender gaps in employment quality**

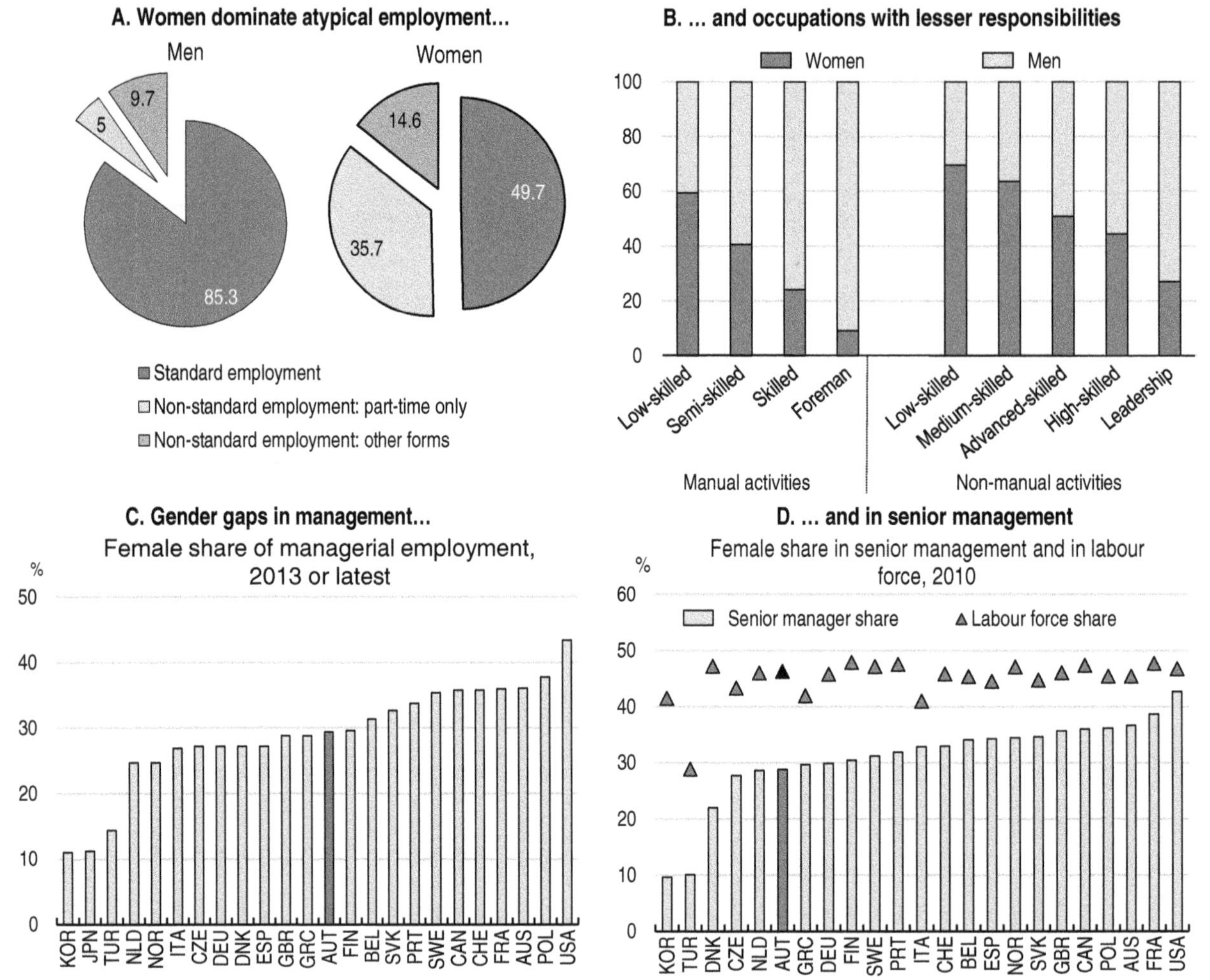

Source: Statistik Austria, Labour Force Surveys 2013; Arbeitmarketservice, Microcensus on labour 2008; OECD (2014), *OECD Family database*, *www.oecd.org/social/family/database.htm*; OECD (2012), *Closing the Gender Gap: Act Now*, OECD Publishing, Paris, *http://dx.doi.org/10.1787/9789264179370-en*.

StatLink http://dx.doi.org/10.1787/888933252052

Administrative Court. Female members of Parliament made up 33% of seats, the same share as in the federal government. Only 6% of town mayors were women. The federal government has recently set quantitative targets for the allocation of senior public positions, as part of gender mainstreaming policies (Chapter 2).

Different entrepreneurial activities

Women are also under-represented among entrepreneurs in Austria. The opportunities and outcomes for women entrepreneurs represent a major dimension in gender equality (OECD, 2013a). In 2012, 65% of entrepreneurs were men, with 9% of the female and 14% of the male labour force being made of entrepreneurs. These proportions are broadly similar to comparable countries (European Commission, 2014a). According to another source, in 2014 58% of start-ups were set up by women and 45% of individual enterprises (*Einzelunternehmen*) were led by women (Wirtschaftskammer Österreich, 2015).

Table 1.1. **Gender employment according to education and occupations**

Education level	All employed	1. Elementary occupations	2. Plant and machine operators	3. Craft workers	4. Skilled workers	5. Service and sales workers	6. Clerical support workers	7. Technicians and associate professionals	8. Professionals	9. Managers
Men										
Compulsory school	100	16.8	14.4	25.8	8.8	14.2	5.1	10.5	2.3	1.6
Apprenticeship	100	5.9	13.2	36.0	4.1	12.1	4.8	16.4	2.8	4.0
Intermediate technical and vocational school	100	2.6	6.0	12.8	18.8	9.7	6.9	29.2	7.3	6.2
Academic secondary school/higher technical and vocational school	100	3.5	3.3	8.2	2.3	10.1	9.0	34.4	19.3	9.7
University, university of applied science, post-secondary college	100	1.4	1.4	2.4	0.5	2.7	3.9	13.2	61.1	12.9
Women										
Compulsory school	100	33.6	4.1	3.0	9.1	32.9	8.4	6.2	1.5	1.1
Apprenticeship	100	11.6	2.4	4.4	4.8	42.5	17.2	12.7	2.6	1.9
Intermediate technical and vocational school	100	5.5	1.4	1.7	7.2	21.9	18.1	34.5	6.9	2.7
Academic secondary school/higher technical and vocational school	100	5.7	0.9	1.4	1.3	18.6	24.4	28.9	15.6	3.3
University, university of applied science, post-secondary college	100	1.6	0.2	0.7	0.7	5.6	6.4	15.3	63.1	6.4

Source: Statistik Austria, Microcensus Labour Force Survey, 2014.

However, female entrepreneurs have a number of specific characteristics in Austria, which seem to make their activities more compatible with separate gender roles (OECD, 2012):

- Most self-employed women have no employees and operate in practice as free-lance workers. In 2012, 72% of female entrepreneurs had no employee, against 51% for men. Women who have employees run smaller firms (Figure 1.14, Panel A).
- Women entrepreneurs' motivations are less "profit oriented" than men's. They are more frequently after "work-life reconciliation" and "flexible activity time". Around 60% of female entrepreneurs mention "combining work and private life" as their main aspiration.
- A high proportion of female entrepreneurs work part-time: 33%, against 9% for male entrepreneurs. In addition, part-time women entrepreneurs work fewer hours than in other European countries. This is in contrast with full-time female entrepreneurs (who are presumably more professionally and financially motivated) who work longer hours than in comparable countries (Figure 1.14, Panel B).
- Women entrepreneurs are almost fully absent from manufacturing. They instead specialise in local services and this asymmetry is deeper than in comparable countries. The proportion of women inventors is also slightly lower than in comparable countries (European Commission, 2014a).

All in all, the profile of female entrepreneurs reveals their preference for smaller size, less time-demanding and financially less rewarding activities than men. These forms of entrepreneurship are more compatible with the prevailing separate roles.

Figure 1.14. **Women have different entrepreneurial activities**

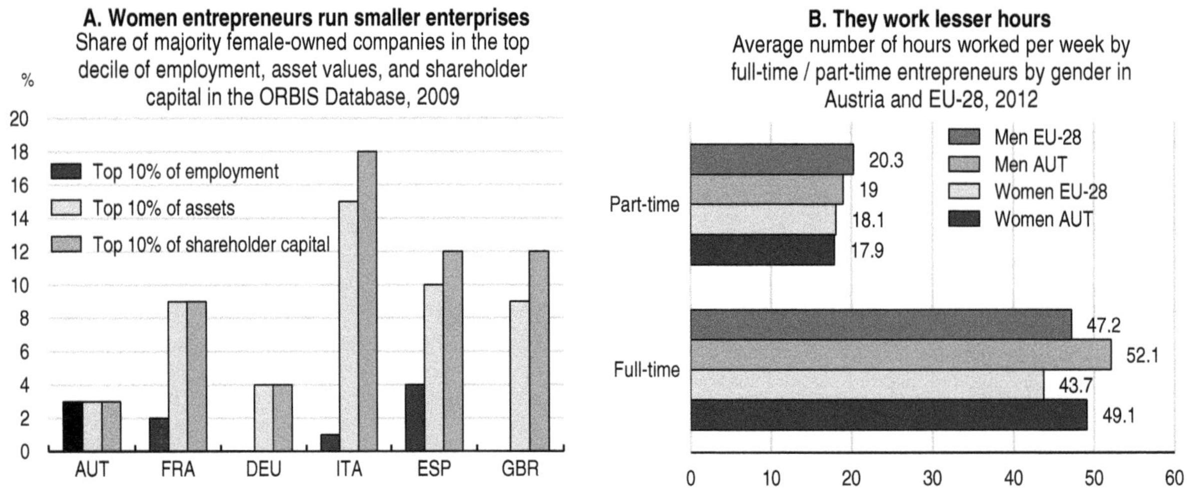

Source: OECD (2012), *Closing the Gender Gap: Act Now*, OECD Publishing, Paris, *http://dx.doi.org/10.1787/9789264179370-en*; European Commission (2014), *Statistical Data on Women Entrepreneurs in Europe – Country Fiche – Austria*, Enterprise and Industry, September, Brussels.

StatLink http://dx.doi.org/10.1787/888933252213

Income and wealth

Income and wealth are important for well-being. The ability to command resources allows everybody to satisfy material needs and pursue other goals that they deem important. Earned incomes enhance people's freedom to choose the lives that they want to live, and protect them against risks.

As most women and men live in couples, the intra-household distribution of resources within the couple delineates both genders' consumption and investment options. However, reliable information is scarce in this area (Box 1.1), hence this Survey focuses on gender differences in separately earned incomes.

Box 1.1. **Intra-household sharing of resources**

As reviewed in detail in OECD (2013b), ignoring the intra-household distribution of resources may lead to important misperceptions of actual inequality between genders. There are no international guidelines on how intra-household allocation of resources should be measured. The European Union Survey on Income and Living Conditions (SILC) introduced some questions on intra-household distribution of resources but this effort is exploratory (European Commission, 2012b).

About two thirds of European households in this EU-SILC Survey declared that they consider individual revenues as a common resource to the family. OECD (2013b) suggests that intra-household sharing of earned incomes is driven by household members' attitude towards the value of unpaid work. International poverty indicators assume on the other hand that all incomes are pooled within households, and therefore all household members reach the same level of material well-being.

In Austria, a lower proportion of all couple families than in comparable countries treat the couple's income as a common resource. About half of Austrian households report such pooling, against more than 70% in Germany, Sweden, Denmark and the Netherlands. This could imply that unpaid work is not seen as fully equivalent to paid work in a significant proportion of Austrian families. Historically, in many households, the breadwinning husband used to give a "household budget and pocket money" to his partner, and the latter did not know the exact level of family income. The information must now be more widely shared, but the "budget and pocket money" practice seems to persist in many families.

In all OECD countries, women's earned incomes are lower to men's on average (or at the median), but the gap is particularly wide in Austria (Figure 1.15). This has three sources: differences in number of hours worked; gaps in hourly wages; and differences in entrepreneurial incomes. The first two components are better documented. *Statistik Austria* reports them on the basis of hourly wages (Geisberger and Glaser, 2014), while the OECD compiles, less frequently, pay gaps for full-time earners.

Figure 1.15. **Gender pay gaps in Austria**

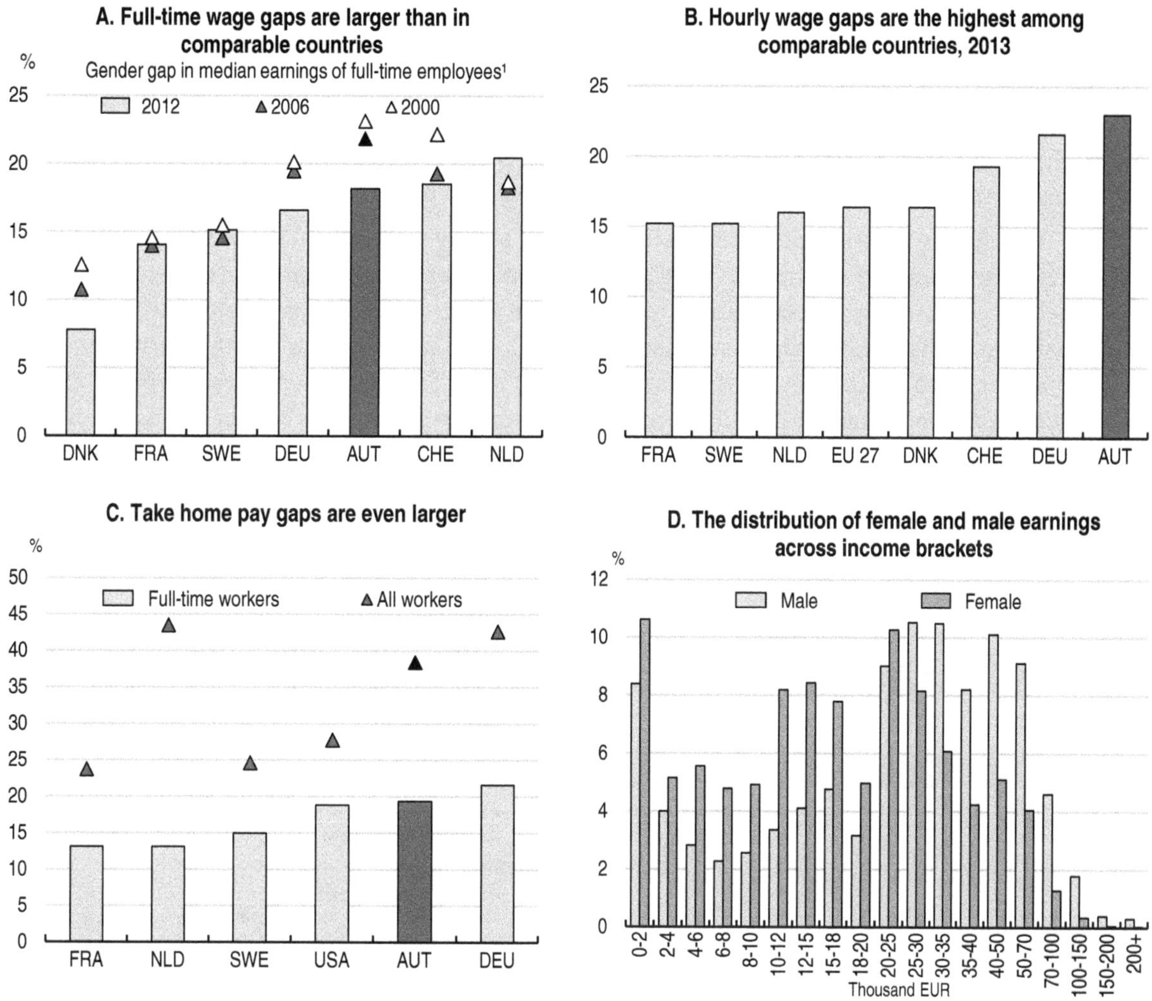

1. The gender wage gap is unadjusted, and is calculated as the difference between median earnings of men and women relative to median earnings of men. Estimates of earnings used in the calculations refer to gross earnings of full-time wage and salary workers. However, this definition may slightly vary from one country to another.

Source: OECD (2014), *OECD Family database*, *www.oecd.org/social/family/database.htm*; Eurostat; OECD (2012), *Closing the Gender Gap: Act Now*, OECD Publishing, Paris, *http://dx.doi.org/10.1787/9789264179370-en*; Statistik Austria.

StatLink *http://dx.doi.org/10.1787/888933252227*

The gender pay gap amounted to 19% for full-time earners in 2011 (Figure 1.15, Panel A) and to 23% for hourly wages in 2013 (Figure 1.15, Panel B). Gaps remained large despite a faster reduction than in most of the similar countries in the 2000s. Compounded by differences in the number of work hours, actual income gaps are higher, attaining about 40% (Figure 1.15, Panel C). The weight of part-time work contributes importantly to income gaps not only because pay is low due to fewer hours, but also because hourly wages are significantly lower in part-time than in full-time jobs (EUR 15.58 vs. 12.43 according to Eurostat, 2010).

Men are also concentrated in higher paying sectors. The wage differential between high and low wage sectors is among the largest in Europe. Although collective agreements generally reduce gender pay gaps (European Trade Union Confederation, 2015), their very large coverage in Austria (95% of the work force is covered) does not suffice to reduce the pay gaps. This arises from two factors: i) differences are large between collectively agreed pay levels across branches and more women than men work in low wage branches; and ii) in high wage branches, supplementary pay above collectively agreed levels is widespread and benefit mostly men in higher hierarchical positions. Women in high wage branches earn more than women in other branches, but the gender pay gap is larger within such branches, as men benefit more from overpay. Otherwise, pay gaps for skilled jobs are narrow in international comparison, as a result of collective agreements.

The latest statistical analysis available of the gender pay gap in Austria (Figure 1.16, Panel A) decomposed the hourly pay gap in 2010 into a set of potential determinants (age, education, sector, region, occupation, full/part-time work, seniority, size of enterprise, etc.) (Geisberger, 2014). The analysis suggests that: i) 3.7 percentage points of the hourly wage gap are related to the sector men and women work in; ii) 2.2 percentage points to differences in occupation; iii) 3.2 percentage points result from the higher incidence of part-time jobs that are less well remunerated; and iv) 2.4 percentage points are related to the higher seniority of men. Enterprise size and region do not play a significant role.

Figure 1.16. **Drivers of the gender pay gap**

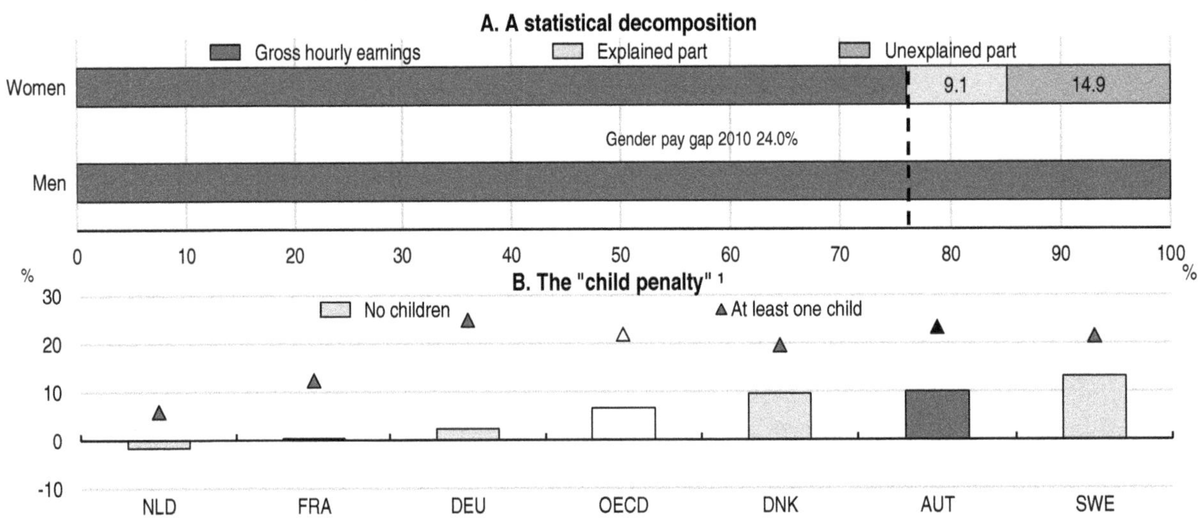

1. Pay gap over men for women with and without children.

Source: Geisberger, T. and T. Glaser (2014), "Geschlechtsspezifische Verdienstunterschiede – Analysen zum Gender Pay Gap auf Basis der Verdienststrukturerhebung 2010", *Statistische Nachrichten* 2014, No. 3, Statistik Austria, Vienna; OECD (2012), *Closing the Gender Gap: Act Now*, OECD Publishing, Paris, *http://dx.doi.org/10.1787/9789264179370-en*

StatLink http://dx.doi.org/10.1787/888933252234

A more complete analysis of the drivers of the gap might shed additional light on the respective influences of objective vs. non-identified sources. Possibly, with more detailed identification and measurement of worker and job characteristics, the explained part of the gap would increase (O'Neill, 2003; Goldin, 2014). An ongoing OECD study aims at re-estimating the gender pay gaps in OECD countries after controlling for a range of structural characteristics. Early results for Austria suggest that, once observable factors are controlled for, the wage penalty for part-time permanent work disappears for women, although there is still a significant penalty for women in part-time temporary work. But the bottom-line is that the gender pay gap remains very large.

One factor that plays an important role in the pay gap is the presence of children. This appears to affect much more women's (mothers') pay than men's. According to existing evidence, and before statistically controlling for other factors, the wage gap is significantly higher for women with children than women without. This penalty appears to be larger in Austria than in similar countries, except Germany (Figure 1.16, Panel B). The Chamber of Labour observes that this source of wage discrepancy varies across *Länder* and is inversely proportional to available child care capacity. The child penalty may be proxying the observed or anticipated reduction in workplace availability, and the commitment of the mother associated with care responsibilities (Lazear and Rosen, 1990; Goldin, 2014).

According to OECD Employment Statistics, the Austrian gender pay gap is particularly large at the low end of income distribution (Figure 1.17, Panel A): despite some narrowing over the past decade, it remains the second largest for low-income earners among all OECD countries (after Korea). The pay gap was 5.5% for civil servants in 2012, 50% for white-collar employees and 57% for blue-collar workers (AMS, 2014). The absence of a national minimum wage, combined with asymmetries between collective agreement

Figure 1.17. **Pay gaps are larger for low income workers**

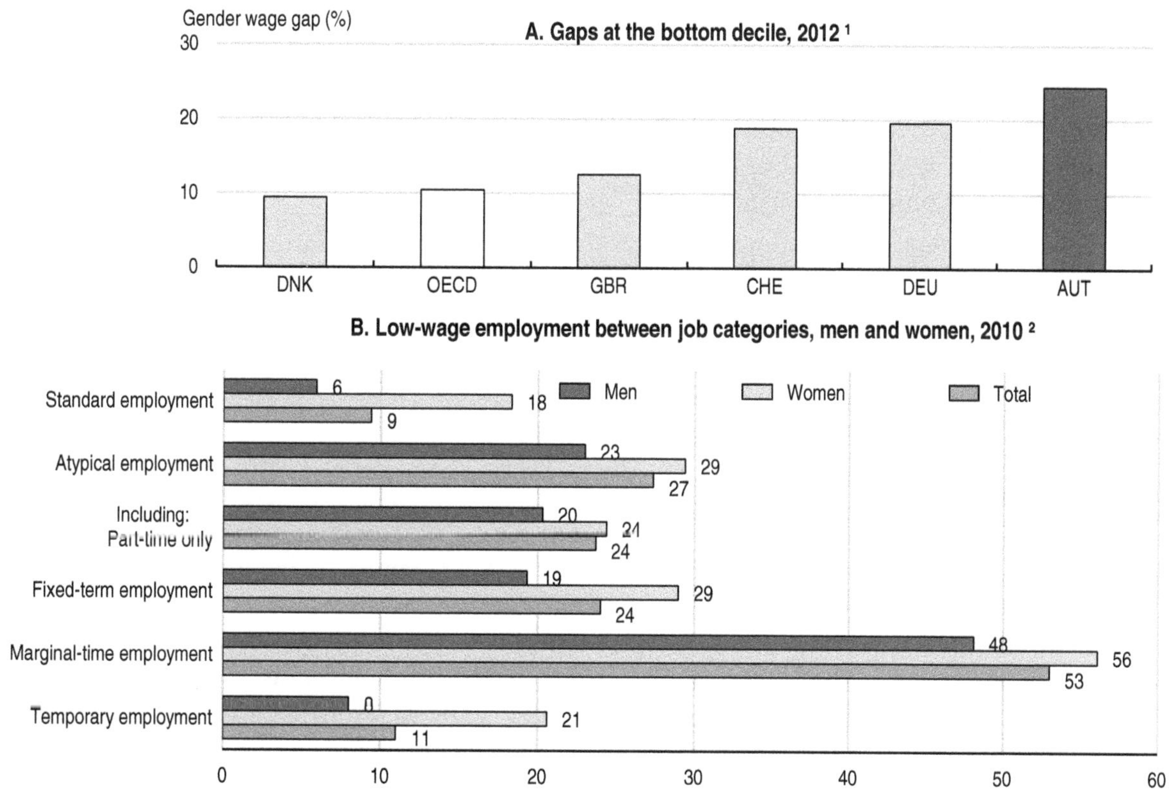

1. 2011 for Germany, 2010 for OECD unweighted average and for Switzerland.
2. Low-wage jobs are defined as those earning less than 60% of the average hourly wage.

Source: *OECD Employment database* as of 11 February 2015 (*www.oecd.org/els/emp/onlineoecdemploymentdatabase.htm*); Statistik Austria.

StatLink http://dx.doi.org/10.1787/888933252241

outcomes in different branches may explain this result. A quarter of all working women are in low-wage jobs (defined as earning less than 60% of the median hourly wage), against 9% for men. This is the largest gap among low-wage earners in EU countries. Women's weight in non-standard jobs is a major driver: almost 30% of fixed-term and nearly 60% of marginal jobs occupied by women are low-paid (Figure 1.17, Panel B). In addition, low-wages are more persistent for women: one out of five women who had a low-paid job in 2000 was in the same position in 2010, while for men the same ratio was 1 out of 10. Between 2000-10, 70% of men changed successfully to a better paid job, while only a quarter of the women managed to do so.

As a result, poverty risks are highest for women. The incidence of absolute poverty is low in Austria as a whole, but relative poverty, which designates the persons earning less than 60% of median income, concerns a majority of women. Poverty risks are highest in single-parent households, the quasi-totality of which (90%) are single-mother households.

Income gaps between genders result chiefly from earned income, but are amplified by gaps in pension entitlements and capital revenues. Around 15% of women at poverty risk are single female pensioners. The low level of women's pensions mirrors their generally discontinuous and part-time contribution histories. Average female pensions attained only 62% of men's in 2014 (EUR 890 per month on average, against EUR 1 430 for men).

Despite significantly lower entitlements in terms of annuities, women's lifetime "pension wealth" is well above that of men, due to lower legal retirement ages, longer life expectancy and generous survivor pensions. Female retirees spend 6 years more than men in retirement, this length reaching 28 years in average – and about 32 years for "middle-class" women (middle-class is defined according to income level, occupation, social insurance status and place of residence) (Marin, 2013). Cross-gender subsidies within the social security system secure these entitlements, without however raising them significantly above the material deprivation floor: average female pensions (EUR 890 per month) are only slightly above that level (EUR 870 per month, i.e. the level of the socially guaranteed minimum income) (Box 1.2).

Women and men have also uneven financial wealth, generating uneven capital revenues. As the majority of people live in couple households, the crucial factor is how ownership of and returns from these assets are shared in the households. This evidence is not available but recent information from European *Household Finance and Consumption Surveys* shed some light on wealth differences between single male and single female households (Box 1.3).

Work-life balance

The OECD's *Babies and Bosses* (2007) and *How's Life?* (2013) underline that obtaining the right balance between work and personal life is a key factor in people's well-being. Insufficient work prevents people from earning enough income to attain the desired standard of living. In contrast, overly absorbing work has a negative impact when health or personal lives suffer. Work-life balances do not only affect the well-being of individuals but also of their family. Notably, children's well-being depends strongly on the capacity of parents to both work and care for them.

Box 1.2. **Pension subsidies to women**

Current pension rules support women through four channels (in addition to earlier opportunities to "purchase" contribution years at about 10% of actuarial value):

- *Childcare years are taken into account:* childcare periods of up to four years per child are credited on the basis of a fictitious pensionable salary of EUR 1 650 per month. Fathers too have such years credited as contributory years if they are the main carer of the child, e.g. as a lone parent or male homemaker living with a working mother.
- *Survivor benefits:* survivors' pensions are fixed according to benefit rules which were revised in 2009. Benefits can reach up to 60% of the income of the deceased person depending on the financial conditions of the survivor. More than 25% of pensioners were drawing survivor benefits in mid-2000s and this proportion is projected to stay above 20% until 2050. The benefit is available to both women and men, but the incidence is smaller for the latter because of the gap in life expectancy and pension entitlements.
- *Working-time reductions:* government subsidies are granted to women above 53 – and men above 58 – to help them reduce working hours and shift to part-time work without losing income (*Altersteilzeit*). Two thirds of the users of this scheme are women.
- *Minimum social assistance:* Elderly people in financial distress can obtain this assistance (*Mindestsicherung*), which ensures a minimum retirement income of EUR 828 per month to each single person, and EUR 1 242 to a couple. There are 14 payments per annum. This is available to men and women alike but a majority of women receive it in practice.

Source: OECD (2013), *OECD Economic Surveys: Austria 2013*, OECD Publishing, Paris, *http://dx.doi.org/10.1787/eco_surveys-aut-2013-en*; and OECD (2013), *Pensions at a Glance 2013: OECD and G20 Indicators*, OECD Publishing, Paris, *http://dx.doi.org/10.1787/pension_glance-2013-en*.

Existing work-life arrangements give rise to four specific tensions in Austria (Figure 1.18): i) the excessively long hours worked by men crowd out their private and family life; ii) a share of women part-timers desire to work longer hours but do not have the necessary service support; iii) households opting for other arrangements confront many practical challenges; and iv) the population as a whole faces a more restricted set of options in work and life arrangements than in comparable countries:

- In Austria 10% of employees work more than 50 hours per week, more than in comparable countries. In 2013, 25% of men worked overtime, against 13.5% for women. According to a survey by the Chamber of Labour, 46% of all full-time working men with children below age 12 regularly work overtime, against 28% for full-time working women (Bergmann et al., 2014). The number of working hours is particularly high when the partner is out of employment: 40% of the full-time employed sole-earners work more than 10 overtime hours per week.
- The OECD report on family policies stresses that "there is a premium to part-time work in terms of control over working time, stress and health, and for the vast majority of part-timers the advantages outweigh the disadvantages" (OECD, 2011a). OECD (2010a) reports that across the OECD 83% of part-time workers declare doing so voluntarily, and that they deliberately accept lower earnings and slower careers "in exchange for better working-time arrangements and less stress". Female part-time work in Austria reinforces this pattern, which is supported by an institutional and infrastructural framework (Chapter 2). According to OECD's *Gender Equality in Employment database* the share of involuntary part-time workers is lower than in comparable countries in Austria, at less than

Box 1.3. **Gender wealth gaps**

According to Mader et al. (2014), who used data from the new European Household Finance and Consumption Survey, the financial wealth gap between genders in Austria is wider than in comparable countries. Comparing single-person households, the authors find that men households are richer than in the rest of Europe, and female households poorer (table below, Panel A). The gap stays large through income deciles (Panel B).

A. Net wealth by household type (EUR thousands)

	Austria		European Union	
	Mean	Median	Mean	Median
Single female households	110	22	127	42
Single male households	194	123	151	39
Couple households	381	170	292	164

B. Net wealth by income distribution (EUR)

Income percentiles	Single female households			Single male households		
	Annual income	Wealth		Income	Wealth	
		Mean	Median		Mean	Median
1	600	39 479	11 300	900	8 322	5 140
10	6 653	49 456	6 913	9 022	243 414	13 535
25	12 538	75 459	12 023	16 240	191 893	5 655
50	19 530	84 930	12 080	24 028	195 444	11 977
75	29 733	88 168	16 135	33 363	142 981	13 990
90	43 857	89 355	17 788	48 560	139 944	16 683
99	83 285	90 412	19 523	120 671	159 874	19 840

Source: Mader et al. (2014).

A recent analysis (Altzinger, 2014) found that financial wealth plays a role only for top earnings. Until the 95th percentile, households live almost entirely out of labour or entrepreneurial incomes. Gaps in financial wealth affect incomes at the highest end of the income distribution.

2% of total employment. However, there is a common perception, as in other OECD countries with a similar experience (e.g. Germany and Switzerland), that if conditions were more conducive for full-time work, a significant proportion of women would shift from part-time to full-time employment to improve earnings and careers. In an earlier survey, only 19% of households with a child below 6 had two full-time breadwinners, but twice as many of them (36%) declared to be willing to do so (Jaumotte, 2003).

- Men and women opting out of disparate gender roles find a relatively unsupportive environment. The "double burden" of job and care duties for full-time working women and sole mothers generate time deprivation and stress, with negative effects on life satisfaction and health. Multivariate analyses suggest that a further child generates a reduction in discretionary time for women of 2.3 hours per week (1.7 hours for men), and an increase of 3.5% in the probability to be time-poor (2.6% for men) (OECD, 2013b). Such households face many practical, organisational and financial strains.

Figure 1.18. **Work and life balances**

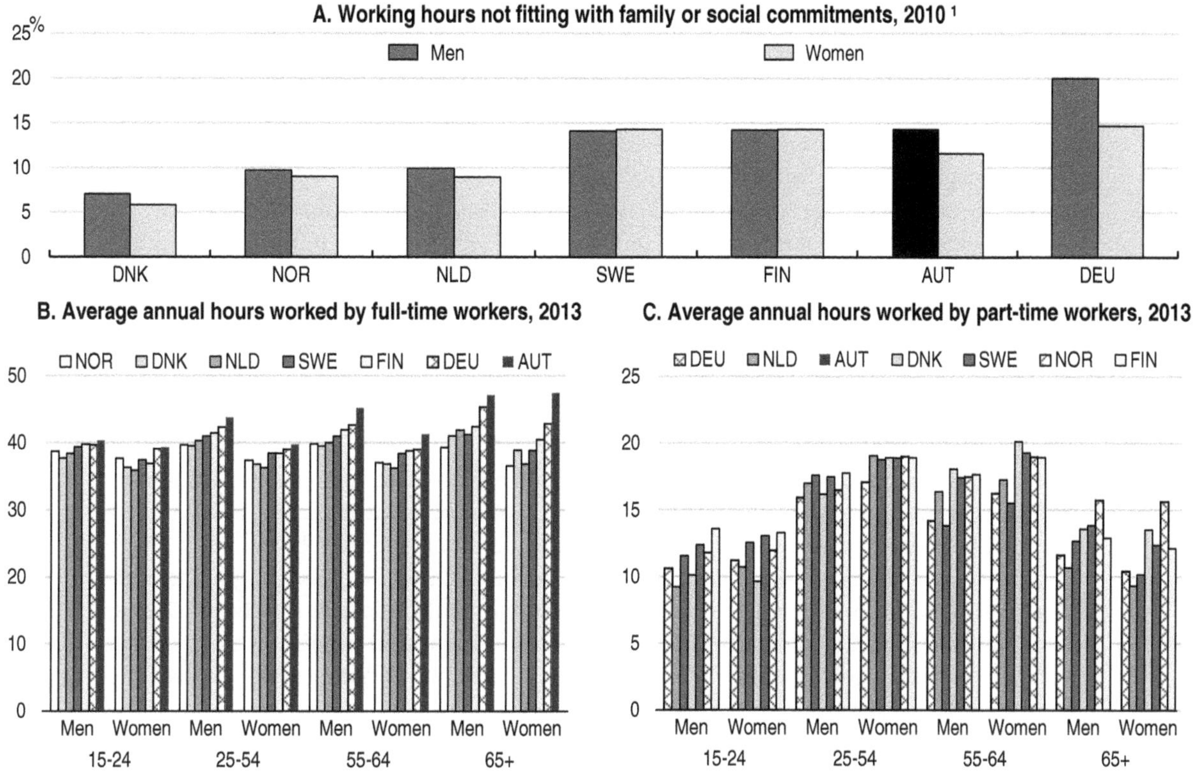

1. Question: In general, do your working hours fit in with your family or social commitments outside work very well, well, not very well, not at all well? Answers included in the graph: "fit not at all" and "fit not very well".

Source: Eurofound, European Working Conditions Survey 2010; OECD, *Labour Force Statistics database*.

StatLink http://dx.doi.org/10.1787/888933252256

- Overall, the Austrian population has fewer options to combine work and life priorities than in comparable countries. Available time and life organisation patterns are more limited, while demand for alternative arrangements expands (Box 1.4). The distribution of workers by weekly work hours suggest that intermediary arrangements have started to spread, but they remain less common (Figure 1.18, Panel A). Austria also lags comparable countries in possibilities to vary work hours according to employee needs (Figure 1.19, Panels B and C). Long-term leave possibilities are unevenly available, according to enterprises. A parent who has been working in a firm with more than 20 employees for three or more years is in principle entitled to part-time work. However, specific aspects of the leave, including scheduling, duration, etc. need to be agreed with the employer. If no agreement is reached, the Labour and Social Court rules "with due regard to the interests of both parties". The entitlements of parents who have been with the same employer for less than three years, and those working in firms with less than 20 employees are subject to bilateral negotiation.

  According to the European Commission (EC, 2014b), Austrian legislation on employee rights for care needs is less generous than in other countries. Half of Austrian enterprises offer long-term parental leave and 20% leave possibilities for other family tasks – the lowest ratios among EU countries. A recent review confirmed that not all legal entitlements available to parents can be utilised in practice (Buchebner-Ferstl, 2014).

Box 1.4. Reconciling work and family life in a competitive economy

A recent survey of "time poverty" reviewed internationally available evidence on the factors modifying the work-life balances of highly educated professionals of both genders (The Economist, 2014). It suggests that over the past three decades European economies tended to trade wages for free time (Blanchard, 2004). However, this model is now coming under pressure, notably for highly skilled professionals. The better educated who face stronger income and career opportunities are putting in more hours, especially in "winner-takes-all" professional settings. A survey of 1 000 executives in the United States confirmed that 95% worked more than 50 hours per week, and 50% more than 65 hours per week. Similar pressures are mounting in the European countries, including in Austria. The fast extension of the so-called "all-in" employment contracts in the recent period, which facilitate overtime work by providing it with more flexible conditions, is a sign of this. They already cover half of all Austrian managers. Furthermore, senior managers are exempt from the Working Hours Act, which allows them to work more than 50 hours per week.

Female professionals with children are recognised as the most time-scarce segment of society "even more so because of the rise in standards for what it means to be a good parent". The tension concerns in principle both fathers and mothers but affect women more severely in practice. Female professionals' desire for time flexibility augments with the arrival of children. According to a review of occupational choices in the United States, many skilled women tend to prefer jobs which put stable and predictable workplace demands on them (Goldin, 2014). This concerns the number of hours to be worked, the particular hours worked, being "on call", etc.

The study finds that the distribution of total employment between jobs involving more or less time pressure is driven by the evolution of technologies. Overcoming tensions in work-life balance "does not necessarily involve government intervention, women's bargaining skills and men being more responsible. It involves alterations in the labour market, in particular changing how jobs are structured and remunerated to enhance temporal flexibility". The gender gap can be reduced and "might even vanish if firms did not have an incentive to disproportionately reward individuals who worked long hours, and who worked particular hours. Such change has already occurred in various sectors, but not in enough". The study also emphasises that this is not a woman's issue: all workers will benefit from structural changes providing greater command on time schedules, although those who do not value the amenity will likely lose from its lower price.

A large-size investigation covering Germany, Switzerland and Austria (Stock et al., 2012) analysed the margins of freedom available to face these pressures. It in particular focused on their impacts on fertility. Child raising is recognised as a prime life aspiration, as well as a key determinant of the long-term balances of ageing societies. The study went through the time sovereignty needs of professionals of both genders and concluded that:

- There is a large diversity in people's time-use priorities. However, each person needs to assume that in certain phases of life he/she will have adequate time for family and care responsibilities.
- Paid and unpaid work should be recognised as having equal importance for families' and children's well-being. Mothers and fathers who prefer part-time work should be permitted to do so.
- "Time policies" are needed to achieve these objectives. They should be compatible with practical conditions in various professions, spheres and fields of economic activity.
- A vast array of lifestyles must be accommodated. Individuals should be enabled to follow various work/life arrangements, which evolve through their life cycle.

Figure 1.19. **Work/life organisation options are more limited in Austria**

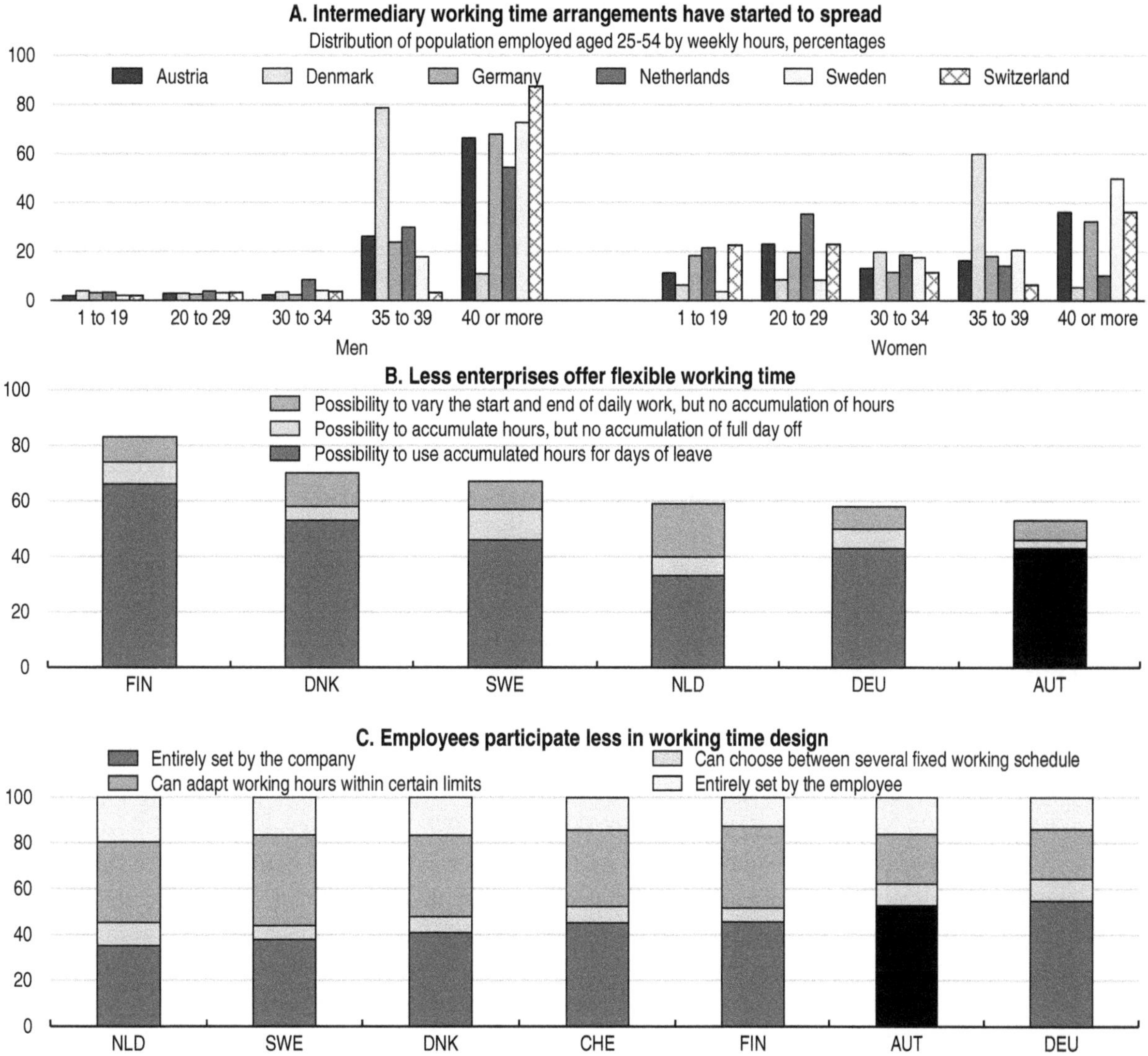

Source: OECD, *Labour Force Statistics database*; OECD (2011), *Doing Better for Families*, OECD Publishing, Paris, *http://dx.doi.org/10.1787/9789264098732-en.*

StatLink http://dx.doi.org/10.1787/888933252264

The current legal framework intended to reconcile work and family tasks appears to face a number of new tensions. The costs that it implies for the flexibility and international competitiveness of firms are more frequently invoked than before. The Ombud for Equal Treatment mentioned companies which report difficulties in complying with the existing gender equality legislation (Mairhuber, 2009). Relatedly, employer organisations propose to reduce the long-term part-time leave option from seven to four years. The enforcement of the recently adopted *Freizeit* agreements face also similar difficulties. Many workers prefer to trade a lower wage for more free time under the choices offered by these agreements, but only part of the employers can go along: 20% of workers applied for more free time in related negotiations, but only 10% of enterprises agreed (Chamber of Labour, 2014).

As a result, the menu of options to help reconcile work and family life is available along a pecking order: it is generally more generous in the public sector, then in international firms, then respectively in large, medium-sized and smaller enterprises. Given the high weight of SMEs in Austria's business sector, this deprives a significant share of the population from the options available in the more advanced parts of the economy (KMU Forschung Austria, 2010).

Health

According to OECD (2013) "being healthy and living a long life free of illness and disability are among the aspects that people value the most. Being healthy affects the probability of having a job, earning an adequate income, and actively participating in social activities". Life expectancy is the most widespread indicator of health outcomes for purposes of international comparison.

Women enjoy a longer life expectation than men in Austria (84 years against 78), and the difference is one of the widest in OECD (Figure 1.20, Panel A). However, the indicator does not provide a full picture of the health status of the population because additional years of life are not necessarily lived in good health. Research on gender gaps in health outcomes brought to light, in particular, the so-called "male-female health-survival paradox": despite having consistently higher life expectancy, women in all countries report worse health than men. They show higher rates of morbidity (life under serious health limitations) for longer periods.

Morbidity is widespread in Austria despite a well-regarded public health system. Both genders suffer from it, but a higher share of women's lifespan is affected by disease and injury (25% of years lived, as opposed to 19% for men). Still, because of the gap in aggregate life expectancy, women live longer healthy years than men (Figure 1.20, Panels B and C).

Men and women's asymmetric work and life trajectories may be contributing to their observed health strains at old age. Some recent research started to investigate this avenue in Austria, with no clear conclusion so far (Leoni and Eppel, 2013). Nonetheless, it revealed that strong strains experienced in life have detrimental impacts on individuals' long-term health. Additional research may confirm, in line with the international literature, that work-life imbalances may negatively affect both life expectancy and morbidity (Darden, 2014; Barney, 2014). Damaging effects of such imbalances on the well-being of employees and the productivity of enterprises start to be better understood at the international level, notably through their effect on mental health (OECD, 2015b). Further research in Austria could shed more light on these effects.

Life satisfaction

OECD (2013) suggests that individuals' subjective well-being should be monitored as a key indicator of a society's welfare "as people are the best judges of how their own lives are going". The headline indicator of subjective well-being, life satisfaction, aims to capture people's evaluation of their life as a whole. Another indicator, affect balance, yields additional information on their emotional situation in the short-term.

Figure 1.20. **Gender gaps in health outcomes**

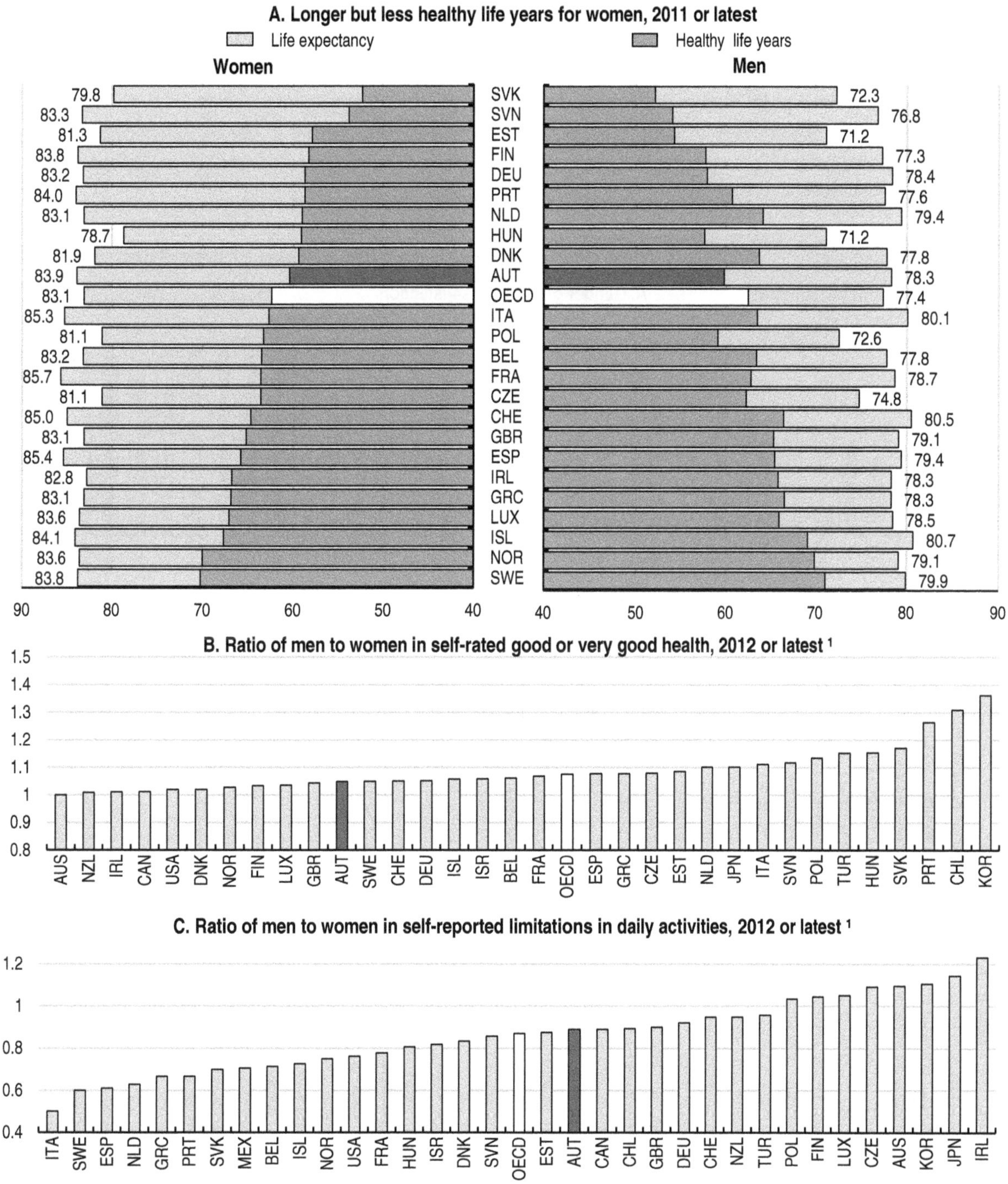

1. Persons aged more than 15.

Source: OECD (2013), *How's Life? 2013: Measuring Well-being*, OECD Publishing, Paris, *http://dx.doi.org/10.1787/9789264201392-en*; and *OECD Health database*.

StatLink http://dx.doi.org/10.1787/888933252275

Austrians report being generally satisfied with their lives. When asked to rate their life satisfaction on a scale from 0 to 10, they assign it an average score of 7.5, higher than the OECD average, but slightly lower than in some countries (Figure 1.21, Panel A). Eighty per cent of respondents to a recent survey reported being very satisfied or satisfied with their lives. Austrians' high level of satisfaction with work conditions appear to contribute to these good outcomes (Figure 1.21, Panel C). Women report a higher degree of life satisfaction than men, despite feeling comparatively less satisfied with their work conditions. This suggests that their sources of life satisfaction may be more varied than men's (Box 1.5).

Figure 1.21. **A generally high degree of work and life satisfaction in Austria**

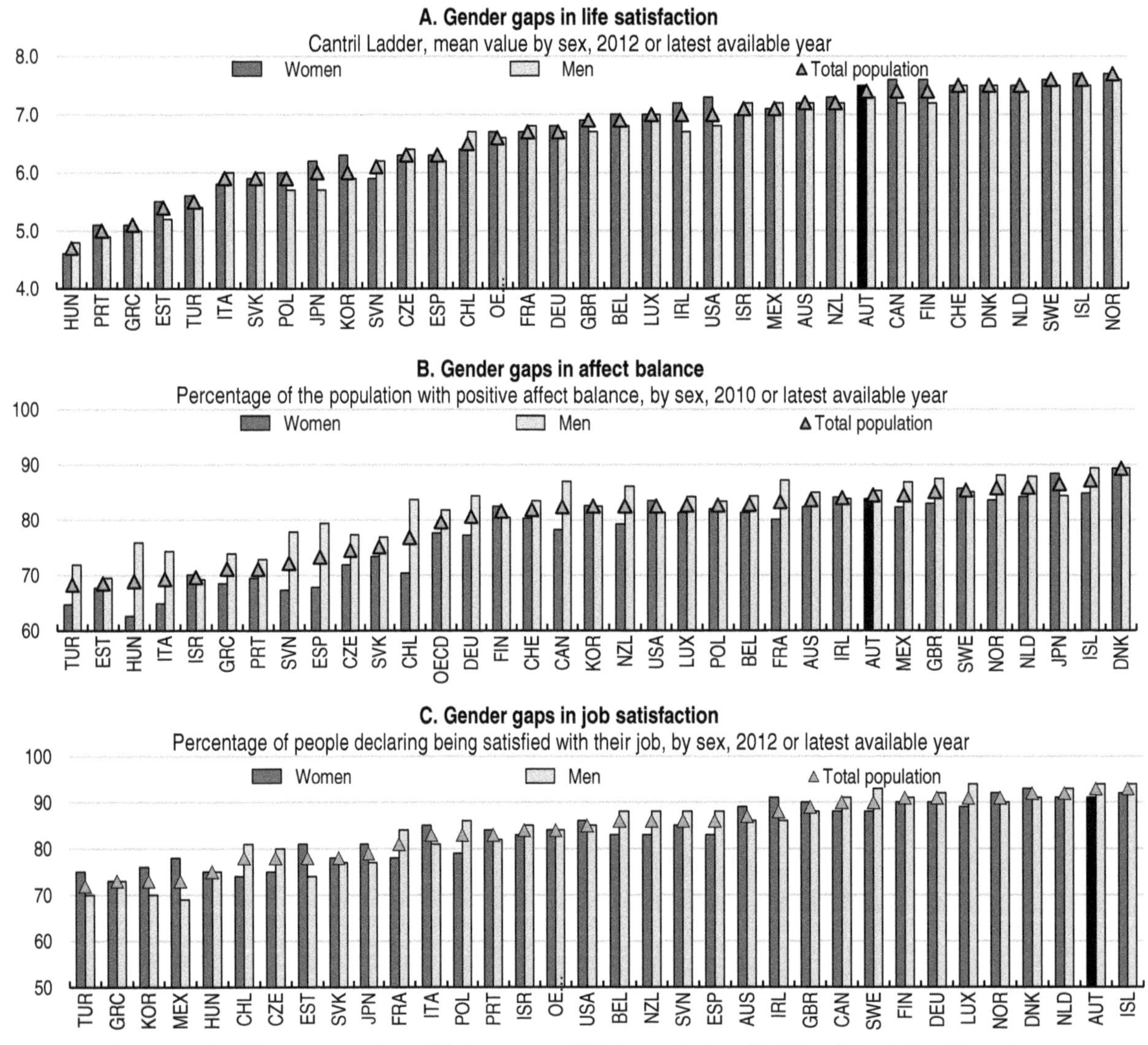

Source: OECD (2013), *How's Life? 2013: Measuring Well-being*, OECD Publishing, Paris, *http://dx.doi.org/10.1787/9789264201392-en.*

StatLink http://dx.doi.org/10.1787/888933252286

Box 1.5. **Gender differences in job satisfaction**

OECD (2013b) confirms the growing interest in member countries in understanding gender divergences in job satisfaction. It discusses the so-called "paradox of the contented female worker", i.e. the fact that "lower wages that women generally receive, as well as the gender bias that they may face through hiring and occupational segregations seem to be at odds with their reported job satisfaction". Research reviewed suggests that, in the OECD area as a whole, job characteristics valued by women and men differ: "Women are less likely to identify earnings as the most important feature of a job. Higher income adds more to the job satisfaction of men than to that of women. Women are more likely than men to identify the flexibility of work schedule, social relations at work, and the significance of the task as the most important aspects".

Source: OECD (2013), *How's Life? 2013: Measuring Well-being*, OECD Publishing, Paris, *http://dx.doi.org/10.1787/9789264201392-en.*

Although Austrian women report a higher degree of life satisfaction than men, as in most other OECD countries, their satisfaction is declining. A review by the OECD of trend declines in women's life satisfaction across the OECD area suggests that this may result from "changes in family structures... and the fact that today's women have to juggle more complicated lives and many more objectives than in the past. These multiple goals compete for women's time and resources" (OECD, 2013b). These forces seem to be at play in Austria.

OECD investigations on the determinants of subjective well-being in member countries (Fleche et al., 2012 and Boarini et al., 2012, which were summarised in the 2013 *OECD Economic Survey of Austria*) have been updated with 2013 data. Gender-specific factors which drive Austrian men and women's life satisfaction are confirmed. Comparisons with similar countries hint at the persistence of, but also tensions in, separate gender roles:

- *Income* is a major driver of well-being in Austria, as in all OECD countries. However, its effect is weaker for women than for men. The difference between the contribution of income to men's and women's life satisfaction is larger than in peer countries.
- Voluntary *part-time work* is associated with higher life satisfaction for women without children. Notably, tertiary educated voluntary female part-timers emerge as a group with particularly high reported life satisfaction, more than in comparable countries.
- As a difference from comparable countries, *the presence of children* reduces reported life satisfaction for Austrian women, except when they are working full-time. This may be seen as a sign of tension in separate gender roles.
- For mothers who are not forced to withdraw from full-time work (either because they have access to full-day child care and schools, or find other solutions via family and/or informal support) there is a positive link between number of children and life satisfaction.
- Life satisfaction is lower among women who work part-time and have children. This suggests that part-time work may be preferable when material needs are limited, but may become detrimental when they increase. A large share of Austrian women feel indeed unhappy with their household income level. These findings hint at the fragility of part-time work as a determinant of life satisfaction.
- *Living in urban areas.* Life satisfaction is higher in urban than in rural areas. This is notably the case of women. In Austria's circumstances, living in a city may be a proxy for wider life options via better access to employment opportunities and support services.

Raising awareness about persisting gender gaps and their causes and consequences

The evidence presented in this chapter identifies Austria as one of the countries with the most distinct gender roles in the OECD. Many aspects of well-being are shaped by this separation, whereby women withdraw fully from the labour force when children are young, and return to the labour market through part-time work as children grow up. Men remain fully devoted to breadwinning. This model puts genders on diverging paths of skill acquisition, careers, incomes and other well-being dimensions.

Making work/life patterns more gender-equal would produce gains in all key well-being dimensions. The society's talent and resources can be better mobilised, and economic growth and fiscal resources, and consequently the material foundations of individual and societal well-being can be strengthened. Gender-specific motivations in education can be reduced and economic participation would increase, including in entrepreneurial activities. Both women and men can then fully use their potential and benefit from the same set of opportunities. Work/life balances would be expected to improve for all. An important gain would be in form of more equilibrated and better resourced families, which would be more able to have as many children as they wish.

Higher awareness of the persisting gender gaps, their sources, and their impact on various dimensions of well-being would help policymakers, families and enterprises focus on the top priorities in "opening-up" the separate roles model. This chapter suggests that the following areas deserve special attention:

- School age girls (and their families) should pay full attention to life opportunity, career and income implications of their study area choices.
- Young women should pay full attention to the long-term consequences of their labour force participation and employment decisions, including on their long-term pension entitlements.
- Men should pay more attention to the impact of imbalanced work/life patterns on families' long-term well-being, children's development and own health outcomes.
- Employers should fully realise the loss of talent and productivity arising from less than full engagement of women with children in professional activities.

Wider evidence, research and information in these areas would help Austrians of all genders, ages, professional positions and managerial responsibilities in the public and private sectors to realise the potential of opening-up the separate roles model for well-being gains and stronger economic growth (Box 1.6).

Box 1.6. **Promote awareness of gender gaps, their sources and consequences**

- Produce and disseminate up-to-date evidence and research on persisting gender gaps in Austria, their sources, and their impact on main dimensions of well-being.
- Publicise information on innovative practices successfully helping open-up the separate gender roles model. Notably:
  - Wider study area choices for schoolgirls and schoolboys.
  - Higher labour force participation of mothers with young children.
  - Better balanced paid and unpaid work duties within families, including in child and elderly care.
  - Workplace innovations to facilitate more purposeful time management by both genders.

Notes

1. *Statistik Austria* has developed an indicator to assess if an individual child care facility is compatible with full time work – the so called "VIF" (Indicator of Reconciliation between Family and Work). To be eligible, a facility must be open at least 45 hours per week, 47 weeks a year, and offer lunch. Only in Vienna is the majority of children in care places meeting the VIF criteria. In other *Länder*, a very small share of enrolled children attends such facilities (see Chapter 2, Figure 2.11).
2. More than 80% of about 450 000 long-term dependents, which together account for 5.4% of total population are taken care of at home. In this population, there are seven levels of care needs recognised by the Austrian social security system: 23% of dependents were at Level 1 in 2013, requiring at least two hours of presence of a carer per day. From Level 4, dependents need continuous surveillance; 30% were in this situation. At Levels 6 and 7, which concern 6% of dependents, they must have day and night intense care.
3. According to the OECD methodology, "rural areas" designate regions with less than 150 inhabitants per sq km. Following this methodology Austria as a whole qualifies as "predominantly rural".
4. Since respectively 1987 and 1993, irrespective of gender, both boys and girls can attend handicraft (*textiles Werken*) or technical (*technisches Werken*) lessons. Since 2012, the two subjects have been merged into one in "New Secondary Schools".

Bibliography

Adema, W. (2013), "Greater Gender Equality: What Role for Family Policy?", *Family Matters*, No. 93.

Adema, W., N. Ali and O. Thévenon (2014), "Changes in Family Policies and Outcomes: Is there Convergence?", *OECD Social, Employment and Migration Working Papers*, No. 157, OECD Publishing, Paris, *http://dx.doi.org/10.1787/5jz13wllxgzt-en*.

Altzinger, W. (2014), "Income and Wealth Distribution in Austria", mimeo, Vienna University of Economics and Business, Vienna.

AMS (2014), *Bericht Gleichstellung am österreichischen Arbeitsmarkt (Report on Gender Equality in the Labour Market)*, Arbeitmarketservice,Vienna.

Arbeiterkammer Wien (2013), *Beschäftigte im Reinigungsgewerbe – Analyse der Beschäftigteninterviews (Workers in the Cleaning Industry – Analysis of Employment Interviews)*, Institut Für Empirische Sozialforschung, Vienna.

Arbeitkammer Wien (2014), *Frauen Management Report*, Vienna, *http://media.arbeiterkammer.at/PDF/AK_Frauen_Management_Report_2014.pdf*

Austrian Court of Audit (2013), *Bericht des Rechnungshofes (Report of the Auditors)*, Vienna, *www.rechnungshof.gv.at/fileadmin/downloads/2013/berichte/einkommensberichte/Einkommensbericht_2013.pdf*.

Barnay, T. (2014), "Health, Work and Working Conditions: A Review of the European Economic Literature", *OECD Economics Department Working Papers*, No. 1148, OECD Publishing, Paris, *http://dx.doi.org/10.1787/5jz0zb71xhmr-en*.

Berghammer, C. (2014), "The Return of the Male Breadwinner Model? Educational Effects on Parents' Work Arrangements in Austria, 1980-2009", *Work, Employment and Society*, Vol. 28, No. 4.

Bergmann, N., L. Danzer and S. Schmatz (2014), "Vereinbarkeit von Beruf und Kinderbetreuung – betriebliche Rahmenbedingungen aus Sicht berufstätiger Eltern" (Reconciliation of Work and Childcare – Framework for Working Parents), *L&R Social Research*, Vienna.

Blanchard, O. (2004), "The Economic Future of Europe", *NBER Working Paper Series*, No. 10310.

Bloom, D., D. Canning, G. Fink and J. Finlay (2009), "The Cost of Low Fertility in Europe", *NBER Working Paper Series*, No. 14820.

Boarini, R. et al. (2012), "What Makes for a Better Life? The Determinants of Subjective Well-Being in OECD Countries – Evidence from the Gallup World Poll", *OECD Statistics Working Papers*, No. 2012/03, OECD Publishing, Paris, *http://dx.doi.org/10.1787/5k9b9ltjm937-en*.

Böheim, R., K. Himpele, H. Mahringer and C. Zulehner (2013), "The Gender Wage Gap in Austria: Eppur si muove!", *Empirica*, Vol. 40, No. 4.

Buber-Ennser, I., N. Neuwirth and M. Testa (2014), *Families in Austria 2009-2013: Descriptive Findings on Partnerships, Fertility Intentions, Childbearing and Childrearing*, Vienna Institute of Demography, Vienna.

Buber-Ennser, I. and R. Panova, (2014), "Attitudes towards parental employment across Europe, in Australia and in Japan", *Working Paper*, No. 5, Vienna Institute of Demography, Vienna.

Buchebner-Ferstl, S., M. Kaindl, R. Schipfer and M. Tazi-Preve (2014), "Familien- und kinderfreundliches Österreich?", *Austrian Institute of Family Studies Forschunbericht*, No. 13, Vienna University, Vienna.

Chamber of Labour (2014), "Labour Market and Reconciliation of Work and Family Life", Background Information for the *OECD Economic Survey*, mimeo, December.

Darden, M. (2014), "Workplace Stress in the United States: Issues and Policies", *OECD Economics Department Working Papers*, No. 1150, OECD Publishing, Paris, *http://dx.doi.org/10.1787/5jz0zb5t4532-en*.

Eder (2012), *Divergence of Pupils Interests in Austria*, unpublished mimeo quoted by Lassnigg (2014).

Eiffe, F. and K. Gärtner (2014), "Distribution and Determinants of Subjective Well-Being in Austria", mimeo based on *Statistische Nachrichten 2014*, No. 1, Statistik Austria, Vienna.

European Commission (2012a), *The Role of Men in Gender Equality – European Strategies and Insights*, DG Justice, December, Brussels.

European Commission (2012b), *2010 Ad hoc EU SILC Module on the Intra-Household Sharing of Resources*, Employment, Social Affairs and Inclusion, November, Brussels.

European Commission (2014a), *Statistical Data on Women Entrepreneurs in Europe – Country Fiche – Austria*, Enterprise and Industry, September, Brussels.

European Commission (2014b), *Family-related Working Schedule Flexibility Across Europe*, Statistical Report, No. 6, April, Brussels.

European Commission (2014c), *Adequate Social Protection for Long-term Care Needs in an Ageing Society*, Brussels.

European Commission (2015), *Country Report Austria*, Commission Staff Working Document, February, Brussels.

European Trade Union Confederation (2015), *Collective Bargaining and Gender Equality*, *www.etuc.org/collective-bargaining-and-gender-equality*.

Eurostat (2010), *Structure of Earnings Survey 2010 – Metadata*, *http://ec.europa.eu/eurostat/web/labour-market/earnings*.

Eurostat (2011), *Adult Education Survey*, *http://ec.europa.eu/eurostat/web/microdata/adult-education-survey*.

Fleche, S., C. Smith and P. Sorsa (2012), "Exploring Determinants of Subjective Wellbeing in OECD Countries: Evidence from the World Value Survey", *OECD Statistics Working Papers*, No. 2012/01, OECD Publishing, Paris, *http://dx.doi.org/10.1787/5k9ffc6p1rvb-en*.

Freisinger, C., A. Palienko and J. Straner (2014), *Zugangsbeschränkungen und Chancen(un)gleichheit im Hochschulsystem*, Arbeitkammer Vienna.

Geisberger, T. and T. Glaser (2014), "Geschlechtsspezifische Verdienstunterschiede – Analysen zum Gender Pay Gap auf Basis der Verdienststrukturerhebung 2010", *Statistische Nachrichten 2014*, No. 3, Statistik Austria, Vienna.

Goldin, C. (2014), "A Grand Gender Convergence: Its Last Chapter", *American Economic Review*, Vol. 104(4).

Huerta, M. et al. (2011), "Early Maternal Employment and Child Development in Five OECD Countries", *OECD Social, Employment and Migration Working Papers*, No. 118, OECD Publishing, Paris, *http://dx.doi.org/10.1787/5kg5dlmtxhvh-en*.

Huerta, M. et al. (2013), "Fathers' Leave, Fathers' Involvement and Child Development: Are They Related? Evidence from Four OECD Countries", *OECD Social, Employment and Migration Working Papers*, No. 140, OECD Publishing, Paris, *http://dx.doi.org/10.1787/5k4dlw9w6czq-en*.

Kaindl, M. and G. Wernhart (2012), "Wie Großeltern ihre Kinder und Enkelkinder unterstützen. Persönliche und finanzielle Hilfe von Großeltern aus Sicht der Großeltern und der erwachsenen Kinder", *Working Papers*, No. 78, Österreichisches Institut für Familienforschung.

KMU Forschung Austria (2010), *Study on Non-legislative Initiatives for Companies to Promote Gender Equality at the Workplace*, Austrian Institute for SME Research, Vienna.

Knittler, K. (2011), "Intergenerationale Bildungsmobiltät" (Intergenerational Educational Mobility), *Statistische Nachrichten*, No. 4, Statistik Austria, Vienna.

Korpi, W., T. Ferrarini and S. Englund (2013), "Women's Opportunities under Different Family Policy Constellations: Gender, Class and Inequality Trade-offs in Western Countries Re-examined", *Social Politics*, Spring.

Lang, S. and B. Sauer (2012), "Does Federalism Impact Gender Architectures? The Case of Women's Policy Agencies in Germany and Austria", *The Journal of Federalism*, Vol. 43, No. 1.

Lassnigg, L., A. Kulhanek and P. Wejwar (2014), "Quantitative Information About Sex and Gender Issues in the Austrian National Education Report", mimeo, Institute for Advanced Studies (IHS), Vienna.

Lazear, E. and S. Rosen (1990), "Male-Female Wage Differentials in Job Ladders", *Journal of Labour Economics*, Vol. 8, No. 1.

Leoni, T. and R. Eppel (2013). "Women's Work and Family Profiles over the Lifecourse and their Subsequent Health Outcomes", *WWW For Europe Working Paper*, No. 28, *https://ideas.repec.org/p/feu/wfewop/y2013m7d0i28.html*.

Lutz, H. and M. Schratzenstaller (2010), "Mögliche Ansätze zur Unterstützung von Familien durch die öffentlichen Haushalte", *WIFO Monatsberichte*, No. 8.

Mader, K., A. Schneebaum, K. Hollan and P. Kopf (2014), "Vermögensunterschiede nach Geschlecht: Erste Ergebnisse für Österreich" (Wealth Differences: First Results for Austria), *Document on Economy and Society*, No. 129, Arbeitkammer, Vienna.

Mairhuber, I. (2009), "The Cost of Non Gender Equality – Report on Austria", Forschungs und Beratungsstelle Arbeitswelt, Vienna.

Marin, B. (2013), *Welfare in an Idle Society? Reinventing Retirement, Work, Wealth, Health and Welfare*, Ashgate, London.

Musset, P. et al. (2013), *A Skills beyond School Review of Austria*, OECD Reviews of Vocational Education and Training, OECD Publishing, Paris, *http://dx.doi.org/10.1787/9789264200418-en*.

OECD (2007), *Babies and Bosses – Reconciling Work and Family Life: A Synthesis of Findings for OECD Countries*, OECD Publishing, Paris, *http://dx.doi.org/10.1787/9789264032477-en*.

OECD (2011a), *Doing Better for Families*, OECD Publishing, Paris, *http://dx.doi.org/10.1787/9789264098732-en*.

OECD (2012), *Closing the Gender Gap: Act Now*, OECD Publishing, Paris, *http://dx.doi.org/10.1787/9789264179370-en*.

OECD (2013a), *Recommendation of the Council on Gender Equality in Education, Employment and Entrepreneurship*, OECD, Paris, 29 May, *www.oecd.org/gender/C-MIN(2013)5-ENG.pdf*.

OECD (2013b), *How's Life? 2013: Measuring Well-being*, OECD Publishing, Paris, *http://dx.doi.org/10.1787/9789264201392-en*.

OECD (2013c), *Government at a Glance 2013*, OECD Publishing, Paris, *http://dx.doi.org/10.1787/gov_glance-2013-en*.

OECD (2013c), *OECD Economic Surveys: Austria 2013*, OECD Publishing, Paris, *http://dx.doi.org/10.1787/eco_surveys-aut-2013-en*.

OECD (2014a), *Education at a Glance 2014: OECD Indicators*, OECD Publishing, Paris, *http://dx.doi.org/10.1787/eag-2014-en*.

OECD (2014b), *Recruiting Immigrant Workers: Austria 2014*, OECD Publishing, Paris, *http://dx.doi.org/10.1787/9789264226050-en*.

OECD (2014c), *Women, Government and Policy Making in OECD Countries: Fostering Diversity for Inclusive Growth*, OECD Publishing, Paris, *http://dx.doi.org/10.1787/9789264210745-en*.

OECD (2015a), *The ABC of Gender Equality in Education: Aptitude, Behaviour, Confidence*, PISA, OECD Publishing, Paris, *http://dx.doi.org/10.1787/9789264229945-en*.

OECD (2015b), *Fit Mind, Fit Job: From Evidence to Practice in Mental Health and Work*, Mental Health and Work, OECD Publishing, Paris, *http://dx.doi.org/10.1787/9789264228283-en*.

OeNB (2014), *Financial Stability Report*, No. 28, Österreichische Nationalbank, December.

O'Neill, J. (2003), "The Gender Gap in Wages, circa 2000", *American Economic Review*, Vol. 93, No. 2.

Plantenga, J., C. Remery, H. Figueiredo and M. Smith (2009), "Towards a European Union Gender Equality Index", *Journal of Europan Social Policy*, Vol. 19.

Queisser, M. (2013), "2013 Demography Forum: Investing in Europe's Demographic Future", *Newsletter*, No. 2/2013, mimeo, OECD, Paris, *www.ce-ageing.eu/index.php?option=com_content&view=article&id=300:2013-demography-forum-investing-in-europe-s-demographic-future-may-6-and-7-2013-brussels&catid=41&Itemid=124*.

Ray, R., J.C. Gornick and J. Schmitt (2010), "Who Cares? Assessing Generosity and Gender Equality in Parental Leave Policy Designs in 21 Countries", *Journal of European Social Policy*, Vol. 20.

Shratzenstaller, M. (2015), "Familienpolitische Leistungen in Österreich im Überblick" (Family Benefits in Austria – An Overview), *WIFO-Monatsberichte*, No. 88(3).

Schwartz, S. and T. Rubel-Lifshitz (2009), "Cross-National Variation in the Size of Sex Differences in Values: Effects of Gender Equality", *Journal of Personality and Social Psychology*, No. 97/1.

Schwarz, P. (2012), "Tax Disincentives and Female Employment in OECD Countries", *Journal of European Social Policy*, No. 22.

Sen, A. (2001), "The Many Faces of Gender Inequality", *The New Republic*, September.

Sparreboom, T. (2009), *Gender Equality, Employment and Part-Time Work in Developed Countries*, Report for the 98th Session of the International Labour Conference, Geneva.

Statistik Austria (2007), *Erwachsenenbildungserhebung (Adult Education Survey)*, Vienna.

Statistik Austria (2009), *Zeitverwendung (Time Use Survey)*, Vienna.

Statistik Austria (2010), *Frauenbericht (Women Report)*, Vienna.

Statistik Austria (2014a), *Vertiefende Analysen der PIAAC-Erhebung 2011/12 (In-depth PIAAC Analyses)*, Vienna, *www.statistik.at/web_de/statistiken/bildung_und_kultur/piaac/vertiefende_analysen_der_piaac_erhebung_2011_12/index.html*.

Statistik Austria (2015), *People, Society, Labour Market, Family and Employment Statistic*, *www.statistik.at/web_de/statistiken/menschen_und_gesellschaft/arbeitsmarkt/arbeitszeit/teilzeitarbeit_teilzeitquote/062882.html*.

Steier, G. (2013), "Womenomics for Nursing Growth: Making the Case for Work Time Flexibility and Mother-Friendlier Workplaces", *Buffalo Journal of Gender, Law and Social Policy*, Vol. 21.

Stock, G., H. Bertram, A. Fürnkranz-Prskawetz, W. Holzgreve, M. Kohli and U. Staudinger (2012), *A Future with Children: Fertility and the Development of Society in Germany, Austria, and Switzerland*, Campus Verlag.

Tesch-Römer, C., A. Motel-Klingebiel and M. Tomasik (2007), "Gender Differences in Subjective Well-Being: Comparing Societies with Respect to Gender Equality", *Social Indicators Research*, Vol. 85, Issue 2.

The Economist (2014), *In Search of Lost Time: Why Is Everyone So Busy?*, 20 December.

Thévenon, O. (2011), "Family Policies in OECD Countries: A Comparative Analysis", *Population and Development Review*, Vol. 37, Issue 1.

Thévenon, O. (2013), "Drivers of Female Labour Force Participation in the OECD", *OECD Social, Employment and Migration Working Papers*, No. 145, OECD Publishing, Paris, *http://dx.doi.org/10.1787/5k46cvrgnms6-en*.

Thévenon, O. and A. Gauthier (2011), "Family Policies in Developed Countries: A 'Fertility-Booster' with Side-Effects", *Community, Work and Family*, No. 14/2.

Thévenon, O., N. Ali, W. Adema and A. Savi del Pero (2012), "Effects of Reducing Gender Gaps in Education and Labour Force Participation on Economic Growth in the OECD", *OECD Social, Employment and Migration Working Papers*, No. 138, OECD Publishing, Paris, *http://dx.doi.org/10.1787/5k8xb722w928-en*.

Weber, A. and C. Zulehner (2014), "Competition and Gender Prejudice: Are Discriminatory Employers Doomed to Fail?", *Journal of the European Economic Association*, Vol. 12, No. 2.

Wernhart, G. and R. Winter-Ebmer (2012), "Do Austrian Men and Women Become More Equal? At Least in Terms of Labour Supply!", *Empirica*, No. 39.

Wirtschaftskammer Österreich (2013a), "Leitfaden Betriebliche Kinderbetreuung" (A Guide to Corporate Child Care), published in co-operation with the Ministry of Economy, Family and Youth, Vienna.

Wirtschaftskammer Österreich (2013b), "Handbuch zur vereinbarkeit von Familie und Beruf" (Handbook on work-life balance), published in co-operation with the Ministry of Economy, Family and Youth, Vienna.

Wirtschaftskammer Österreich (2015), "Jahrbuch" (Yearbook), *http://wko.at/statistik/jahrbuch/ng-geschlecht.pdf*.

World Economic Forum (2014), *The Global Gender Gap Report 2014*, Geneva.

Chapter 2

Towards more gender equality

Chapter 1 provides empirical evidence for strong and persistent patterns of separated gender roles in Austria. While this model is generally considered to have worked well in the past, it faces important challenges arising from societal and economic changes in Austria. Hence, gender mainstreaming with the aim of more gender equality ranks high on the agenda of Austrian policy makers. An integrated policy framework to make Austria more gender-equal should build on 3 pillars: i) make the tax and benefit system more employment friendly; ii) extend the care service infrastructure; and iii) encourage more flexible workplace practices. Streamlining family policies across regions and levels of government would entail efficiency gains for all pillars. Long-run simulations suggest that achieving more gender equality in Austria could boost GDP by 13 percentage points until 2060. In addition, promoting more gender equality in the Austrian Society will improve Austrians' well-being.

The rationale of promoting gender equality

Despite important progress and increasing attention of policy makers, gender equality remains a largely unachieved goal, in Austria and elsewhere. Chapter 1 provides evidence on the prevailing family patterns that involve separate and asymmetric gender roles in Austria. Aspirations for more gender equality call for change. It is by now widely accepted that gender equality requires more than equal opportunities and equal access to institutions. Women also need the decisional autonomy to develop the capabilities to make use of equal opportunities and live up to their aspirations. Therefore, achieving gender equality requires a flexible approach with a dedicated mix of objectives that eliminate barriers to equal opportunities and objectives that prescribe equal outcome targets for women and men (Box 2.1).

Many Austrian women with family tasks, notably child care, work part-time. The vast majority of them declare doing so voluntarily, but there is a common perception, as in other OECD countries with a similar experience (e.g. Germany and Switzerland) that if conditions were more conducive for full-time work, a significant proportion of women would shift from part-time to full-time employment to improve earnings and careers. Entrenched social norms and prevalence of stereotypes often implicitly reduce the set of opportunities that are effectively available to women (Box 2.1) which may bias their perception. For instance, Nordenmark (2013) shows that women who live in an egalitarian gender regime (e.g. Sweden, Denmark, Norway) more often report disagreement about the division of household work and work-family conflicts than women who live in traditional gender regimes, in particular in Austria and Switzerland. Against this background, the provision of equal opportunities in a legalistic sense may not be sufficient to achieve gender equality as women's access is limited *de facto*. One example is the option for parents to work part-time until the child's 7th birthday. While this option addresses both fathers and mothers, it is mostly taken up by women (Chapter 1).

But even if individual choices are made under autonomy and with an equal set of opportunities, they may still give rise to suboptimal outcomes, individually and collectively. For instance, while reduced working time may be individually preferable, myopic behaviour may not fully internalise long-term effects on pension entitlements and risk of old-age poverty. Collectively, the decision to work less also affects the viability of social security institutions owing to reduced contributions and lower growth potential. The inadequate use of human capital represents a cost to the family through lower income but also exerts a negative externality on society as a whole. A second example of an adverse externality is low fertility. It undermines growth potential and jeopardises the intergenerational balance underlying social institutions through increasing dependency ratios. While child bearing is a profoundly intimate matter and choice, raising the awareness of negative spill-overs and fostering a more child-friendly environment can be seen as a part of public policy so as to internalise negative externalities of individual choices and correct for market failures.

Box 2.1. **Different concepts of gender equality**

Equality of outcomes

Equality of outcomes seeks identical outcomes in terms of societal and economic indicators such as income, wealth or other well-being aspects. The major caveat is that the concept denies differences in individual preferences, choice and efforts (Philllips, 2006). Further, delivering equality in one measure does necessarily create inequalities in other measures as the individual preferences differ (e.g. with respect to income and leisure). On the other hand, affirmative action by imposing gender quotas in the labour market can entail greater efforts of firms to identify qualified women (Holzer and Neumark, 2000) and can encourage more women to participate in the competition for jobs (Niederle et al., 2013).

Equality of opportunity

Equality of opportunity acknowledges the freedom of personal choice and differences in preferences. It distinguishes between "legitimate" differences in outcomes due to different choices made and "illegitimate" differences in outcomes that arise from discrimination or other impediments beyond one's control (Robeyns, 2006). The pursuit of equality of opportunities between the genders means to strive for equal access to education, health and the labour market, and, in a nutshell, the elimination of any barriers that may hamper men and women to realise their individual aspirations. Similar to the goal of equality of outcomes, it also requires a certain amount of redistribution in order to neutralise the inequitable distribution of initial resources. The major caveat of the concept of equal opportunities is the fine line that it draws between the inequality the agent should be accountable for and the inequality that results from exogenous factors, in particular as individual choices are influenced by social norms, cultural perceptions, habits and asymmetric information.

Equality of autonomy

It is by now widely accepted that gender equality requires more than equal opportunities (Seguino, 2013). In his seminal work on the aspects of freedom, Amartya Sen (1993) extents the concept of equal opportunities by distinguishing between the opportunity aspect of freedom and the process aspect of freedom. Its combination is referred to as *equality of autonomy* and can be described as not only having a sufficiently large set of opportunities available but also benefiting from decisional autonomy in choosing among them and immunity from interference by others. To this extent, a redistribution of resources or incentivising certain outcomes can be warranted to level the playing field and to allow all agents to acquire equal capabilities and have equal access to resources. As such, promoting equality of autonomy can be seen as a hybrid between the goal of equality of outcomes and the goal of equality of opportunities. The balance between the two latter concepts depends on the domain and the extent of biases inherent in values and preferences. For instance, it is reasonable to pursue equality of outcomes when focusing on the health status of individuals. On the contrary, educational choices may be better targeted through equality of opportunities, subject to the impacts of gender socialisation (e.g. prevalent stereotypes) that may require pro-active action to neutralise its biases.

Gender equality improves well-being

Pursuing the goal of gender equality is an aim in itself. But it is also likely to generate improvements across a wide range of well-being dimensions. Table 2.1 summarises the tentative impacts of a more gender-equal Austrian society on the various dimensions of well-being and suggests corresponding channels. Modifications to early life education,

Table 2.1. **Well-being implications of more gender equality**

Well-being dimensions	Outcomes	Channels
Education and skills	Increase in educational attainment	Open up educational tracks
	Improvement in intergenerational mobility	Open up educational tracks
	Better preservation and more diversification of skills	More post-formal education and on-the-job training for women
Jobs and earnings	Reduction of the gender pay gap	Reduction in structural asymmetries in the labour market
	More innovations	More gender diversity in managerial and entrepreneurial positions
	Creation of personal service sector jobs	Market supply of household services
	New work organisation challenges in enterprises	Reduction in hours worked by men
Income and wealth	Increase in family income	Stronger and more ambitious involvement of women in the labour market
	More financial independence for women	Higher earnings for women and a more even distribution of wealth
Health	Impact on women's health uncertain	Additional risks of stress for women, but also relief from care duties and less mental retirement
	Improvement in men's health	Fewer working hours for men and more time spent with the family
Work-life balance	Better work-life balance for both genders	Convergence in time spent on paid and unpaid work between genders
	Reduced strains at work and at home	Family-friendly work organisation and more formal childcare
	Improved child well-being, notably in vulnerable families	Stronger presence of father and better socialisation through kindergarten access
Life satisfaction	Realisation of broader life choices	Broader options for economic participation, earnings and family organisation
	Realisation of initial child rearing desires	Better reconciliation of child raising and professional aspirations

including gender-sensitive curricula and better guidance throughout the schooling period, may break down cultural and traditional barriers that have so far restricted intergenerational educational mobility (Scheebaum et al., 2013; and OECD, 2014a). In particular girls and children with an immigrant background are likely to benefit from the greater set of opportunities that opening up of the educational system would provide. More diversification in the choices of fields of study would enlarge the set of opportunities for both genders and facilitate better matches between talent and skill formation (Musset et al., 2013). Beyond school, better work-life balances would allow more women to enrol in on-the-job training and professional courses.

A better reconciliation of work and family life would enable parents to maintain or increase their employment commitment and have the number of children they would like to at the time of their choosing. Women could better pursue their individual and professional aspirations. Improved job satisfaction exerts a protective role on physical health and shields against mental disorder (Barnay, 2014). In addition, women would be less restrained by caregiving activities which are found to induce psychological stress, strain and overall health deterioration. Recent evidence suggests that the prevalence of mental health problems is 20% higher among carers than among non-carers (OECD, 2011b). Moreover, Adema et al. (2014) suggest that enrolment in formal Early Childhood Education and Care (ECEC) facilities has a negative effect on infant mortality rates, possibly related to the fact that such environments help to identify health issues at an earlier stage. Formal childcare is also shown to be positively associated with the child's cognitive development, in particular for children in disadvantaged households (Huerta et al., 2011). At the same time, very early enrolment outside home (before 6 months) impedes the opportunity of extended breastfeeding and deprives the child of the continuity in infant care and attention which may have adverse effects on its emotional well-being (OECD, 2011c).

From the employer's perspective, committed male and female workers that can remain in the workforce makes them regardless of gender – and this is key to avoiding discrimination – equally attractive and deserving of investment in their training and career development, which enables men and women to pursue careers. A greater use of flexible work and leave arrangements by both genders would make parental leave periods less penalising. A convergence in hours worked between women and men and more ambitious career trajectories for women would further reduce the gap in take-home pay. Stronger female labour participation, in particular in full-time jobs, increases family income and improves career prospects for women. Higher income for women fosters their financial independence, reduces individual, family and child poverty risks, improves resilience against adverse financial shocks and increases retirement entitlements and wealth. Financial independence gains more and more importance owing to rising numbers for one-person and single-parent households.[1]

Macroeconomic implications of more gender-equal work-life arrangements

This section uses the OECD's in-house growth model (Johansson et al., 2013) to offer long-term simulations of alternative family and work arrangements in Austria. The model is based on a growth accounting framework that allows for adjustments in structural parameters that reflect changes in the work-life balance between women and men, namely the transition towards a more balanced dual-earner dual-carer model (Box 2.2).

Labour force participation and labour intensity

Thévenon (2013) studies the impact of policies and institutions on female labour participation, distinguishing between full-time and part-time participation. Results suggest that full-time employment of women is likely to benefit most from spending on leave and birth grants, spending on childcare services in general and an the increase in the coverage of formal childcare facilities for children aged 0-2 years in particular. He also argues that an estimation of individual effects of the aforementioned institutional and policy features, including the tax and benefit system, care infrastructure and an enabling work organisation, is difficult due to the likely interaction of these features. For instance, the impact of an extension of the maternal or parental leave systems depends on the availability of formal childcare facilities and family-friendly workplace practices. Thévenon (2013) recognises that the evaluation of the impact of individual policies is burdensome and, given the low degrees of freedom resulting from multiple interactions, econometrically questionable.

The present simulation approach is based on a convergence of part-time patterns and participation in Austria towards those observed on average in selected countries.[2] Currently, the incidence of part-time among Austrian women is 5 times higher than the incidence of part-time among Austrian men. In the more gender-equal scenario it is assumed that this ratio convergence towards the OECD and peer country average of 3 until 2025. While participation rates for men (81%) are close to those observed in peer countries, female participation (71%) still lags behind rates observed in the selected countries (75%). On the other hand, men engaged in full-time work spend considerably more time at work with respect counterparts in peer countries (43.5 hours per week

Box 2.2. **OECD's long-term growth projection model**

The model provides a projection of potential output and is based on the supply-side of the economy. The different long-term growth determinants (physical capital (K), human capital (H), potential employment (N), labour efficiency (E)) are aggregated trough a standard Cobb-Douglas production function with constant returns to scale:

(1) $$y = \alpha (n + e + h) + (1 - \alpha) k$$

where lower case letters denote natural logarithms and α the wage share. Each component is projected out to 2060 according to long-term dynamics and convergence patterns between the countries. Changes to per capita GDP can be decomposed into changes trend productivity and changes in labour utilisation:

(2) $$\Delta(y - p) = \Delta(y - n) + \Delta(n - p)$$

where P denotes the total population based on Eurostat (for European countries) and UN (for non-European countries) projections. By rearranging (1), three drivers of changes in trend productivity can be distinguished:

(3) $$\Delta(y - n) = \Delta e + \Delta h + \{(1 - \alpha)/\alpha\} \Delta(k - y)$$

- Labour efficiency (Δe) is projected based on convergence towards the technological frontier. Speed of convergence depends on the initial position and structural factors such as product market regulation.
- Human capital (Δh) is a function of average years of schooling with decreasing rates of return. The baseline specification assumes that these returns to education are the same for all countries and that educational attainment (measured by average years of schooling) of the 25-29 age cohorts improves by 1% per year over the projection horizon.
- Physical capital intensity [$\Delta(k - y)$] is affected by changes in interest rates and has a mean-reverting component so that the capital-output ratio (K/Y) stabilises over the long run.

Labour utilisation can be rewritten using labour force (LF) and working age population (PWA), the latter being defined as the population aged 15 years and older. This decomposition reveals three drivers for changes in labour utilisation:

(4) $$\Delta(n - p) = \Delta(n - lf) + \Delta(lf - pwa) + \Delta(pwa - p)$$

- Structural unemployment [$\Delta(n - lf)$] is assumed to converge to its lowest level observed between 2007 and 2014.
- Labour force participation [$\Delta(lf - pwa)$] is projected based on a cohort model. Participation rates of older workers are adjusted in line with implemented pension reforms. In addition, future increases in the pensionable age are assumed by indexing it to projected life expectancy.
- Active population ratio [$\Delta(pwa - p)$] follows directly from the population projection and is affected by underlying assumptions concerning fertility, mortality, net immigration and life expectancy.

against 41.8). Accordingly, the more gender-equal scenario assumes the following convergences to take place between 2016 and 2025:

- Increase in female labour participation rate from 71% to 75%.
- Reduction in the incidence of female part-time work from 33%[3] to 21%.
- A reduction in hours worked per week for full-time working men from 43.5 to 41.8.

All other things equal, these effects would increase total hours worked by 3.5% by 2025. Convergence is assumed to be linear which translates into annual increases in total hours worked of 0.35% per year from 2016 to 2025 with respect to the baseline scenario. In terms of the growth accounting framework (Box 2.2), increases in hours worked per person translate one-to-one into increases in labour efficiency (Δe) while increase in female labour participation increase labour utilisation [$\Delta(n - p)$].

Human capital

More gender equality would also lead to more diversified choices of fields of study across genders. Enrolment and duration in higher education are likely to increase and pave the way for a higher accumulation of human capital. In the OECD growth modelling framework (see Box 2.2), human capital is indeed measured as a function of average years of schooling with a decreasing rate of return. Currently, Austria lacks behind comparable countries. The more gender-equal scenario assumes that the average number of years in schooling will converge towards the one observed in Denmark by 2060 (Figure 2.1).

Figure 2.1. **Assumed convergence in years of schooling**

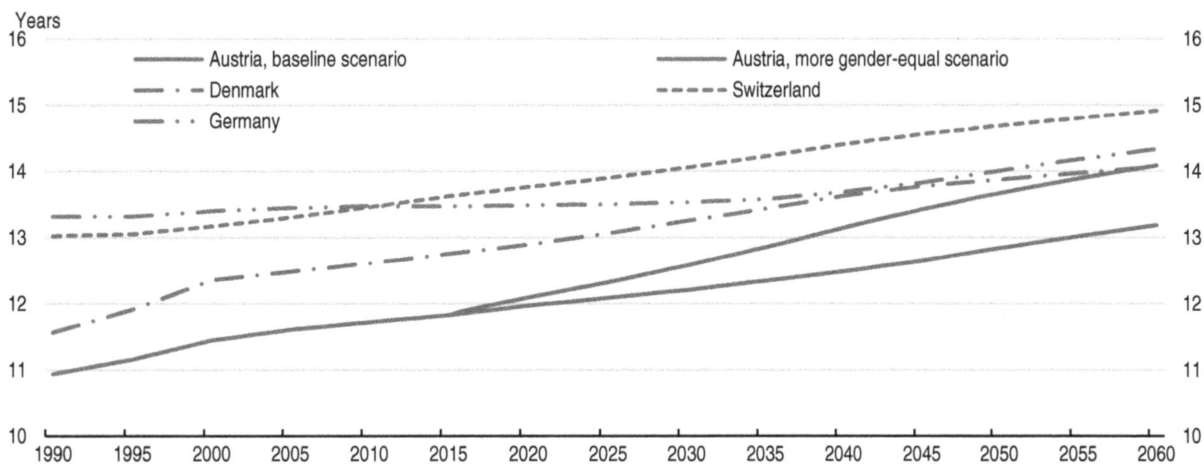

Source: OECD projections and calculations based on *OECD Economic Outlook*.

StatLink http://dx.doi.org/10.1787/888933252294

The modelling framework assumes that the return to schooling has the same functional form for all countries and across scenarios. As a result, some potentially positive effects on human capital of a more gender-equal society cannot be captured. For instance, a better transition from school/university to work and a reduction in the incidence of part-time work is likely to increase human capital and reduce hysteresis effects. Indeed, full-time work coincides with more on-the-job-training, higher participation in regular professional education and training courses as well as better job opportunities and careers. Additionally, a more gender-equal work environment would reduce the incidence of over-qualification and over-skilling. Mussat et al. (2013) revealed that Austria exhibits the highest incidence of over-skilled workers across OECD countries and over-skilling is particularly high for Austrian women.[4] Especially the use of information-processing skills is strongly gender-biased. The incidence of under-exploiting skills at work is particularly high among part-time employees which may be one explanation for the fulltime dividend that contributes to the gender pay gap. Better matches would further increase the return to education.[5] The simulated effect of less segregated educational and job-market patterns for human capital (Figure 2.2) can therefore be seen as a lower boundary for the expected total effect.

Figure 2.2. **Human capital improvement induced by more gender equality**

Percentage point increase in human capital from the baseline scenario to the more gender-equal scenario

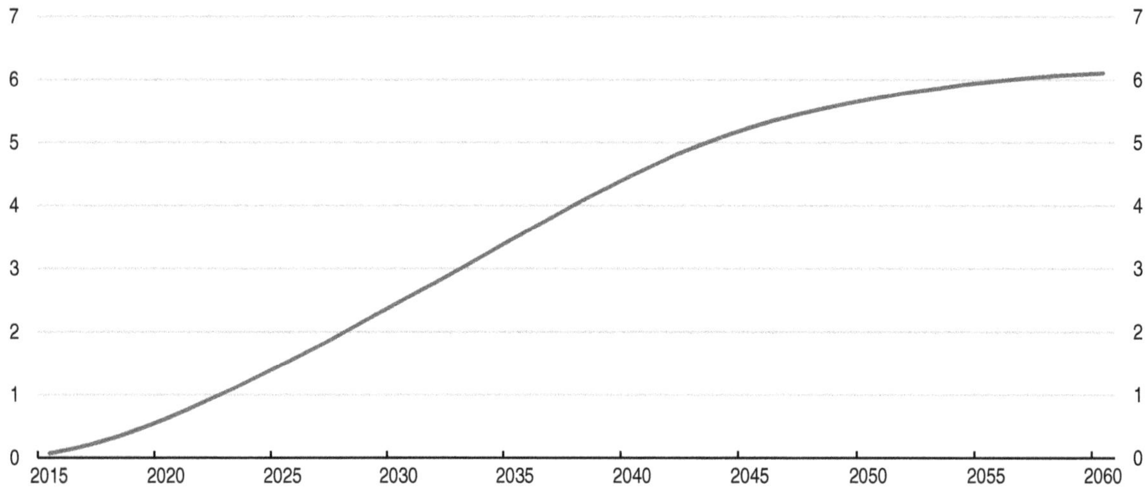

Source: OECD calculations.

StatLink http://dx.doi.org/10.1787/888933252303

Fertility

A recent study based on long-term time trends (Adema et al., 2014) identifies fertility as one of the three main indicators of family and child well-being, the others being female employment and infant mortality. According to the authors, cross-country differences in total fertility rates reflect, at least to some extent, difficulties in combining work and family commitments. The lack of adequate formal childcare and enabling workplaces makes it difficult to reconcile family and career aspiration for women. As a result, many couples have fewer children than intended and are pushed to abandon or postpone parenthood (Adema, 2012).

While the decision to have a child is an entirely private one, a more gender-equal society is likely to increase child bearing for several reasons. First, an enabling infrastructure, namely full-day early childhood care and family-friendly workplaces, mitigate the tension between work and family life and break with the current practice of having to choose between the two (Box 2.3). Ideally, the birth of a child would not interfere with medium- and long-term career plans of women, which facilitates the decision to have children. Second, a higher prevalence of dual-earner families increases average family income, makes child bearing financially more affordable and reduces the likelihood of child poverty. Third, a more balanced distribution of unpaid work at home ensures an equal sharing of the burden of child care tasks (Huerta et al., 2013). Sullivan et al. (2014) argue that the recent upturn in fertility rates in some low-fertility countries coincides with an increase in the contribution of fathers, in particular younger and highly educated fathers, to childcare and domestic tasks. De Laat and Sevilla-Sanz (2011) find evidence that men's involvement in home production explains the positive cross-country correlation

Box 2.3. **Drivers of low fertility in Europe**

Several researchers have stressed the importance of welfare state regimes for family and fertility outcomes. Neyer (2013) identifies "commodification", "de-familialisation" and "de-gendering of employment and care" as the main welfare-state principles that shape fertility patterns across Europe. These three principles materialise in policies that i) allow to form and maintain a household and a family; ii) deliver an enabling set of opportunities and the capability to choose; and iii) ensure fairness in the gender distribution of family work and care. Opponents to this view often claim that fertility is more likely to be driven by social norms than by family policies (e.g. Sobotka and Testa, 2008). Klüsener et al. (2013) find evidence for a disconnection between inherited social norms and family policies with respect to fertility. They compare fertility rates in a German-speaking community in Belgium, close to the German border, with fertility rates in the rest of Belgium and Western Germany. This community shares social norms with Western Germany and the family policy framework with the rest of Belgium. The results show that the community's fertility pattern is much closer to the one observed in the rest of Belgium than to the one of Western Germany which suggests that family policies settings prevail over social norms. Again, the striking difference between the 2 countries in terms of family policy resides in the coverage of external early childhood care and preschool facilities. The provision of external child care indeed perfectly illustrates the extent to which public policy can be constraining or enabling for the child-raising process. Lesthaeghe and Permanyer (2014) identify two distinct low fertility clusters In Europe. On the one hand, Southern European countries that face matching problems on the partnership market, leading to "pronounced partnership and parenthood postponement"? On the other hand, German-speaking countries fail to allow parents to reconcile work and family which delays or even hinders the formation of a family. The insufficiently developed care infrastructure is put forward as the main obstacle in these countries.

between female labour participation and fertility. Similarly, Buber-Ennser et al. (2014) finds a strong positive correlation between a mother's satisfaction with the division of childcare tasks and her intention of bearing a second child.

Eurostat population projections provide both a baseline and a low-fertility scenario. By extrapolating the differences for each age cohort, a high-fertility scenario is obtained for Austria. It entails a gradual increase in the average fertility rate from 1.45 births per woman in 2013 to 1.9 in 2060, against 1.6 in the baseline and 1.3 in the low-fertility scenario. Figure 2.3 illustrates the changes with respect to the baseline for the total population and the working age population.

Public investment and government spending

A necessary condition for the transition towards a more balanced dual-earner dual-carer model and greater employment participation of sole parents is better access to quality early childhood education and care facilities. The Austrian Federal Chamber of Labour (2013) estimates a gap of 35 000 places in care facilities for children aged 0-2 years (day-care centres). Filling this gap would lift the enrolment rate for 0-2 years above the Barcelona target of 33%. The construction of the missing places is projected to cost about EUR 100 million per year over 3 years. In addition, an improvement in the quality of childcare is modelled via the reduction of the child-teacher ratio and a general increase in opening hours. This would lift share of full-day care centres from currently 44% to close to

Figure 2.3. **A high-fertility scenario for Austria**

Percentage point increase from the baseline scenario to the more gender-equal scenario

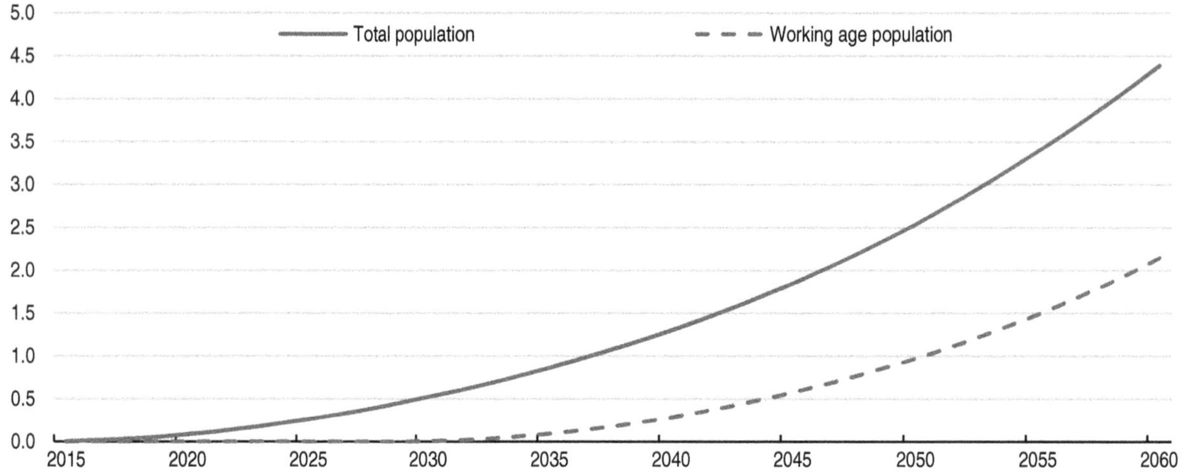

Source: Eurostat population projections and OECD calculations.

StatLink http://dx.doi.org/10.1787/888933252313

70% over the next 3 years. Total additional personnel costs are assumed to amount to EUR 200 million in the first year, EUR 350 in the second and EUR 500 million in the third year increasing with inflation and productivity thereafter. Table 2.2 summarises the derived fiscal implications for the more gender-equal scenario.

Table 2.2. **Fiscal costs of quantitative and qualitative childcare infrastructure improvements**

	2016	2017	2018	2016	2017	2018	2019-60	2016	2017	2018	2019-60
	In EUR million			% of component				% of GDP			
Government investment	100	100	100	1.05	1.05	1.05	0.00	0.03	0.03	0.03	0.00
Government current disbursements	200	350	500	0.13	0.22	0.31	0.31	0.06	0.11	0.16	0.16
Government total disbursements	300	450	600	0.19	0.28	0.38	0.31	0.09	0.14	0.19	0.16

Source: OECD calculations inspired by numbers provided by the Austrian Federal Chamber of Labour.

These numbers are considerably larger than the investment that is currently envisaged. Government expenditures do not directly enter the growth accounting framework, which is based on supply-side components (see Box 2.2). It is implicitly assumed that the debt-to-GDP ratio converges to 60% with a maximum fiscal consolidation effort of ½ percentage point of GDP per year. In absence of offsetting effects from spending cuts or additional revenues, increases in government spending therefore imply a longer period of fiscal consolidation with respect to the baseline. In their assessment, The Austrian Federal Chamber of Labour (2013) assumes that the mere increase in female labour participation auto-finances the investment projects within an estimated time of 7 years (average of the 2 scenarios presented).

Potential output

Trend productivity is affected by increases in labour efficiency due to higher hours worked per person and by increases in human capital. Taken together, trend productivity is projected to increase by close to 10% until 2060 of which 3.5% result from gains in labour efficiencies (see above) and a little more than 6% from gains in human capital (Figure 2.4).

Figure 2.4. **Trend productivity with respect to the baseline scenario**

Percentage point increase in trend productivity from the baseline scenario to the more gender-equal scenario

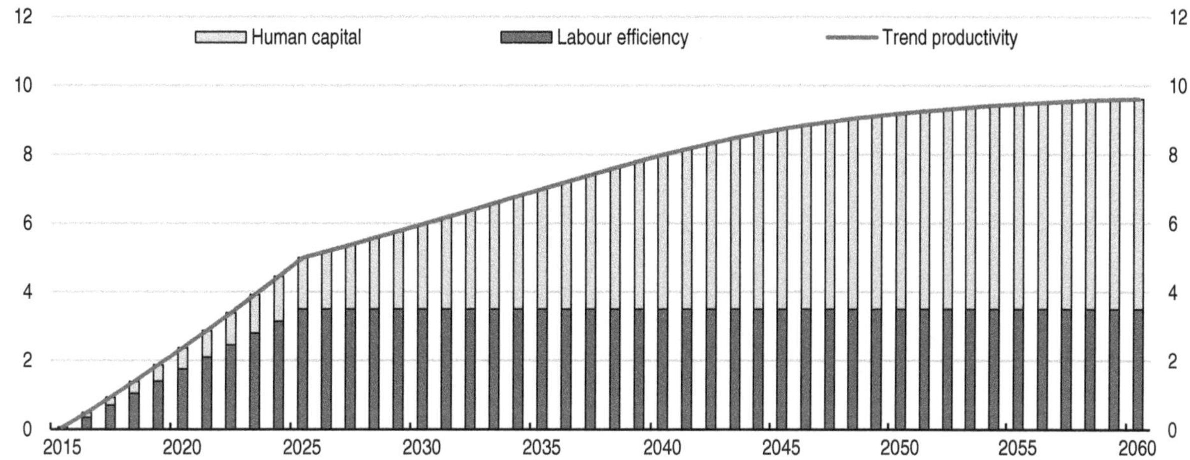

Source: OECD calculations.

StatLink http://dx.doi.org/10.1787/888933252328

In addition to the higher working age population induced by higher fertility, potential employment would benefit from a rising participation rate. First, this is due to the assumption of gradual increases in the female participation rate. Second, it is induced by a demographic effect as younger age cohorts exhibit relatively higher participation rates than older ones, and their share in the work force would gradually increase. By 2040, the simulation exhibits a 1pp increase of potential employment with respect to the baseline. This gap increases to 2pp in 2050 and to close to 4pp in 2060 (Figure 2.5) when demographic

Figure 2.5. **Implications for potential employment**

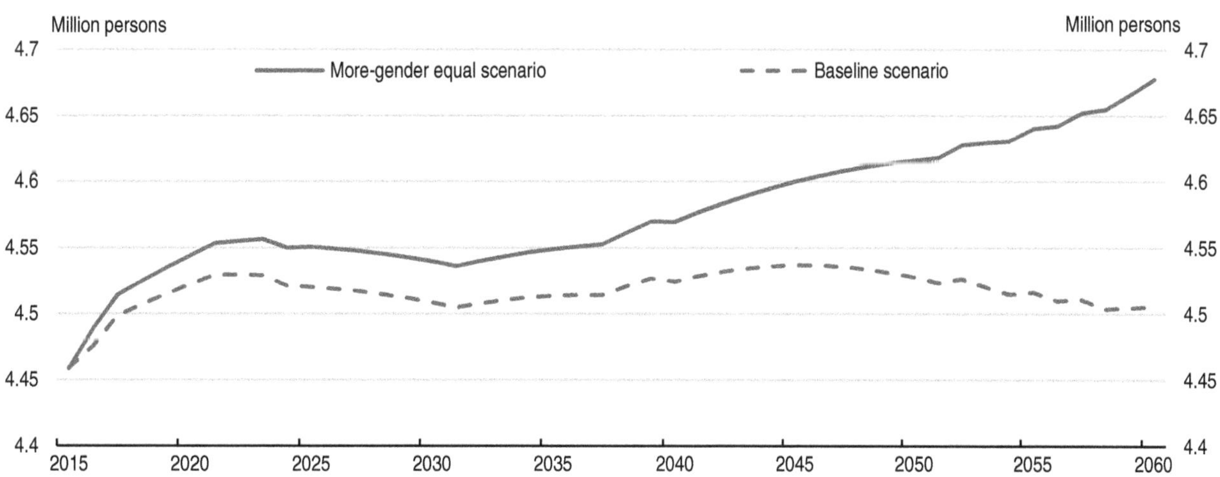

Source: OECD calculations.

StatLink http://dx.doi.org/10.1787/888933252339

effects from an increase in fertility have materialised in all age-cohorts, in particular those with relatively high participation rates.

Taken together, potential GDP is simulated to rise by about 13 percentage points in the more gender-equal scenario with respect to the baseline until 2060. Per capita GDP would increase by 8 percentage points and total population by approximately 4.5 percentage points, respectively (Figure 2.6).

Figure 2.6. **GDP implications of more gender-equality**

Percentage point increase from the baseline scenario to the more gender-equal scenario

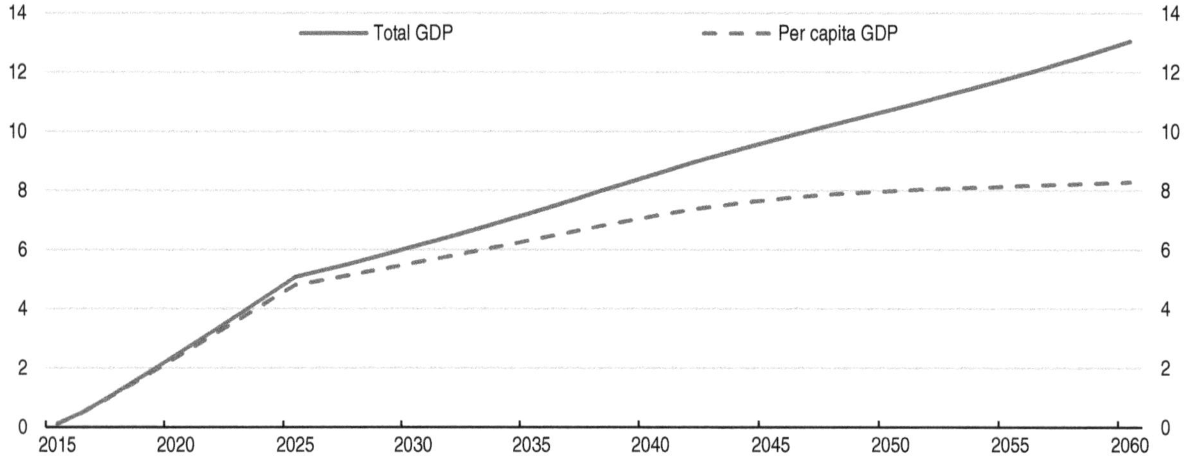

Source: OECD calculations based on OECD's long-term growth model (Box 2.2).

StatLink http://dx.doi.org/10.1787/888933252349

An integrated policy framework to promote gender equality in Austria

The Austrian government has launched a set of initiatives to raise awareness for gender inequalities and highlight the government's willingness to tackle them (Box 2.4). The gender mainstreaming agenda is underpinned by a Committee on Gender Equality, elected by parliament, that deals with all bills and legislative proposals related to gender equality, including women's and men's empowerment and the prevention of gender discrimination in all policy areas. Despite these efforts, some evidence calls for a stronger whole of government approach in Austria, including more robust processes for collecting gender-specific data, better and more systematic integration of gender analysis into the policy making process and a strengthening of monitoring, auditing and accountability measures (OECD, 2014b).

Raising awareness for the existence of gender inequalities and for the potential benefits of a more gender-equal society is a prerequisite for broad support for a gender mainstreaming policy agenda. Bringing in gender issues in the public debate through information campaigns or disseminating best practices can contribute to dismantling stereotypes such as the belief that a working mother is a bad mother (*Rabenmutter*) or that technical professions are male professions. It would help to motivate and underpin an integrated policy framework to achieve more gender-equality based on the following principles: i) make the tax-and-benefit system less gender role biased; ii) reconcile work and family lives by extending the service infrastructure; and iii) encourage more flexible workplace practices.

Box 2.4. **Current gender mainstreaming initiatives**

One of the prime examples for public action to foster gender equality in Austria is the gender budgeting project. It allows gender initiatives to make use of resources that go beyond the Federal Ministry of Education and Women's Affairs and can induce cultural change at the administrative and political level. Critics refer, however, to limited co-ordination across different bodies and levels of government. Objectives differ substantially in terms of quality and ambition, and the monitoring provided by the Federal Performance Management Office and the Parliamentary Budget Office has only limited power. It co-ordinates measures and targets across the different ministries by organising workshops, building up know-how and providing quality assessments and feedback. However, the budgetary impact of specific targets is not assessed. To remedy to this situation, the monitoring of spending associated with gender targets shall be provided by an independent gender budgeting council. Schratzenstaller (2014) further encourages a better link between medium-term gender objectives and gender-related long-term strategies at the EU level.

An initiative that extends awareness of gender inequalities beyond the public sphere is the requirement for income reports for companies with more than 150 employees. These compulsory reports result from the "National Action Plan for Gender Equality in the Labour Market" (2008-13) and are a legal requirement under the Equal Treatment Act. The reports seek to improve income transparency and inform about gender-specific pay differences. They are also likely to trigger self-correction mechanisms as part of the dissemination process. Finally, the income reports reduce the extent of asymmetric information during the individual wage negotiation processes for both incumbent employers and outsiders. According to a survey jointly conducted by the Chamber of Labour (AK) and Austrian Trade Union Federation (ÖGB) and published in 2014, 71% of the interviewed works councils found the income reports relevant and 63% affirmed that the content of the reports is useful. As a reaction to the income reports, 23% of the employers declared to deal with the apparent gender pay gap and 21% showed the willingness to concrete action such as training, measures to better reconcile work and family, female promotion plans or support for fathers in taking over family commitments.

In the absence of legislated regulation against sexist advertising, an advisory board on anti-sexism was created within the Austrian Advertising Council in 2011. The benefits of such a board are twofold. First, it allows for the monitoring of commercial audio-visual communication with respect to gender discriminatory advertising and enables the Advertising Council to stop campaigns if norms are violated.* Second, it raises awareness in the advertising industry and may help to promote non-discriminatory portrayal of genders. To foster such progress, in 2012, the "Gender Award Advertising" initiative has been launched which rewards gender-sensitive advertising campaigns according to their extent of promoting gender equality by representing women and men in atypical roles and professions and thus overcoming gender stereotypes.

* In 2012, among the 278 complaints received by the Council more than a half dealt with gender discriminatory advertising and 13 campaigns have eventually been stopped.

Make the tax and benefit system less gender role biased

In many respects, the Austrian tax and benefit system is rather dual-earner friendly. Income taxation is individual which means that the entry tax rate for the second earner is smaller, all other things equal, than in joint or family-based taxation system. In addition, basic family allowances are rewarded universally, that is, independent from the level or distribution of earnings. On the other hand, certain characteristics of the tax and benefit system distort incentives in favour of the one bread-winner or the "1½ model". In particular, the high marginal tax wedge for medium incomes is supportive of part-time work. The arrival of children reinforces this model through means-tested childcare allowances, sole-earner deductions, long parental leaves and a family benefit system largely tilted towards cash benefits.

Eliminate work disincentives in the tax system

Despite a significant reduction owing to the recent tax reform, Austria still has one of the highest bottom statutory rate in the OECD (declines from 36.5% to 25% in 2016, Box 1 and Figure 3, Panel A). In combination with a large zero-tax zone this leads to a substantial threshold effect at the point where the first tax bracket sets in. The transition from the zero-tax zone to the first income bracket merely concerns part-time employees and causes a considerable disincentive to extend working hours for employees whose income is close to but below the threshold of about EUR 17 000 of annual gross earnings.[6] Indeed, many female employees are concentrated in this part of the earning distribution (Chapter 1, Figure 1.15, Panel D).

The sole-earner deduction, which has not been addressed by the tax reform, provides disincentives for marginally employed second earner spouses. This tax allowance depends on the number of children and is rewarded to families whose second earner's annual taxable income does not exceed EUR 6 000 (Box 2.6). For average hourly wages this threshold corresponds to approximately 9-10 hours per week. A marginal increase in the spouse's working time above 10 hours per week would effectively reduce the family's disposable income. This explains the local peak in the distribution of female earnings in the EUR 4 000-6 000 range (Figure 1.15, Panel D).

A further disincentive for marginally employed workers is set by the threshold of currently EUR 405.98 below which no social security contributions are due. Above this limit, social security contributions are payable on the total amount of earnings resulting in an effective decrease in disposable income. Indeed, an employee earning EUR 477 per month actually ends up with the same net income of EUR 405 as an employee earning EUR 405 the difference being the social security tax liability (15.1% or EUR 72 for the former, 0% for the latter). This threshold reinforces the effect of the sole earner tax credit and supports the male breadwinner model as well as the 1½ model.

Employee's and commuter tax credits (Box 2.5) are refundable and paid out as negative taxes to non-commuting (commuting) employees with an upper limit of 10% (18%) of paid social security contributions for a maximum of EUR 110 (EUR 400). At current contribution rates this means that incomes of non-commuting (commuting) employees below EUR 7 300 (EUR 14 700) gradually loose entitlement to negative taxes. Below these thresholds, the negative tax has the effect of an in-work benefit. While the 2015/16 tax reform is foreseen to lift the ceiling to EUR 400 (EUR 500) as of 1 January 2016, the fact that, the tax credits will be capped at 50% of paid social security contributions reduces the in-work benefit character as the ceiling will be hit earlier than before.

Box 2.5. **Main features of Austria's personal income tax system**

Since 1973 individuals are taxed separately rather than jointly as a household. Annual gross earnings are usually divided into 14 equal monthly instalments of which 12 correspond to current monthly payments and the other 2 to holiday and Christmas bonuses. The tax schedules for these payments are different:

Tax schedule for personal income

Until 31 December 2015		From 1 January 2016		Holiday and Christmas bonus in EUR	Marginal rate in %
Current taxable income in EUR	Marginal rate in %	Current taxable income in EUR	Marginal rate in %		
0-11 000	0.0	0-11 000	0.0	0-620	0.0
11 001-25 000	36.5	11 000-18 000	25.0	620-25 000	6.0
25 001-60 000	43.2	18 000-31 000	35.0	25 000-50 000	27.0
60 001 +	50.0	31 000-60 000	42.0	50 000-83 333	35.75
		60 000-90 000	48.0	83 334 +	50.0
		90 000-1 million	50.0		
		1 million +	55.0		

Current taxable income is obtained as the sum of the 12 current monthly payments reduced by the employee's social security contributions and various tax allowances:

- Work related expenses for commuting, clothes, language courses, phone, etc. (lump sum of EUR 132).
- Special expenses: lump sum of EUR 60 or a quarter of expenses related personal insurance schemes, renovation or acquisition of principal residence. Maximum of EUR 2 920 for singles and EUR 5 840 for couples, with an additional EUR 1 460 from three children onwards. Maximum allowance is limited to annual earnings up to EUR 36 400. Above EUR 36 400 maximum allowance reduces gradually to reach EUR 60 at annual earnings of EUR 60 000 and beyond. This part of special expenses relief will be abolished as of 1 January 2016. The lump sum of EUR 60 and costs related to contracts concluded before 2016 will be paid until 2020.
- Additional pay for overtime hours (up to 50% of the supplementary hourly wage) are exempt from income tax for the first 10 overtime hours (max. EUR 86 per month). Until 2009 only 5 overtime hours' allowances were tax-exempt.

The tax liability is obtained by applying the tax schedule to taxable income. Several tax credits then reduce the tax liability:

- Employee's tax credit: EUR 54. All employees are entitled.
- Commuter tax credit: EUR 291. Depending on availability of public transport and commuting distance, an additional commuter tax credit is paid. Thresholds are 2 km without public transport and 20 km with public transport available. The additional tax credit can reach up to EUR 3 672 for commuting distances exceeding 60 km with no suitable public transport available.

Tax credits are non-wastable and paid out as negative tax up to 10% of paid social security contributions with a maximum of EUR 110 per year. Employees eligible for the additional commuting tax credit (see above) for long distances are entitled to an additional EUR 290 of non-wastable tax credits (EUR 400 in total) limited at 18% of paid social security contributions. As of 1 January 2016, tax credits will be granted up to EUR 400 for all employers and up to EUR 110 for pensioners limited at 50% of paid social contributions. For low-income commuters who do not pay income taxes, the negative tax credit can amount to maximal EUR 500.

Box 2.6. **The current system of family benefits**

The bulk of spending on family benefits is paid out in cash (74.6%) most of which non-means-tested. Tax breaks only represent 1.5% and in-kind benefits 23.9% of total spending on family benefits.

Cash benefits

Family allowances are granted universally for each dependent child independent from the number of earners or the level of earnings in the family. Dependent children are all children aged 18 years or younger, or between 19 and 24 as long as their income does not exceeding EUR 10 000 per year. Allowances are decomposed in a basic allowance of EUR 109.70 per child and month, an age supplement and a sibling supplement (table below). Family allowances will be augmented by 1.9% in 2016 and again by 1.9% in 2018.

Monthly family allowance per depend child and month

Child's age	Total number of dependent children						
	1	2	3	4	5	6	7
0-2 years	109.7	116.4	126.3	135.2	140.5	144.0	159.7
3-9 years	117.3	124.0	133.9	142.8	148.1	151.6	167.3
10-18 years	136.2	142.9	152.8	161.7	167.0	170.5	186.2
19-24 years	158.9	165.6	175.5	184.4	189.7	193.2	208.9

Source: Federal Ministry for Family and Youth. As of October 2014. Currency: EUR.

Additionally, a "school supplement" of EUR 100 is rewarded every September for children aged between 6 and 15. Families are further entitled to a non-wastable tax credit of EUR 58.40 per month and child. This tax credit is paid out independently from the income tax regime and meets the condition of a cash benefit. The only means-tested cash benefit is a "multiple child" supplement of EUR 20 per month, granted for the 3rd and any additional child provided that the family's taxable income does not exceed EUR 55 000. A supplement for families in need is available at the *Länder*-level. Eligibility criteria and amount of these means-tested cash transfers vary substantially from one Land to another.

Tax allowances

- Sole earner deduction: single parents and couples where the second earner's income does not exceed EUR 6 000 per year are entitled to a deduction from their taxable income: EUR 494 per year for the first child, 175 for the second child and EUR 220 for the 3rd and any additional child.
- A single parent tax payer can deduct EUR 220 per child from the annual taxable income while two parents have the choice between deducing EUR 220 for one parent or EUR 132 each. To be eligible, the tax payer must be entitled to the children tax credit (EUR 58.40 per month, see above) for the corresponding child for more than 6 months during the reference year. In the course of the 2015/16 tax reform, it is planned to double the tax allowance per child to EUR 440.

In-kind benefits

In-kind benefits include direct financing of childcare or subsidising providers of childcare facilities. It amounts to 0.65% of GDP, that is, approximately a fourth of total spending on family benefits. Since 2009, employers can grant a childcare subsidy to the employee of up to EUR 500 per year for children under ten years of age conditional on the use of an formal childcare facility or a licensed child minder. The subsidy can be paid either directly to the facility or to the care giver either in cash or as a voucher to be cashed in at a facility of her choice. The subsidy is exempt from taxation and social security contributions.

The tax exemption for the supplement awarded for overtime hours (Box 2.5) is another tax measure that encourages an unequal distribution of paid work between the two partners as it provides an incentive to increase working time beyond the regular working hours. Indeed, in Austria, the male bread winners bear the bulk of overtime hours and Austrian men are the OECD champions of weekly hours worked. This obviously makes them less available at home and reinforces the separate gender role model (Chapter 1).

Family benefits need to be better targeted to offer real choice

In sharp contrast to the OECD average, spending on family benefits as a share of GDP has declined in Austria since the beginning of the 2000's. As of 2011, overall spending on family benefits in Austria amounted to 2.7% of GDP which was only slightly above OECD average of 2.6% of GDP and substantially below spending by countries of the top third (3.7%) (Figure 2.7). The breakdown into spending categories varies substantially across countries. While the average OECD country allocates about half of its spending to cash benefits, cash transfers account for three quarters of the family related spending in Austria. Tax breaks are barely used at all and benefits in-kind fall significantly short of what can be observed in peer countries and the OECD as a whole.

Figure 2.7. **Public spending on family benefits**

In per cent of GDP, 2011

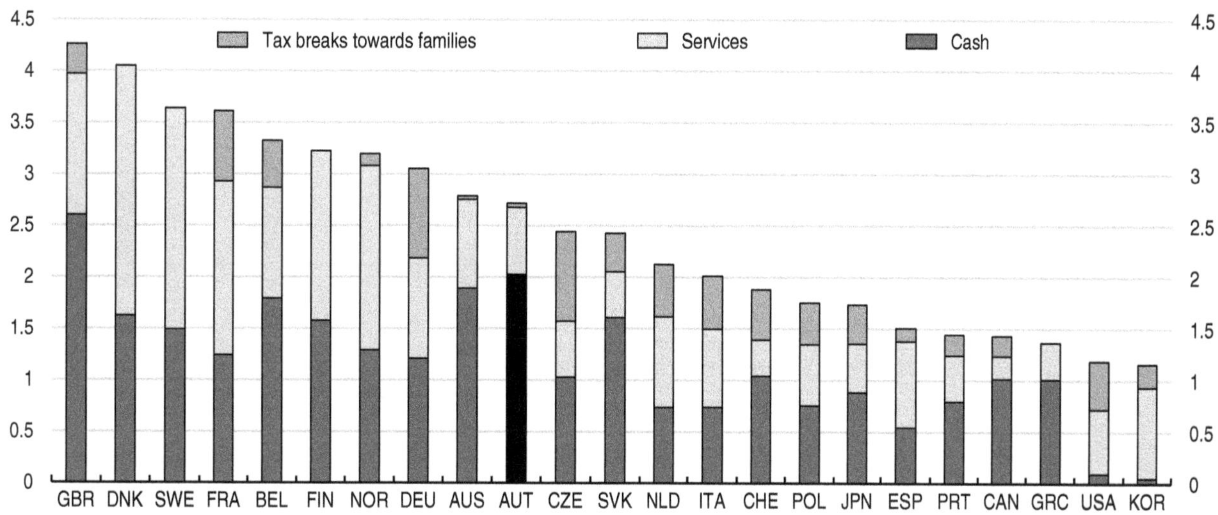

Source: OECD (2014), *OECD Family database, www.oecd.org/social/family/database.htm.*

StatLink http://dx.doi.org/10.1787/888933252356

On the one hand, cash benefits prove to be an effective tool to reduce child poverty and inequality (Förster and Verbist, 2012). On the other hand, they are less effective in pursuing other policy objectives such as maximising labour force participation, in particular, if, as is the case in Austria, none of the cash transfers are conditional on the use of childcare services. Against this background, a shift from cash towards in-kind benefits and tax-breaks could rebalance the provision of family benefits in favour of parents in employment and support the compatibility of career and family life, in particular for mothers of young children.

The voucher system that supports families that make use of formal ECEC services should be extended to all parents and streamlined with the general scheme of public childcare allowances (Box 2.6). Currently, the maximum amount of the voucher that employers can grant to their employees is EUR 500 per year, while the unconditional childcare allowance ranges from EUR 436 to EUR 2 000 per month. Especially for low-income families, the costs of formal childcare may exceed earnings prospects for the second earner, in particular, if regularly provided formal childcare facilities are not available or do not cover the full day. More in-kind benefits would give a stronger focus on earlier years of the child's development for which Austria spends a considerably lower share than other OECD countries (Figure 2.8). This lowers return on investment in human capital that is found to be highest for the earliest years (Heckman, 2006).

Figure 2.8. **Public spending on family benefits and education by age**

In per cent of GDP

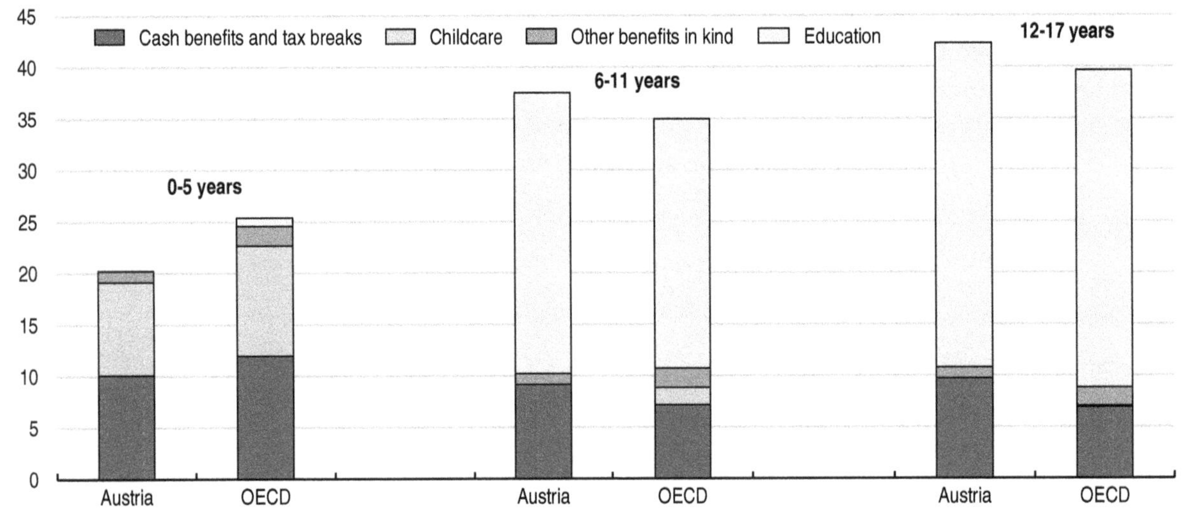

Note: The indicator is calculated using the Age-Spending Profiles methodology used in *Doing Better for Families* (OECD, 2011). Preliminary 2011 data for Austria. Data for the OECD refer to 2009.

Source: OECD, *Social Expenditure database* and OECD *Education database*, 2014.

StatLink http://dx.doi.org/10.1787/888933252363

In its 2013-18 work programme, the Austrian government has acknowledged the need to provide "more transparency and simplification regarding family benefits". The 2013 OECD Economic Survey's review of the system of family benefits has highlighted the complexity of the system. The wide range of instruments across different levels of governments, with regional differences, can lead to inequalities due to lack of information or simply due to the place of living. In 2012, *Länder*-specific transfers to families in need amounted to 7% of total spending on family benefits at the federal level (among recipient families the share of *Länder* transfers is much higher). Eligibility criteria and amount varied considerably across the *Länder* which, *inter alia*, leads to regional inequalities, in particular, among poor families. A general effort to streamline benefits across different levels of government, horizontally and vertically, would reduce inequalities and inefficiencies, in particular, as financing responsibilities and provision of the benefits often do not lie in the same hands.

De Boer et al. (2014) evaluate the impact of fiscal stimuli likely to support working parents (Box 2.7). They use a structural model calibrated on recent reforms in the Netherlands and administrative data for hours worked and the use of formal childcare. The results suggest that a combination of means-tested in-work benefits for secondary earners and targeted subsidies for childcare services have the strongest potential to support working parents in a cost-efficient way. The findings are likely to bear interest among Austrian policymakers and may give rise to discussion about innovations in the tax and benefit system.

Box 2.7. **Estimating the efficiency of support policies for working parents**

The Netherlands Bureau of Economic Policy Analysis produced a pioneering analysis of the efficiency of alternative support schemes for working parents (de Boer et al., 2014). The researchers suggest that their "findings are relevant for the effectiveness of these policies in other developed OECD countries".

The Netherlands' highly varied experience with support schemes for working parents (following several reforms over the past decade), and the availability of high quality information on households' labour market position, tax liabilities, social benefits and child care practices over the same period permitted to estimate a large structural model, which helps simulate the responses of different types of households to alternative policy schemes. Only couple families with children less than 12 year old are covered. The model simulates their decisions in the face of different incentives, and helps calculate "net employment gains per euro of public spending" under different schemes. It takes into account second round fiscal effects from changes in workers' behaviour and seems to have a good fit with actual experience so far.

The model has been used to estimate likely gains from a fictitious EUR 100 million support package for working parents. The impacts of three main types of policy schemes currently in use in OECD countries (and which have been utilised in the Netherlands in the past) were investigated: i) a rise in childcare subsidies (cutting the childcare fees for dual-working parents); ii) in-work tax credits granted to all working parents; and iii) in-work benefits granted to all second earners. Two variants of each scheme have been tested: i) universal benefits at a flat rate, granted to all families; and ii) income-dependent benefits reserved to mid- to high-income households. Simulation results differ significantly between policy options, in all respects, and the net fiscal cost of an additional full-time job ranges from EUR 29 000 to EUR 180 000. The most significant findings are:

- *A strong increase in universal childcare benefits* enhances total work hours, but is costly. It has little impact on men's total labour supply (slight increase in their labour force participation, to qualify for benefits, but also a reduction in work hours). Impacts on women's labour force participation and work hours are both significant and positive. Yet, the impact on child care use is even stronger, suggesting that part of the increase in subsidised child care does not directly support labour force participation. In this scheme, a high share of child care costs end up being publicly funded (76% in average, up to 96% for low-income households), explaining the high budget cost of EUR 50 000 per full-time job created.
- *An increase in childcare benefits for middle-to-high income families* increases total work hours in the same proportion, but at a lower fiscal cost. Women's labour supply increases less than above (there is an income effect for higher earning women, which slows their participation), but high earning men's labour supply is resilient. As childcare costs are in the first place less subsided for these households (by about 40%), their broader recourse to additional care after this incentive is less fiscally costly. Moreover, these families' higher work hours generate higher tax revenues. This second variant of childcare support is more efficient (EUR 40 000 per full-time job created) but comes at an equity cost. Income inequality increases, and children from low income families participate less in formal child care.

Box 2.7. **Estimating the efficiency of support policies for working parents** *(cont.)*

- The allocation of the EUR 100 million into flat *in-work benefits for all working parents* has a very weak simulated impact. The bulk of transfers go to men, who have a largely inelastic labour supply. Effects on second earners are more positive, but are diluted (subsidies are spread thin). When in-work benefits are targeted to mid-to high income families, the effects are more tangible, but in both cases the schemes are highly inefficient from a fiscal viewpoint: each full-time job costs EUR 180 000 in the first variant and EUR 140 000 in the second.
- When *in-work benefits are targeted to second earners alone*, behavioural responses are stronger. They differ however between two variants. If benefits are flat, they have a positive effect on labour force participation (as more 2nd earners want to qualify) but a negative effect on average number of hours worked (only an income effect operates for those qualified). In the second variant, as in-work benefits are income dependent, both labour force participation and work hours increase. This second variant has the lowest fiscal cost per full-time job created, at EUR 29 000, against EUR 50 000 in the first variant.

This simulation focuses on the likely fiscal efficiency of alternative schemes and is highly informative. Implications for income distribution are also well documented. However, impacts on other well-being dimensions are not incorporated in the analysis. For example, implications for the long-term well-being of children (participating or not participating in formal child care according to their family circumstances) is a prime issue, and needs to be taken into consideration in the design and selection of support schemes. The Netherlands Bureau of Economic Policy Analysis plan to extend future work towards such dimensions.

Promote a more gender-equal parental leave system

Parental leave policies are in general complex and vary considerably across countries. The main discriminant parameters of parental leave systems are: i) the duration; ii) wage replacement rates; and iii) eligibility and transferability criteria for mothers and fathers. Generous parental leaves can facilitate child bearing decisions but also affect other outcomes, in particular the child's development and the parents' employment pattern. Maternal and paternal presence until a child has reached at least 6 months is generally judged as positive for the child's psychological and cognitive development, not the least related to breastfeeding. Beyond the 6 months, effects of in-house versus formal childcare on the child's cognitive and non-cognitive depend, *inter alia*, on the educational background of parents and their parenting skills (Huerta et al., 2011). In terms of employment outcomes, leave schemes can strengthen the mother's tie to paid work and uphold women's employment rate. This is usually associated with rather short leave durations of below 1 year. On the other hand, absence from work can have adverse consequences for the parent's, mostly the mother's, human capital and future employment opportunities. Such hysteresis patterns typically increase with the duration of the leave taken. Since parental leaves, especially longer spells of absence, are generally taken up by women, longer durations are likely to sharpen gender-inequalities in the labour market.

After the obligatory maternity leave (8 weeks before and 8 weeks after the birth), the Austrian system grants a parental leave to parents that lasts at most until the 2nd birthday of the child. The leave is a family entitlement and can be shifted from one parent to the other twice for a total of three distinct spells, each of which has to last at least 2 months. It cannot be taken simultaneously. There is no specific paternity leave entitlement except for public sector workers who can take 1 month of unpaid leave.[7] The childcare allowances (Table 2.3) are in principal independent from the parental leave entitlement. However, periods of childcare allowance entitlements do in general coincide with parental leaves

Table 2.3. **Distinct childcare allowance variants in Austria**

	Model 30+6	Model 20+4	Model 15+3	Model 12+2 A	Model 12+2 B
Payment	EUR 436	EUR 624	EUR 800	EUR 1 000	80% of average of last months' salary; max. EUR 2 000
Entitlement for 1 parent	30 months	20 months	15 months	12 months	12 months
Additional entitlement for 2nd parent	6 months	4 months	3 months	2 months	2 months
Max. authorised additional income	60% of annual salary of reference year; min. EUR 16 200	60% of annual salary of reference year; min. EUR 16 200	60% of annual salary of reference year; min. EUR 16 200	60% of annual salary of reference year; min. EUR 16 200	EUR 6 400
Additional state aid for low income families	EUR 180 during max. 12 months	EUR 180 during max. 12 months	EUR 180 during max. 12 months	EUR 180 during max. 12 months	-

Note: The state aid supplement is conditional on earnings being below EUR 6 400 for the recipient *and* below EUR 16 200 for the spouse.
Source: Austrian Federal Ministry of Families and Youth.

due to the eligibility criteria of the former. Other than the actual parental leave, each childcare allowance variant has a, albeit short, non-transferable component for the 2nd parent, usually the father.[8] Although less so than in the past, the vast majority of Austrian parents still opt for childcare allowance variants lasting at least 2 years, hence longer than the job-protected leave entitlement (Table 2.4).

Table 2.4. **Take up distribution of childcare allowance variants**

	Year of the child's birth				
	2010 %	2011 %	2012 %	2013 %	2014 %
Model 30+6	53	49	44	40	37
Model 20+4	25	26	26	27	27
Model 15+3	6	6	6	6	6
Model 12+2 A	5	5	6	6	7
Model 12+2 B	12	14	18	21	23

Source: Federal Ministry for Family and Youth. As of March 2015.

Official statistics on the take up of parental leaves by mothers and fathers are not available but the distribution of childcare allowances by gender is likely to reflect the distribution of leave taken (Table 2.5). The numbers illustrate that only a small share of Austrian fathers take parental leave. In addition, those who do typically take not much more than the duration defined by the non-transferable amount of months of the chosen variant. Fathers also tend to participate more in shorter better remunerated variants. In total, only 18% of fathers participate in parental leave arrangements. Fathers usually take not much more than the months reserved for them, between 2 and 8 months, according to the chosen variant (Table 2.5). This is consistent with international evidence that fathers make little use of parental leave when it is provided as a family entitlement (Moss, 2012) and that they make more use of it in countries with individual and well-paid entitlements, such as in the Nordic countries.

In sum, mothers tend to choose longer durations of leave while fathers tend to do the opposite. Back on the job, the resulting adverse consequences for women with respect to men are sustainable and widely documented (Riesenfelder, 2013). The share of women

Table 2.5. **Fathers' involvement in parental leave**

	Year of the child's birth					Father's share in months (averages)
	2009 %	2010 %	2011 %	2012 %	2013 %	
Model 30+6	12	11	11	-	-	7.8
Model 20+4	18	19	18	18	-	5.2
Model 15+3	26	28	28	27	-	4.2
Model 12+2 A	35	30	30	29	28	3.5
Model 12+2 B	26	26	26	27	29	2.7

Source: Federal Ministry for Families and Youth. As of March 2015.

(men) that earn more than EUR 2 000 drops from 45% (52%) the year prior to parental leave to 3% (34%) during the first year of parental leave and only recovers to the level of 17% (50%) during the fourth year following the start of the parental leave. A great part of this long-lasting negative impact on mothers' earnings is related to the transition to part-time subsequent to the parental leave. If they have a tenure of 3 years prior to the birth of the child, parents working in companies with at least 20 employees are entitled to part-time work until the child turns 7 years old. As discussed above, the tax and benefit system encourages the use of part-time or marginal employment for one parent while the other is working full-time. To the extent that mothers take longer leave, the interplay of leave policies, childcare allowance eligibility criteria and fiscal incentives explains the significant wedge between part-time prevalence of mothers and fathers of young children documented in Chapter 1.

Transforming the parental leave entitlement into a more flexible time account that would allow parents to return earlier to work and save some of their entitlement for later stages of the child's education (pre-school or early school years, for example) would be welcome. Childcare allowance and parental leave schemes could be transformed into a unique childcare allowance account that allows parents to allocate subsidised absence from work flexibly over time. A sizeable part of this account, at least 33%, should be reserved to the exclusive use of fathers to strengthen labour market attachment of both fathers and mothers without jeopardising care and family commitments.

For instance, the account could be calibrated to a total absence of 18 full-time months, at least 6 of which are reserved to the father, with a total entitlement of up to EUR 30 000 (which would make it slightly more generous than the current income-dependent variant). Monthly allowances could be limited to 80% of the earnings of the highest earner's income prior to the birth of the child (max EUR 1 667) for full absence from work (adjusted in pro-rata terms for part-time work/absence). Work intensity, allocation across partners and across time can then be chosen by the parents subject to agreements with their employers. Some possibilities of its use, all equivalent in terms of total absence and transfers received,[9] are illustrated in Table 2.6. Importantly, absences from work can coincide between the 2 parents without a loss in entitlement. Further, absences could be split in several spells until, for instance, the child's 8th or 15th birthday. These options are outlined to illustrate the flexibility and potential of the single account concept, which lends itself to additional possibilities and features according to evolving consensuses in society and practical experience.

Table 2.6. **Possible use of a unique childcare allowance account**

Variant	Father			Mother		
	Reduction of working time %	Duration (months)	Monthly allowance (EUR)	Reduction of working time %	Duration (months)	Monthly allowance (EUR)
Standard parental leave	100	6	1 667	100	12	1 667
Standard part-time leave	50	12	833	50	24	833
Equal-shared parental leave	100	9	1 667	100	9	1 667
Equal-shared part-time leave	50	18	833	50	18	833
Mother works 4 days after initial shared 6 months parental leave	100	6	1 667	100 + 20	6 + 30	1 667 + 333
Father works part-time during the mother's 1 year leave	50	12	833	100	12	1 667
Both work 4 days	20	45	333	20	45	333
Both work 3 days	40	22.5	667	40	22.5	667

Note: Based on the proposed design of a unique childcare allowance account calibrated to 18 months of fulltime absence from work and an allowance amounting to 80% of the highest earner's income prior to the birth of the child (max. EUR 1 667). The illustrated amounts assume that the highest earner's income exceeded EUR 1 875 which entitles the parents for a monthly allowance of EUR 1 667 in case of a complete absence from work (EUR 833 for part-time absence, etc.). Cumulated allowances received in all variants sum up to EUR 30 000.

Reconcile work and family lives by extending the service infrastructure

Promote more efficient supply of childcare services

The availability of formal childcare is a precondition for combining full-time work with care chores induced by the presence of young children, in particular following parental leaves. Opening-up work-life patterns by waiving the aforementioned work disincentives is indeed not sufficient to reduce the burden of having to choose between work and family if external care is not available. Childcare infrastructure, in particular for children under 3-years of age, is largely underdeveloped in Austria (Figure 2.9). As of 2010, enrolment rates for under 3-years are among the lowest in the OECD and coverage of 3-5 years olds also stays far behind most peer countries.

From 2010 to 2013, enrolment rates have increased, with very significant progress made in Vienna (Figure 2.10), but the rates are still far below those reached in other OECD countries in general and in peer countries in particular. As already shown in Chapter 1, the numbers also reveal important regional differences both in terms of level of participation and in terms of catch-up velocity. Overall, the extent of enrolment in early childhood care and education facilities is consistent with the observed long durations of parental leaves, generally taken up by the mother.

Enrolment rates for 3-5 year olds in formal childcare are closer to the OECD average but still far lower than what is observed in comparable countries (Figure 2.9). In addition, with the exception of Vienna, the vast majority of facilities are not compatible with a dual-earner full-time family as opening hours and days are very restricted (Figure 2.11). Especially in rural areas, where commuting distances are longer, this represents a genuine obstacle for working parents. In 2008, a specific agreement between the federal state and the *Länder* has defined government support criteria for day-care centres according to the level of compatibility with both parents' fulltime work. Day-care centres are categorised in 3 groups according to the degree of compatibility with fulltime working parents:

- Half-day: min. 30 weeks per year; min. 4 hours per day on average; min. 20 hours per week.
- Full-day: min. 30 weeks per year; min. 6 hours per day on average; min. 30 hours per week; includes lunch.
- Full-time-work-compatible (VIF label): min. 47 weeks per year, min. 45 hours per week, each week min. 9½ hours on at least 4 days; includes lunch.

Figure 2.9. **Participation rates in childcare among children aged 0-5**

In per cent of the age group population

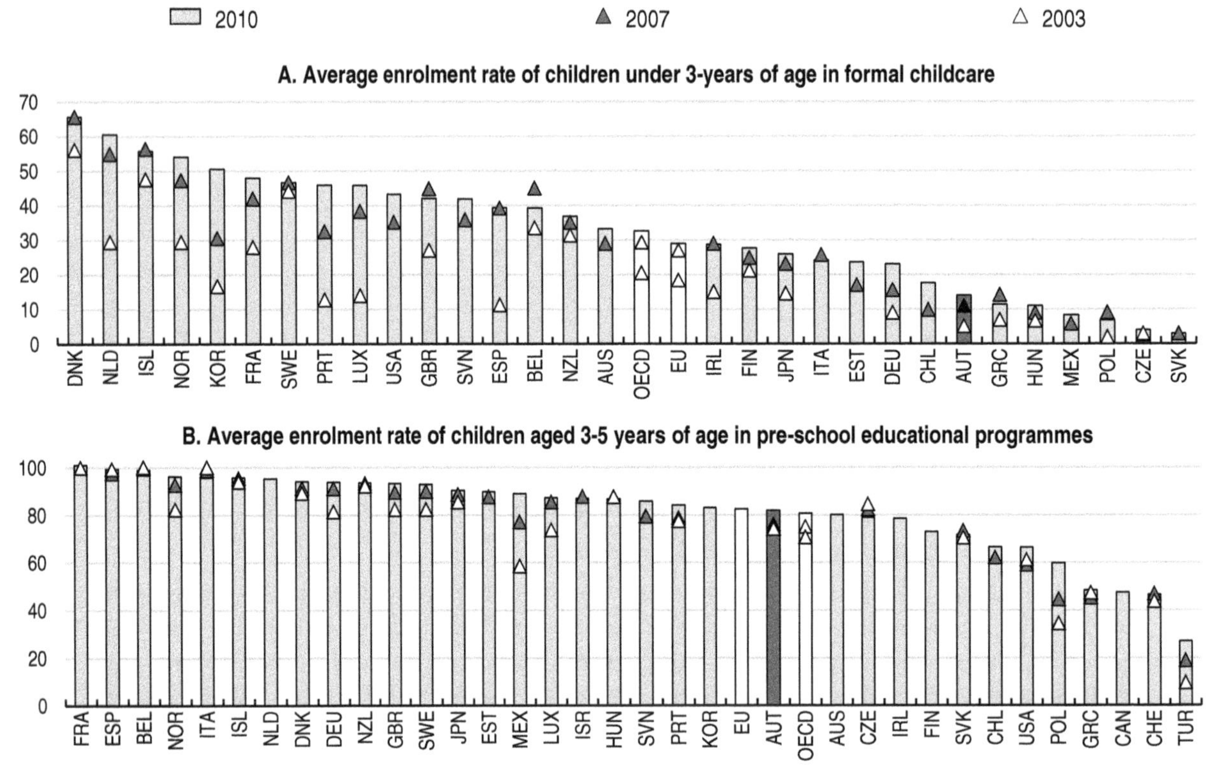

Source: OECD (2014), *OECD Family database, www.oecd.org/social/family/database.htm.*

StatLink http://dx.doi.org/10.1787/888933252370

Figure 2.10. **Participation of under 3-year-olds in formal childcare services**

Enrolment rates, in per cent of population under 3-year-olds

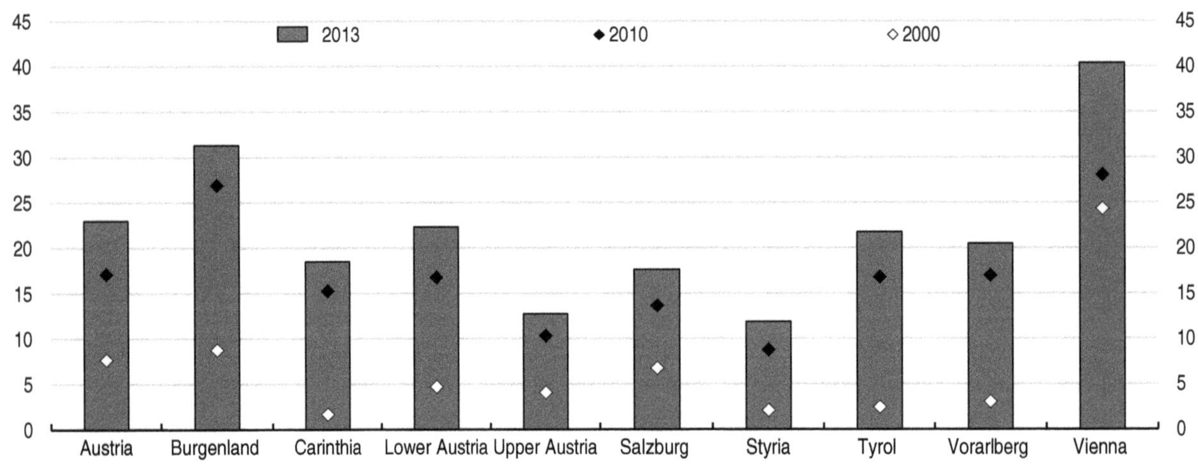

Source: Statistik Austria.

StatLink http://dx.doi.org/10.1787/888933252382

Figure 2.11. **Enrolment of children by type of care facility, age, region and degree of urbanisation**

In per cent of the age group population, 2011

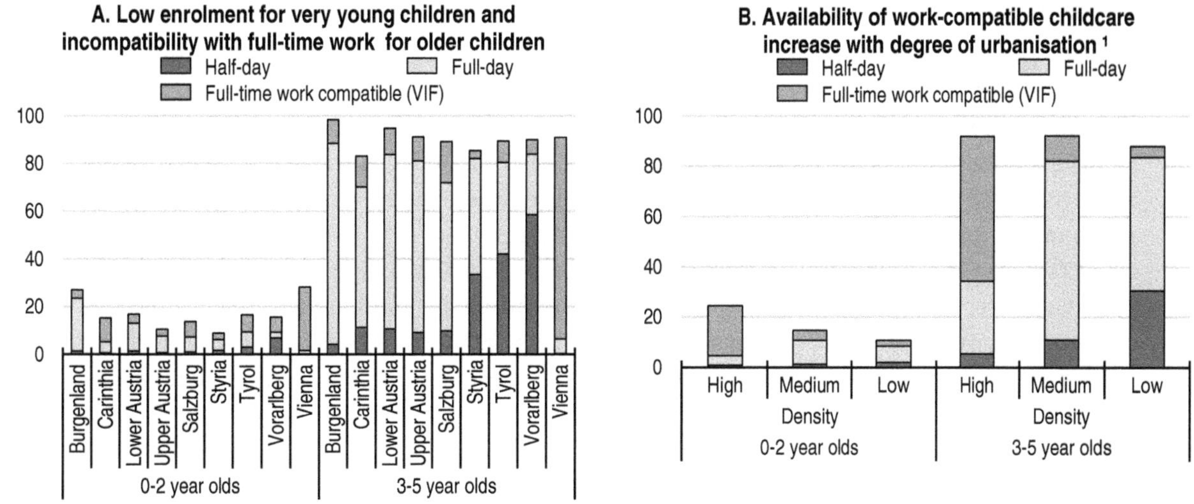

Note: Day-care centres are categorised in 3 groups according to the degree of compatibility with fulltime working parents:

- Half-day: min. 30 weeks per year; min. 4 hours per day on average; min. 20 hours per week;
- Full-day: min. 30 weeks per year; min. 6 hours per day on average; min. 30 hours per week; includes lunch;
- Full-time-work-compatible (VIF label): min. 47 weeks per year, min. 45 hours per week, each week min. 9½ hours on at least 4 days; includes lunch.

1. High, medium and low refer to the population density in the respective municipality according to the Eurostat definition.

Source: Statistik Austria.

StatLink http://dx.doi.org/10.1787/888933252396

The alignment of subsidies with the degree of compatibility with fulltime work is a welcome initiative. As of 2011, only the city of Vienna offered sufficient supply of formal childcare facilities that were compatible with dual-earner families where both parents work fulltime (Figure 2.11, Panel A). So far, annual reports on childcare facilities (Kindertagesheimstatisik) do not provide the breakdown in VIF and non-VIF day-care centres but the report 2014/15 is expected to contain a corresponding table. The dissemination of such a statistic is important as it raises the awareness for the need to reconcile work and family and can foster inter-regional emulation.

Weak demand for formal childcare, while partly driven by traditional beliefs that children should be taken care of at home, is sometimes also explained by the low level of social recognition of public childcare institutions (Austrian Institute for Youth Research, 2004). First, the socio-economic consideration of childcare workers is undermined by the fact that Austria is the only OECD country where pre-school teachers are not required to undergo tertiary education (OECD, 2011d). Qualification requirements could be aligned with those in peer countries in order to increase quality and acceptance of formal childcare services and education and to make the profession more attractive. Second, despite the low enrolment, the child-to-staff ratio in Austria is among the highest in the OECD, which may discourage some parents to send their child to day-care centres. Austria only spends 0.65% of GDP on services for families with children, notably early childhood education care facilities. This is far below the spending in the upper third of OECD countries (1.04%). Nordic countries spend more than 2% of GDP on financing or subsidising childcare facilities. Investing in early childhood care and education is arguably one of the public investments with the highest rates of return for the society. It sets the base for cognitive and non-cognitive developments of the children, allows parents to reconcile family and work and may even encourage child-bearing decisions.

In total, substantial improvement in the coverage of early childhood care and education both at the extensive margin (number of places) and at the intensive margin (opening hours of care facilities) is necessary in order to provide an enabling infrastructure for parents that allows for the combination of work and family duties. A cost-benefit analysis provided by the Austrian Federal Chamber of Labour (2013) analyses the expenditures and revenues of a gradual increase in the number of 35 000 childcare places, extended opening hours for 70 000 places and an increase in teaching personal for 70 000 places in order to decrease the child-to-carer ratio. In terms of indirect employment of the mothers the study presents 2 scenarios: the pessimistic (optimistic) one assumes that 25% (50%) of the women whose children benefit from new childcare places will enter the labour market. Additional revenues from the direct and indirect employment created (income tax, social security contributions) and lower transfer payments outweigh additional running costs for wages, training, maintenance and financing within 5 years in both scenarios. Including the initial investment costs, the break-even point occurs 7 years after the start of the programme in the average scenario (37.5% of mothers newly employed).

The use of childcare fees would help to cover the running costs of childcare facilities. At present, Austria exhibits the lowest childcare fees (as a share of average earnings) of all OECD countries. More cost-based pricing of services could further boost private supply. As in peer countries, tax breaks and rebates for low income families and targeted subsidies could be used to reduce net costs of childcare and reduce inequalities. Indeed, net childcare costs for sole parent families are actually lower in no less than 8 OECD countries notably due to means-tested benefits and rebates (Figure 2.12).

Figure 2.12. **Net childcare costs for a sole-parent family with earnings of 50% of the average wage**

Out-of-pocket childcare costs for a sole parent: Full-time care at a typical childcare centre, 2012

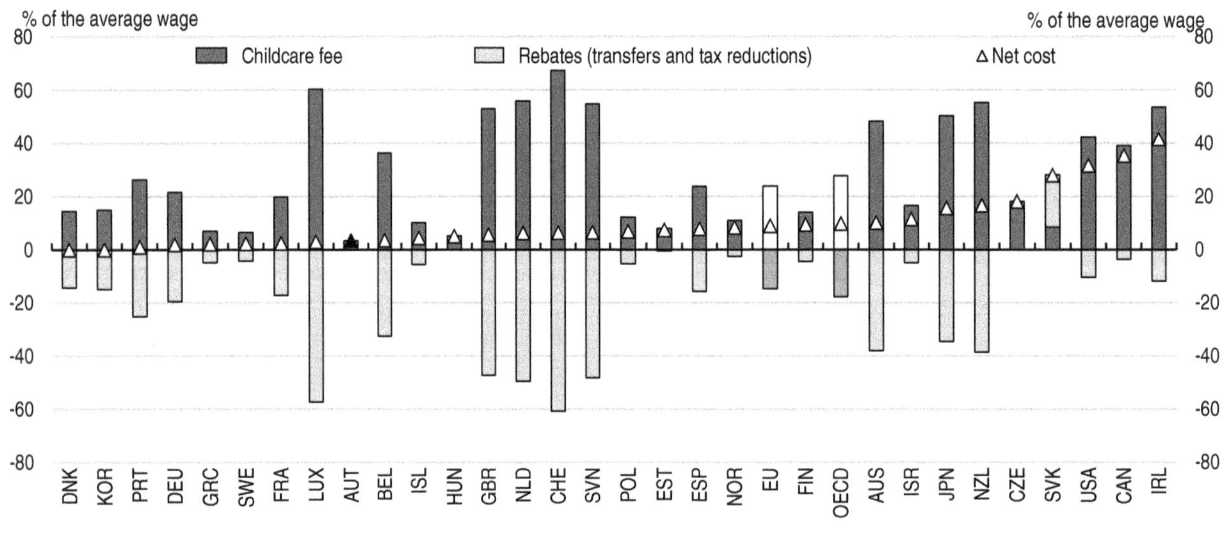

Note: Austria is represented by parameters for Vienna.

Source: OECD (2014), *OECD Family database*, *www.oecd.org/social/family/database.htm*.

StatLink http://dx.doi.org/10.1787/888933252400

A national investment plan for childcare infrastructure could be linked to a legal entitlement for a place in formal childcare facilities for young children. Such a legal right has recently been introduced in Germany for 1 to 3 year olds and would substantially reduce regional inequalities with respect to the ability of combining work and family life. Investment in childcare infrastructure might further benefit from new regulations with respect to spending on social infrastructure. The European Economic and Social Committee (EESC) has proposed to exclude such expenditures from the EMU's fiscal rules for the calculation of government debt and public deficits.

The government could also encourage the installation of more corporate childcare facilities. According to a study conducted by the Austrian institute for families (ÖIF) in corporation with the University of Vienna (Kaindl, 2011), the share of corporate childcare facilities in the total supply is only 2% in Austria. Less than half of the existing facilities have received public support, mostly provided by the *Länder*, but nearly half of them declare that they would not have introduced the facility without public financial support. Administrative burdens for the grants seem to be very high and there are no clear criteria for the provision of public support neither at the federal nor at the regional level. The advantage of corporate childcare facilities is that opening hours can be better aligned to the working hours of employees and that commuting distances are reduced. Surveys results suggest that the availability of corporate reduces the duration of parental leave as it encourages parents to re-enter the workplace more swiftly. Indeed, enrolment rates for the 0-2 year olds largely exceed the ones observed in external day-care centres. More than 80% of the children enrolled in the surveyed corporate facilities entered before the age of 2. Streamlining and making the eligibility criteria more transparent could increase take-up rates of public support.[10]

Elderly care

As in other OECD countries, Austria faces a strong rise in old-age dependency ratios driven by increasing longevity and declining fertility rates. The ratio of persons 65 or older over the working age population is expected to double by 2060 and reach 50%. Additionally, Austria exhibits a rather high share of persons aged 75 years and older who report limitations in daily activities (OECD/European Union, 2013). Accordingly, ensuring and improving the quality and provision of long-term care (LTC) has become a major policy objective.

In Austria, nearly four fifth of the elderly are cared for in family environments, either in their families' home or in their own home under family surveillance (cf. Chapter 1). This is particularly relevant for the gender equality policy objective as the vast majority of working-age informal care-givers are women. Going forward, the ratio of caregiving cohorts (40-59 years) with respect to the population older than 70 (80) years will pass from 2.3 (6.0) in 2014 to 1.5 (3.7) in 2030 and 1.1 (2.1) in 2050. As a consequence, the demand for care places and other formal LTC services is additionally fuelled by a necessary shift from informal to formal care. Famira-Mühlberger and Firgo (2014) project that care expenditures will more than double between 2012 and 2030 with large discrepancies between the regions mainly driven by different starting conditions with respect to the provision of external care.

The Austrian LTC system encompasses universally provided cash benefits for persons in need of care on the one hand (Box 2.8), and publicly provided services and benefits in-kind on the other. Recent reforms have streamlined the process of providing LTC cash

Box 2.8. **Long-term care cash benefits**

Long-term care benefits are non-means-tested benefits, awarded to dependants in need of care. Its amount depends on the hours of effective care need determined by a medical expert.* Women claim long-term benefits significantly more often than men. In 2012, 10.1% of the women and 7.8% of the men aged 61-80 received long-term care benefits. For the age-group 81 years and above, take-up rates were 67.7% for women and 44.6% for men. LTC cash benefits are not linked to actual spending on care services and their amount is usually not sufficient to cover costs of formal long-term care services. As a result, a large part of long-term care is provided on an informal basis by family members. In 2013, 59% of the claimants did not make use of any professional care or nursery service and were taken care of at home by relatives.

Long-term care benefits

Care category	Monthly benefit (EUR)	Care need in hours	Number of claimants	Share of care category %
1	154.20	More than 65 hours	104 393	23
2	284.30	More than 95 hours	130 803	29
3	442.90	More than 120 hours	78 170	17
4	664.30	More than 160 hours	63 463	14
5	902.30	More than 180 hours[1]	46 089	10
6	1 260.00	More than 180 hours[2]	18 806	4
7	1 655.80	More than 180 hours[3]	9 206	2

1. Exceptional care requirements.
2. Permanent presence of caregiver is necessary due to unpredictable care needs.
3. Serious disability impeding the use of hands and feet. No precise movements are possible.

Source: Federal Ministry of Social Affairs. Numbers refer to 2013.

* As of 2016, monthly benefits increase by 2%.

benefits. Until 2012, executive powers were at the *Länder*-level which led to considerable administrative costs and regional discrepancies. In 2012, all responsibility in granting the benefits has been transferred to the federal level, which reduced the numbers of decision makers from 300 to 5. This is likely to increase the transparency of the care benefit enforcement procedures and to ensure inter-regional equity among dependants. It also aligns financing and granting responsibilities which is bound to improve efficiency and financial sustainability.

Several measures provide support to caregiving family members of dependants. Employees who have to give up their job in order to provide care to relatives that are eligible for LTC of at least Category 3, are offered preferential terms for self-insurance or continued insurance under the statutory pension system for an unlimited period of time. Employers' and employees' contributions are paid by the state. Workers or employees who care for relatives are entitles to take unpaid care leave or to work part-time with prorated wage payments for a period between 1 and 3 months, renewable once. During the leave period, care-givers are entitled to care leave benefits that are essentially equal to replacement rates of the unemployment benefit scheme (55%).[11]

Apart from LTC cash benefits, and care leave, the 24-hour care aid constitutes the third pillar of government support for home care. Financial support to care-taking persons amounts to EUR 550 (EUR 275) per month and employed (self-employed) caregiver for a maximum of EUR 1 100 (EUR 550). Entitled are claimants of long-term care benefits of Category 3 or beyond whose monthly net market income (excluding long-term care benefits and other transfers) does not exceed EUR 2 500.[12] To complement the provision of home care support, mobile care, day-care and in-patient services have recently gained importance in Austria. The institutionalisation of 24-hour has put an end to growing grey market where LTC cash benefits have been used to employ informal care-givers, mostly migrants, without appropriate monitoring and qualification management. Their work is now legally framed which ensures the quality of the care and provides social insurance coverage to the caregivers.[13]

In contrast to the universally provided LTC cash benefits, LTC services are not free of charge. Fees are cost-based and the dependant is liable with her personal disposable income including cash benefits and with assets that may be monetised.[14] Only once these resources are exhausted, costs get financed by the *Länder* via the Social Assistance and the Guaranteed Minimum Income Schemes. Provision and monitoring of institutional care is the sole responsibility of the federal provinces in Austria which means that there are no common quality standard or outcome documentations. This makes it difficult to compare service provision across regions, but large differences occur in terms of beneficiaries, gross spending and receipts (Figure 2.13), and minimum quality requirements.[15] The Federation of Care Homes and the Federal Ministry of Labour, Social Affairs and Consumer Protection engaged in a voluntary National Quality Certificate (NQZ) that can be obtained by care homes, which have successfully implemented an accredited quality management system. Since 2013, an independent NQZ organisation was established to administer and further develop the certification procedure. Such certificates foster competition between the regions, ensure common standards across *Länder* and are an encouraging example for achieving independent monitoring of legislation that is delegated to subnational government bodies in a decentralised system.

Figure 2.13. **Provision of long-term care services by *Länder***

In 2013, for population aged 65 and more

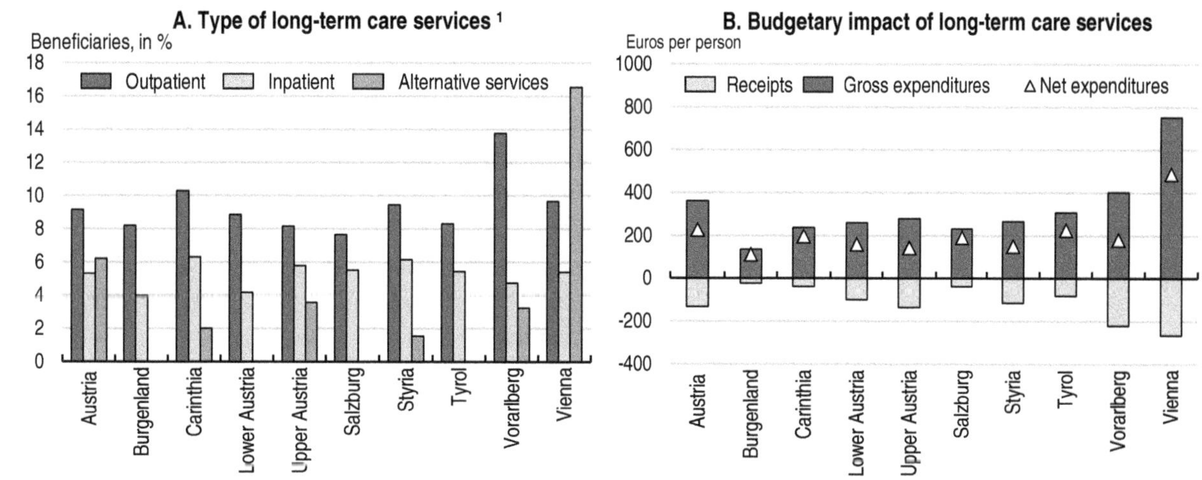

1. In-patient services include semi-in-patient services. Alternative services comprise short-term care, alternative living facilities and case and care management.

Source: Statistik Austria.

StatLink http://dx.doi.org/10.1787/888933252416

The number of beds in residential care facilities is lower than the OECD average and much lower than in many countries (Figure 2.14). This reflects the substantial bias towards home care and a general praise for satisfactory innovations, in particular, alternative living facilities and case and care management services, although the provision of such services shows substantial regional differences (Figure 2.13). Indeed, only in Vienna the coverage of such innovative solutions is currently sufficiently to substitute or complement home care provided by relatives where formal residential care is not available or not affordable.

Figure 2.14. **Number of beds in residential long-term care facilities**

2012, per 1 000 population aged 65 years old and over

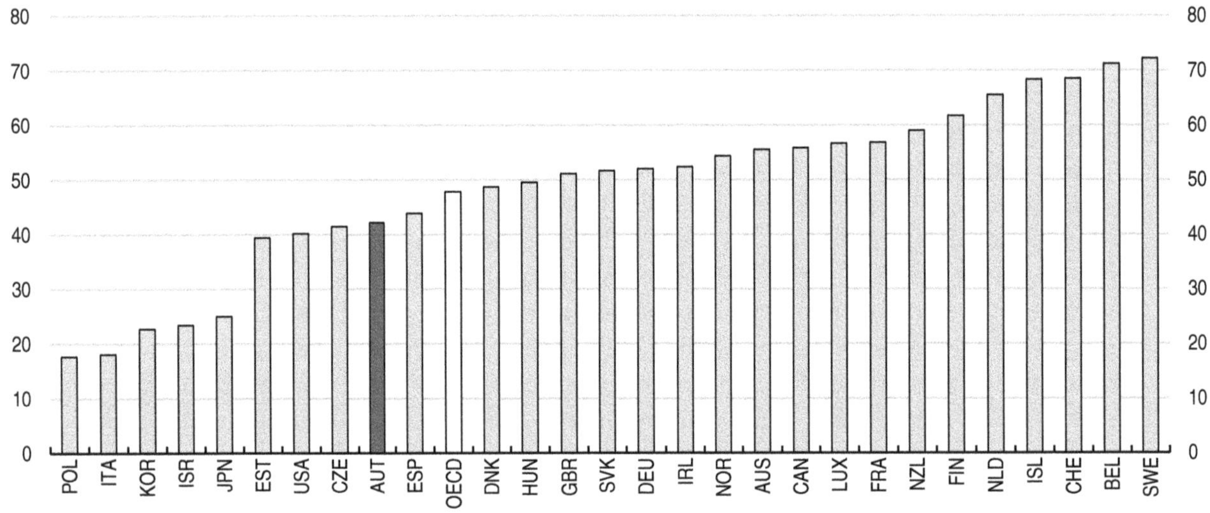

Source: *OECD Health Statistics database.*

StatLink http://dx.doi.org/10.1787/888933252420

Going forward, the current care arrangements face several challenges. First, due to an ageing society fewer family members will be available per dependant, which will put pressure on the sustainability of home-care provision by relatives. Second, convergence towards more gender-equality also implies that elderly care, similar to childhood care, needs to gradually shift towards external care provision. This could require investment in residential facilities and spending on subsidies to mobile care, in-patient care providers or other innovative solutions (alternative living facilities, case and care management, etc.). This would be partly self-financed by higher employment rates of women who formerly partly or fully withdrew from the labour market to provide care. The vast majority of elderly related spending is currently provided as a lump-sum cash transfer. With the transition from informal towards formal elderly care, spending efficiency may benefit from a higher extent of targeted and means-tested transfers.

Encourage more flexible workplace practices

Fostering family-friendly workplaces

Empirical evidence suggests that there are important benefits from a more gender-equal worker structure (Weber and Zulehner, 2014). A family-friendly work environment fosters the motivation and loyalty of employees and makes firms more attractive for skilled young workers with realised or potential family duties. International experience suggests that, in the global open economy, such work conditions are also a major precondition to attract high-level international workers. At the same time, these environments should be designed without jeopardising the competitiveness of enterprises. Mandatory legislation and negotiated collective agreements and voluntary enterprise initiatives will need to be used complementarily. It should be recognised, however, that for small and medium sized enterprises the implementation of more flexible workplaces is more challenging which calls for targeted support policies.

The work and family audit organised by the Austrian government (Box 2.9) enables employers to benefit from external assessment and tailor-made solutions to improve the work environment for employees with family duties. The involvement of the Federal Ministry of, Families and Youth, that provides merits-based certificates, fosters visibility and significance of the auditing and evaluation process. It also allows firms to benefit from best practices and experiences of other firms. The audit further raises awareness and sensibility of the gender issue and triggers competition between the firms so as to converge to high standards in terms of reconcilability of work and family life.

Box 2.9. **Work and family audit**

Since 1998, the Austrian government subsidises and supports "work and family audits" that assess the compatibility of a company's work environment with family related needs. Through discussions with management and employees, the auditor first identifies current setups and needs and then defines targets based on well-performing peer enterprises. A corresponding company plan with dedicated goals and defined time spans is established. Relevant indicators are working hour flexibility, organisation and place of work, information and communication policy, management culture, personnel development, remuneration aspects, services for families, parental leave characteristics and health promoting measures. All Austria-based firms with a minimum of 5 employees are eligible. Auditing and expert fees are partly subsidised by the Austrian government (between EUR 2 000 and EUR 5 000 depending on the size of the company). Every 3 years, and subject to validated improvements, the Austrian Federal Ministry for Families and Youth awards a certificate that attests the quality of a family-friendly work environment. Annual reports and periodical re-assessments ensure the sustainability of the auditing and certifying process. A special "compact" audit was recently developed for the needs and challenges of small firms employing 5 to 50 employees.

In addition, the "university and family audit" is geared to requirements of family-friendliness in tertiary education and the "work and family for nursing and care institutions audit" was developed to deal with the challenges faced by health care institutions. The "family-friendly community audit" addresses villages, small towns and cities aiming at identifying and enhancing existing family-friendly measures.

Well-designed, professionally attractive up-skilling programmes draw the interest of both genders. A Ministry of Labour scheme helping middle-age women to change professions has been oversubscribed. A "Committee on New Skills" elaborates, in co-operation with social partners, new curricula for such programmes. These innovations may help overcome the further entrenchment of skill biases in post-formal adult education.

Other initiatives, such as the INQA (Initiative New Quality of Work) in Germany, could serve as a benchmark for Austrian businesses. The project targets SME's and brings together social partners and employers. It focusses on communicating and developing best practices in the fields of personnel management (e.g. life-cycle orientation), equal opportunities and diversity (e.g. heterogeneous teams), health (e.g. accounting for stress) and knowledge and competencies (e.g. internal share of acquired knowledge).

A growing desire to better align career aspirations with family prospects also calls for innovative working time models. A recent *Freizeitoption* (leisure option, Box 2.10) has been implemented in some collective agreements. Subject to approvals at the plant and the individual level, it enables the employee to exchange the annual pay increase against a reduction in working time. According to Soder (2014), 10% of the concerned employees in the electronic and electrical engineering industry have exercised the option for 2014 subsequent to the collective agreement in 2013. The leisure option can only be used once and reduces the working time on a permanent basis. More flexible options that allow both sides to adjust working time dynamically, by taking competitiveness and order-book considerations on the one hand and changing family duties over the life cycle on the other hand into account, could be envisaged. It would make full-time employment more conceivable for mothers and it allows fathers to take up a bigger share of family duties.

Box 2.10. **"Die Freizeitoption" – a recent instrument to rebalance family and work life**

In spring 2013, as part of the collective agreement in the electrical and electronics industry, a new instrument to facilitate the implementation of flexible working was introduced. The *Freizeitoption* (leisure option) responded to a growing desire of employees to reduce working time to achieve a better balance between family, leisure and work. It allowed the employee to trade the agreed pay increase of 3% against a reduction in annual working time of 60 hours. The option was not a legal entitlement and required prior agreements at the firm and individual level. Employees whose income would fall below the minimum wage in case of exercising the leisure option were not eligible. According to survey results, 73% of the companies covered by the collective agreement have refused to implement the option as part of their company agreements (Soder, 2014). In more than half of the cases the refusal was due to a rejection from the executive board mainly on the grounds of uncertainty regarding the implementation in general and the accounting procedures in particular. Within the companies that ultimately offered the option, roughly 10% of the workers and employees have reached an agreement with their employer and exercised the leisure option. While the steel, metallurgic and mining industries as well as the automotive industries have followed the example by introducing the leisure option in their collective agreements, others have refused to do so. The machine and metal goods industry, for instance, has rejected the implementation of the *Freizeitoption* amid fears over impaired cost competitiveness and reduced flexibility in responding to order fluctuations and uncertainty.

Improving gender-equality in corporate and public decision making

The share of women on boards or in executive management positions is substantially below the European Union average (Chapter 1). The government has launched the "Women are top" initiative that is co-financed by the European Commission. The initiative has two legs. The first focusses on nomination processes for the assignment of board members. The aim is to simulate good and current practices in order to understand and reveal gender-stereotypical patters in assignment processes. The second leg will deliver a catalogue of measures that have been proven to foster gender equality in management positions in selected companies. According to first results, the measures will concentrate on areas such as working time, mobility, recruitment processes and life-phase sensitive career tracks. In line with the leadership-programme "Zukunft.Frauen", another initiative of the government, eight training courses with 176 participants have already been completed – the ninth is starting in autumn 2015. A key element of this initiative is the establishment of a publicly accessible data base for female supervisory boards, where currently more than 410 women are registered.

In political decision making, the situation is slightly different. Market forces are not the main drivers and a certain degree of pro-active outcome equalisation is needed to correct the under-representation of women in public institutions that are meant to mirror and represent the society. In Austria, self-imposed or voluntary quotas have been introduced in 2 out of 6 political parties present in parliament. As of 2014, 30.6% of the members of Parliament were women. Similar shares are observed for female participation in government (4 out 14 ministers and chancellor). In 2011, the government decided to impose gender quotas for the state delegates sent to boards of the 55 companies in which the state holds a majority of the shares. The initial target is 25% in 2013 and the quota will be raised to 35% by 2018. According to a report of the Ministry for Science, Research and Economy and the Ministry of Education and Women's affairs, the 2018 target has already been reached in 2014 as the share of women of state delegates in these boards has reached 36% (after 16% in 2008 and 26% in 2011).

In public services, following the introduction of the Federal Equality Treatment Act, quotas for female employment have progressively been raised to 50%. These targets are far from met as the overall share of women in public service positions remains broadly constant at around 40% since 1999 (Austrian Federal Ministry for Education and Women's affairs, 2014). At high level positions, the women's share, though largely below the 50% target, has constantly increased and reached 33.7% in 2013 up from 18.2% in 1999 and 27.2% in 2005. Similar quotas exist in Public Broadcasting (ORF) and universities.

Streamline family policies across regions and levels of government

Differences in legislation and implementation across *Länder* lead to weak synergies and create inefficiencies and inequalities. On the other hand, they may be a source of emulation and innovation. The challenge is to make the Austrian federal system a support and not an obstacle to gender mainstreaming efforts. Executive, spending and financing authorities are often associated with different levels of the administration which leads to inefficient spending.[16] Most envisaged reforms related to the supply of childcare services may require redistribution and clear division of competencies between the State, the *Länder* and the local governments. In particular the consolidation of competencies with respect to schools, pre-schools and day-care services has been identified as a necessary condition to make progress (Pitlik et al., 2010).

There is also a need for more co-ordination at the federal level to ensure a coherent and sustainable child development policy across the country.[17] On the financing side, arrangements should be optimised on the basis of past domestic experience and international good practices. On the executive side, for each policy target, and depending on constitutional constraints, policy makers have to decide whether a centralised or decentralised implementation is most effective. Reforms should aim at extending autonomy of schools and care institutions combined with superordinate monitoring (state monitors *Länder*, *Länder* monitor communities, and communities monitor schools). A working group entitled "Verwaltung neu" ("Administration new") under the umbrella of the Court of Auditors, the IHS, WIFO and the KDZ have worked out proposals for a comprehensive reform of the federal administration.

In terms of innovations with regard to care services, there may be a case for decentralisation. Successful projects could be implemented and transferred to other regions. There may also be scope for a differentiated approach that takes regional characteristics into account. Regional competition could also trigger convergence towards best practices in terms of gender mainstreaming and reduce the substantial inter-regional disparities currently observed (Bock-Schappelwein, 2013).

Recommendations to promote gender equality

Key recommendations

- Spur investment in high quality childcare facilities. Enhance the availability of full-day schools and care centres. Consider introducing legal entitlements for these services.
- Reduce the implicit taxation of transition from marginal and part-time to full-time employment and replace the sole-earner tax deduction by targeted transfers to families in need.
- Transform childcare allowance and parental leave schemes into a unique childcare account that allows parents to allocate subsidised absence from work flexibly over time. Reserve a sizeable part of this account, at least 33%, for the exclusive use of fathers.
- Raise awareness by publicising more information on innovations in study area choices of schoolgirls and schoolboys, earlier return to full-time work of mothers, and fathers' participation in care and household duties.
- Develop a comprehensive data base on social transfers or a comprehensive panel survey to assess the impact of alternative family policy schemes on labour supply, child care use and net budget costs, and adjust policy packages in the light of this information.
- The private sector should offer more family-friendly workplaces and more enabling working time options to employees of both genders. Policymakers should continue to support auditing and information campaigns to disseminate good practices.

Other recommendations

- Social partners should help develop practices that facilitate the reconciliation of family obligations and work responsibilities while preserving the enterprises' productivity and competitiveness.
- Wage negotiations should aim at reducing the gender wage gap.
- Promote gender diversity in leadership positions in private companies.
- Widen access of part-timer workers to active labour market programmes.

Notes

1. OECD (2011a) projects an increase of 29% for the former and 10% of the latter in Austria from the early-mid-2000s to 2025-30.
2. Selected countries are Northern European Countries and France. This group of countries seems to offer better work-life balances as evidenced by stronger female labour participation combined with higher fertility rates.

3. The common OECD definition based on a 30-usual-hour cut-off in the main job is used. National definitions vary considerably and are therefore not adequate for comparisons and convergence assumptions.
4. Adalet and Andrews (2015) suggest that Austria could increase its labour productivity by 6% by reducing the skill mismatch to best practices, observed in countries such as Sweden.
5. The modelling framework offers potentially two ways of introducing a positive human capital effect in the simulation. The direct approach would be to expand the return to schooling equation by introducing indicators for the incidence of part-time, over-qualification and youth unemployment. Compared to the current equation that derives human capital solely from years of schooling, these parameters would capture the effectiveness of the transition between school and work, and hence serve as a proxy for the mis-use or the destruction of human capital. The second, an indirect method would be to assume that the distance to the labour efficiency frontier is to some extent driven by the way a country makes use of and preserves its initial human capital. As such, the dual-earner model would result in a faster convergence to the frontier as compared to the *status quo*.
6. Taking specific tax rates on holiday and Christmas bonuses and the deduction of social security contributions and standard tax allowances (Box 2.4) into account, the transition from the zero-tax zone to the first income bracket occurs at around EUR 17 000 of gross annual earnings. Median gross annual earnings for full-time jobs amounted to slightly more than EUR 38 000 in 2013 in Austria.
7. Some collective agreements contain provisions for 1 month of paid or unpaid paternity leave.
8. In case of hardship, sole parents can benefit from 2 additional months but do not have access to the months reserved for the second parents.
9. Assuming that the highest earners' income prior to the birth of the child was at least EUR 1 875 (80% of which correspond to the ceiling of EUR 1 500).
10. Specific rules could be laid out to not penalise SME's with insufficient space (facilitating the set-up of a childcare facility for several surrounding firms, etc.).
11. In total, for the same family member in need of care, the number of monthly care leave benefits cannot exceed 12 months to be shared among care-giving family members unless the leave is transformed in hospice leave for the purpose of nursing a dying close family member or a seriously ill child.
12. This threshold rises by EUR 400 for each dependant relative and by EUR 600 for each dependant relative with disabilities.
13. Since 2009, caregivers need to complete dedicated training or, alternatively, they need to prove that they have cared for the caretaker in satisfactory manner for at least 6 months.
14. In addition, the so-called "Familienregress" obliged relatives to co-finance long-term care costs of family members with their respective incomes and assets. This scheme has been abolished over time by all *Länder*. Styria re-introduced the co-payments of children (for their parents) and parents (for their children) in 2011 before abolishing it again in July 2014.
15. For instance, minimum room sizes vary substantially across regions from 24 m^2 in Vorarlberg 13.48 m^2 in Salzburg. Similar differences can be observed for staff-to-patient ratios.
16. For instance, local governments pay the total wage bill for teachers, but are completely reimbursed by the federal state. In such a situation, local government have no incentive to act in a cost-benefit efficient manner.
17. The implementation of standardised accounting practices, as currently announced by the Finance minister, is a necessary condition for such progress.

Bibliography

Adema, W. (2012), "Setting the Scene: The Mix of Family Policy Objectives and Packages Across the OECD", *Children and Youth Services Review*, Vol. 34, No. 3, pp. 487-498.

Adema, W., N. Ali and O. Thévenon (2014), "Changes in Family Policies and Outcomes: Is there Convergence?", *OECD Social, Employment and Migration Working Papers*, No. 157, OECD Publishing, Paris, *http://dx.doi.org/10.1787/5jz13wllxgzt-en*.

Austrian Federal Chamber of Labour (2013), "Social Investment Growth, Employment and Financial Sustainability: Economic and Fiscal Effects of Improving Childcare in Austria", *AK Position Paper*.

Austrian Federal Ministry for Education and Women's affairs (2014), "10. Gleichbehandlungsbericht des Bundes 2014", Vienna.

Austrian Institute for Youth Research (2004), "Österreichischer Hintergrundbericht zur OECD-Länderprüfung" "Starting Strong".

Barnay, T. (2014), "Health, Work and Working Conditions: A Review of the European Economic Literature", *OECD Economics Department Working Papers*, No. 1148, OECD Publishing, Paris, *http://dx.doi.org/10.1787/5jz0zb71xhmr-en*.

Bock-Schappelwein, J. (2013), "Genderindex. Arbeitsmarktlage und Lebenssituation von Frauen und Männern auf regionaler Ebene in Österreich", Study commissioned by Austrian Federal Ministry of Agriculture, Forestry, Environment and Water Management.

de Boer, H.W., E. Jongen and J. Kabátek (2014), "The Effectiveness of Fiscal Stimuli for Working Parents", *CPB Discussion Paper*, No. 286, CPB Netherlands Bureau for Economic Policy Analysis.

Buber-Ennser, I., N. Neuwirth and M. Testa (2014), *Families in Austria 2009-2013: Descriptive Findings on Partnerships, Fertility Intentions, Childbearing and Childrearing*, Vienna Institute of Demography, Vienna.

Famira-Mühlberger, U. and M. Firgo (2014), "Die Entwicklung des öffentlichen Aufwandes für Pflegedienstleistungen. Projektion für die österreichischen Bundesländer", *WIFO-Monatsberichte*, 2014, Vol. 87, No. 9, pp. 643-652.

Förster, M.F. and G. Verbist (2012), "Money or Kindergarten? Distributive Effects of Cash Versus In-Kind Family Transfers for Young Children", *OECD Social, Employment and Migration Working Papers*, No. 135, OECD Publishing, Paris, *http://dx.doi.org/10.1787/5k92vxbgpmnt-en*.

Heckman, J. (2006), "Skill Formation and the Economics of Investing in Disadvantaged Children", *Science*, Vol. 312, No. 5782, pp. 1900-02.

Holzer, H.J. and D. Neumark (2000), "What does affirmative action do?", *Industrial & Labor Relations Review*, Vol. 53, No. 2, pp. 240-271.

Huerta, M. et al. (2011), "Early Maternal Employment and Child Development in Five OECD Countries", *OECD Social, Employment and Migration Working Papers*, No. 118, OECD Publishing, Paris, *http://dx.doi.org/10.1787/5kg5dlmtxhvh-en*.

Huerta, M. et al. (2013), "Fathers' Leave, Fathers' Involvement and Child Development: Are They Related? Evidence from Four OECD Countries", *OECD Social, Employment and Migration Working Papers*, No. 140, OECD Publishing, Paris, *http://dx.doi.org/10.1787/5k4dlw9w6czq-en*.

Johansson, Å. et al. (2013), "Long-Term Growth Scenarios", *OECD Economics Department Working Papers*, No. 1000, OECD Publishing, Paris, *http://dx.doi.org/10.1787/5k4ddxpr2fmr-en*.

Kaindl, M. (2011), "Betriebliche Kinderbetreuung in Österreich Angebotsstruktur sowie Motive und Erfahrungen der Unternehmen im Bereich der betrieblichen Kinderbetreuung", *Working Paper*, No. 75, Austrian Institute for Families.

Klüsener, S., K. Neels and M. Kreyenfeld (2013), "Family Policies and the Western European Fertility Divide: Insights from a Natural Experiment in Belgium", *Population and Development Review*, Vol. 39, No. 4, pp. 587-610.

de Laat, J. and A. Sevilla-Sanz (2011), "The Fertility and Women's Labor Force Participation Puzzle in OECD Countries: The Role of Men's Home Production", *Feminist Economics*, Vol. 17, No. 2, pp. 87-119.

Lassnigg, L., A. Kulhanek and P. Wejwar (2014), "Quantitative Information about Sex and Gender Issues in the Austrian National Education Report – overview and assessment", *8th European Conference on Gender Equality in Higher Education*, Vienna University of Technology, Vienna, 3-5 September 2014.

Lesthaeghe, R. and I. Permanyer (2014), "European Sub-Replacement Fertility: Trapped or Recovering?", *Population Studies Center Research Report*, No. 14-822.

Moss, P. (ed.) (2012), "International review of leave policies and related research 2012", *International Network on Leave Policies and Related Research*.

Müllbacher, S., H. Hofer and G. Titelbach (2014), "Verteilungswirkung und Anreizstruktur des Österreichischen Steuer- und Transfer-Systems", *Institute for Advanced Studies*, Vienna.

Musset, P. et al. (2013), *A Skills beyond School Review of Austria*, OECD Reviews of Vocational Education and Training, OECD Publishing, Paris, *http://dx.doi.org/10.1787/9789264200418-en*.

Neyer, G. (2013), "Welfare States, Family Policies, and Fertility in Europe", in *The demography of Europe*, Springer, Netherlands, pp. 29-53.

Niederle, M., C. Segal and L. Vesterlund (2013), "How costly is diversity? Affirmative action in light of gender differences in competitiveness", *Management Science*, Vol. 59, No. 1, pp. 1-16.

Nordenmark, M. (2014), "Disagreement about Division of Household Labour and Experiences of Work-Family Conflict in Different Gender Regimes", *GÉNEROS – Multidisciplinary Journal of Gender Studies*, Vol. 2, No. 3, pp. 205-232.

OECD (2011a), *The Future of Families to 2030*, OECD Publishing, Paris, *http://dx.doi.org/10.1787/9789264168367-en*.

OECD (2011b), "The Impact of Caring on Family Carers", in F. Colombo et al., *Help Wanted? Providing and Paying for Long-Term Care*, OECD Health Policy Studies, OECD Publishing, Paris, *http://dx.doi.org/10.1787/9789264097759-8-en*.

OECD (2011c), *Doing Better for Families*, OECD Publishing, Paris, *http://dx.doi.org/10.1787/9789264098732-en*.

OECD (2011d), *Starting Strong III: A Quality Toolbox for Early Childhood Education and Care*, OECD Publishing, Paris, *http://dx.doi.org/10.1787/9789264123564-en*.

OECD (2013a), *Recommendation of the Council on Gender Equality in Education, Employment and Entrepreneurship*, OECD, Paris, 29 May, *www.oecd.org/gender/C-MIN(2013)5-ENG.pdf*.

OECD (2013b), *OECD Skills Outlook 2013: First Results from the Survey of Adult Skills*, OECD Publishing, Paris, *http://dx.doi.org/10.1787/9789264204256-en*.

OECD (2014a), *Education at a Glance 2014: OECD Indicators*, OECD Publishing, Paris, *http://dx.doi.org/10.1787/eag-2014-en*.

OECD (2014b), *Women, Government and Policy Making in OECD Countries: Fostering Diversity for Inclusive Growth*, OECD Publishing, Paris, *http://dx.doi.org/10.1787/9789264210745-en*.

OECD/European Union (2013), *A Good Life in Old Age? Monitoring and Improving Quality in Long-term Care*, OECD Health Policy Studies, OECD Publishing, Paris, *http://dx.doi.org/10.1787/9789264194564-en*.

Phillips, A. (2006), "'Really' Equal: Opportunities and Autonomy", *Journal of Political Philosophy*, Vol. 14, No. 1, pp. 18-32.

Pitlik, H. et al. (2010), *Verwaltungsmodernisierung als Voraussetzung für nachhaltige Effizienzgewinne im öffentlichen Sektor*, Wifo.

Riesenfelder, A. (2013), "Wiedereinstiegsmonitoring Ein Überblick über die Ergebnisse der Kohorten 2006 bis 2010 in Österreich und in der Bundeshauptstadt Wien", *L&R Social Research*.

Robeyns, I. (2006), "The Capability Approach in Practice", *Journal of Political Philosophy*, Vol. 14, No. 3, pp. 351-376.

Schneebaum, A., B. Rumplmaier and W. Altzinger (2013), "Gender and Migration Background in Intergenerational Educational Mobility", *Working Paper Series*, No. 156, Vienna University of Economics and Business.

Schratzenstaller, M. (2014), "Gender Impact Assessment in Austria", European Union Programme for Employment and Social Solidarity – PROGRESS (2007-13).

Seguino, S. (2013), "Toward gender justice: Confronting Stratification and Unequal Power", GÉNEROS – *Multidisciplinary Journal of Gender Studies*, Vol. 2, No. 1, pp. 1-36.

Sen, Amartya K. (1993), "Capability and Well-being", in Martha C. Nussbaum and Amartya K. Sen (eds.), *The Quality of Life*, Oxford: Clarendon Press, pp. 30-53.

Sobotka, T. and M.R. Testa (2008), "Attitudes and intentions toward childlessness in Europe", in *People, Population Change and Policies*, Springer, Netherlands, pp. 177-211.

Soder, M. (2014), "Die Freizeitoption in Kollektivverträgen", *Materialien zu Wirtschaft und Gesellschaft*, No. 127, Austrian Chamber of Labour, Vienna.

van Staveren, I. (2014), "The Lehman Sisters Hypothesis", *Cambridge Journal of Economics*, Vol. 38, No. 5, pp. 995-1014.

Sullivan, O., F.C. Billari and E. Altintas (2014), "Fathers' Changing Contributions to Child Care and Domestic Work in Very Low-Fertility Countries: The Effect of Education", *Journal of Family Issues*, Vol. 35, No. 8, pp. 1048-1065.

Thévenon, O. (2013), "Drivers of Female Labour Force Participation in the OECD", *OECD Social, Employment and Migration Working Papers*, No. 145, OECD Publishing, Paris, *http://dx.doi.org/10.1787/5k46cvrgnms6-en*.

Weber, A. and C. Zulehner (2014), "Competition and Gender Prejudice: Are Discriminatory Employers Doomed to Fail?", *Journal of the European Economic Association*, Vol. 12, No. 2, pp. 492-521.

ORGANISATION FOR ECONOMIC CO-OPERATION AND DEVELOPMENT

The OECD is a unique forum where governments work together to address the economic, social and environmental challenges of globalisation. The OECD is also at the forefront of efforts to understand and to help governments respond to new developments and concerns, such as corporate governance, the information economy and the challenges of an ageing population. The Organisation provides a setting where governments can compare policy experiences, seek answers to common problems, identify good practice and work to co-ordinate domestic and international policies.

The OECD member countries are: Australia, Austria, Belgium, Canada, Chile, the Czech Republic, Denmark, Estonia, Finland, France, Germany, Greece, Hungary, Iceland, Ireland, Israel, Italy, Japan, Korea, Luxembourg, Mexico, the Netherlands, New Zealand, Norway, Poland, Portugal, the Slovak Republic, Slovenia, Spain, Sweden, Switzerland, Turkey, the United Kingdom and the United States. The European Commission takes part in the work of the OECD.

OECD Publishing disseminates widely the results of the Organisation's statistics gathering and research on economic, social and environmental issues, as well as the conventions, guidelines and standards agreed by its members.

OECD PUBLISHING, 2, rue André-Pascal, 75775 PARIS CEDEX 16
(10 2015 16 1 P) ISBN 978-92-64-23819-0 – 2015

www.ingramcontent.com/pod-product-compliance
Ingram Content Group UK Ltd.
Pitfield, Milton Keynes, MK11 3LW, UK
UKHW051240300926
15471UKWH00015B/1444

9 789264 238190